THE ROAD TO APPLEDORE

OTHER PROSE BY TOM WAYMAN

TOM WAYMAN

THE ROAD TO APPLEDORE

or HOW I WENT BACK TO THE LAND WITHOUT EVER HAVING LIVED THERE IN THE FIRST PLACE

HARBOUR PUBLISHING

HARBOUR PUBLISHING CO. LTD.
P.O. Box 219, Madeira Park, BC, VON 2H0
www.harbourpublishing.com

EDITED by Noel Hudson
TEXT DESIGN by Libris Simas Ferraz / Onça Publishing
PRINTED AND BOUND in Canada
PRINTED on 100% recycled paper

HARBOUR PUBLISHING acknowledges the support of the Canada Council for the
Arts, the Government of Canada, and the Province of British Columbia through
the BC Arts Council.

LIBRARY AND ARCHIVES CANADA CATALOGUING IN PUBLICATION
Title: The road to Appledore : or, How I went back to the land without ever having
    lived there in the first place / Tom Wayman.
Other titles: How I went back to the land without ever having lived there in the
    first place
Names: Wayman, Tom, 1945- author.
Identifiers: Canadiana (print) 20240298543 | Canadiana (ebook) 20240298780 |
    ISBN 9781990776632 (softcover) | ISBN 9781990776649 (EPUB)
Subjects: LCSH: Wayman, Tom, 1945- | LCSH: Mountain life—British Columbia—
    Slocan River Valley. | LCSH: Slocan River Valley (B.C.)—Social life and
    customs—21st century. | LCGFT: Autobiographies.
Classification: LCC FC3845.S595 Z49 2024 | DDC 971.1/62—dc23

CONTENTS

ACKNOWLEDGEMENTS

Just as every tale is both true and fiction, some names here are real and some have been changed to protect the bearer or myself.

I was helped both to live here and to write this book by numerous people whose marvellous stories for various reasons don't appear in these pages. Among them: Jeremy Addington and Margaret Parker, the late Larry Caesar, Victoria Carleton and Steve Monteer, Anne DeGrace, Nina George and Raynald Losier, Rabi'a Gonzalez, Ernest Hekkanen, Mabel Kabatoff, David Lawson, Peter Martyn, Barbara Curry Mulcahy and the late Mike Mulcahy, Greg Nesteroff, Verna Relkoff, Julian and Ruth Ross, Joanne Taylor, the late Ron Welwood, and Calvin Wharton. A tip of the ball cap to the Duck Stop, Hungry Wolf, Cedar Creek Café, Kayu's Café, and Mama Sita's. Also: Sleep Is For Sissies, Fomi's Bakery, and the Frog Peak Café. My thanks, too, to Jennifer Day for her usual highly perceptive editorial suggestions, and to Noel Hudson for his inspired and meticulous editing.

Excerpt from "The Mountains Have Not Yet Entered" by David Zieroth reprinted by permission of the author.

"Cuttings" copyright © 1948 by Theodore Roethke; copyright © 1966 and renewed 1996 by Beatrice Lushington; from *Collected Poems* by Theodore Roethke. Used by permission of Doubleday, an imprint of the Knopf Doubleday Publishing Group, a division of

Since they never saw Appledore, this book is dedicated to Dennis Saleh (1942–2020) and Stuart Peterfreund (1945–2017).

And to Fran Brafman, who, in her own way, has lived through the years depicted within.

Part 1

THE DESTINATION...

Chapter One

NO GOING BACK

I LOST REVERSE GEAR IN GRAND FORKS, BRITISH COLUMBIA, about five in the afternoon. For seven hours, I'd been steering a rented Ryder truck through the hot August day. The vehicle's 16-foot box was crammed nearly to the roof with most of my belongings, atop which I had managed to squeeze in at an angle a brand-new Old Town 16 canoe. Despite the weight of the truck's load, its unfamiliar size, and my sense of blindness having to change lanes with the aid of only side mirrors, I had found that morning that I could readily navigate the freeway traffic from Vancouver to Hope and the two-lane after. But 500 kilometres east of my starting point, suddenly something had gone wrong with the transmission.

Several minutes behind me down Highway 3, my long-time partner Bea was driving my little Toyota Corolla also jammed with more boxes of my stuff. Bea had graciously agreed to help me move to my new house in BC's West Kootenay region, even though my decision to find a place to live for a while in the province's southern Interior constituted a sort of trial separation. My goal was to attempt to resolve a 15-year relationship that had become stuck: "comfortable, but not satisfying," as a Vancouver marriage counsellor we had gone to had categorized it.

Over a late lunch an hour and a half ago at Osoyoos, we had agreed to next rendezvous at a Shell self-serve gas station I was aware of beside the highway in downtown Grand Forks. Since Bea still hadn't appeared by the time I refuelled the truck, I decided to park across a side street from the gas bar until she arrived.

Keeping a wary eye out for other traffic, I lumbered out of the pump area and turned left onto the street. My plan was to wheel across until I reached the other shoulder, then reverse so as to park facing the highway, ready to resume travel when the Corolla was gassed up. The street wasn't wide enough for me to turn and park along the shoulder in one forward motion.

I cut across the pavement, checked my mirrors in case anything had driven up behind, slipped the automatic shift into R and tapped the accelerator. No response.

A flush of anxiety heated my face. The truck was stopped so that its box blocked the side street. "Keep calm, keep calm," I admonished myself. "Probably you've done something out of sequence. Or the gears are a little worn." I jerked the lever to Drive again, depressed the accelerator slightly, shifted the truck forward a foot. Then I pulled the gear wand back to R once more and gave the engine gas. No response.

Through the windshield, I saw a car signalling to turn off the highway, waiting for me to stop obstructing the street. I felt simultaneously vulnerable and stupid. If I continued my swing ahead so the car could proceed, I'd collide with the stop sign. I fiercely shifted in and out of R twice more. After glancing desperately about, I yanked the wheel hard right and gunned the truck up onto a field of tall grass. I hoped this was a vacant lot rather than the uncut lawn of the neighbouring house.

Once I guessed the rear of the box had cleared the asphalt, I shut off the motor and climbed down, peering around to check if anybody stood glaring at me for parking a truck on their lawn. Across the side street, cars and pickups were arriving and departing from the gas station as though a rental truck halted in the field across from it was an everyday occurrence. Nobody was in sight close by. I climbed back into the cab, fired up the engine, and attempted a few more times to induce the R to engage. My anxiety increased as the truck stubbornly refused to move backwards. How was I going to deal with this development?

A few minutes later I saw Bea pull the Corolla into the gas station. After I went over to explain the dilemma to her, she filled up and relocated the Corolla to the street. Aware of my inclination to become flustered when unexpected serious difficulties arise, Bea tried herself to get the R to engage, without success.

I wasn't sure what we should do next. Keep driving with a crippled truck and hope I didn't ever have to back up? Or find a place to stay overnight in a strange small town in the hope that somebody local could repair the transmission the next day?

I mentally reviewed the road ahead, weighing whether circumstances would arise that required reverse gear. I knew from previous trips that our route east from here on Highway 3 stays in a valley bottom most of the way to the resort community of Christina Lake. Then the road climbs steeply up through the southern Selkirk Mountains to the Blueberry–Paulson Pass. That summit, at 1,450 metres elevation, is only about 150 metres short of the highest point on the Trans-Canada, far to the north, the Kicking Horse Pass.

From the Paulson summit, Highway 3 descends eventually to Castlegar, a pulp mill town alongside the Columbia River. The Kootenay River joins the Columbia here, having flowed past Nelson a half-hour drive upstream. Midway between Castlegar and Nelson, the road west through the Slocan Valley, where my new house was located, T's at the only stoplight between the two towns. Our ultimate destination lay 25 minutes along that westbound route, Highway 6.

Where I now stood with Bea beside a gibbled truck on a patch of overgrown grass, we were still about 150 kilometres away from our goal. I told Bea that, if all went well, I felt we could navigate to my new place without me having to back up. On the other hand, if reverse was required for any reason, we'd have a significant problem. I wasn't sure whether it was best to trust to luck, or at least my truck-driving skills, or play it safe and ask back at the service station whether Grand Forks had a transmission specialist.

The day was waning, and Bea soon tired of my dithering over the pros and cons of remaining where we were or hitting the road again. She refused after a while to offer her opinion. Nervously I announced we'd resume travelling.

My decision was based in large part on my reluctance to stop driving. I'd experienced this inclination of mine during many long-distance trips. I call the syndrome "highway hypnosis": after a few hours behind the wheel, I enter a state of needing to keep those tires turning, a conviction that stopping even for gas or food is wrong. I recognize that highway hypnosis represents a sort of addiction, a workaholism of the wheel: roadaholism. My decision to keep going was also influenced by not knowing how long a repair might take here, given that transmission components might have to be shipped in from a larger centre.

Bea was familiar with my affliction, having travelled with me several times up and down the West Coast as far as California and also to and from Alberta numerous times. Thus, before leaving Grand Forks, we settled that our next stop would be at the junction with Highway 6, where we could grab some supper at a nearby roadhouse, the Dam Inn, before the final leg of our journey.

While Bea headed for the Corolla, I clambered up into the truck cab, started the engine, and geared into low. Once an opening in traffic appeared on the highway, I bumped and lurched out onto pavement again, mud and tufts of greenery spurting behind my rear wheels. Through my side mirrors I could see two deep ruts the truck had left across the grassy patch. I guiltily floored the accelerator and headed on into the evening.

Earlier that day, at my insistence, we had driven five hours straight from Vancouver to Osoyoos, the southern end of the Okanagan Valley, before halting for lunch. My excuse for not taking a break, if one had been demanded, would have been that the route from the Coast to the West Kootenay is conducive to not stopping. The scenery, always spectacular, keeps changing as the road crosses through one ecosystem after another. Curiosity about what's around the next curve would cause anyone to want to continue travelling.

No matter how many times I had followed the highway from Vancouver to the Koots before, or how many times I've navigated it since, I've never tired of motoring the route, whatever the season and weather. Entering the eastbound Highway 1 freeway at the edge of Vancouver, I'm instantly one of hundreds of sedans, pickups, delivery vans and tractor-trailer rigs travelling at a breakneck pace through suburbs: hillsides and river flats crammed with houses, clusters of residential towers, shopping malls, industrial plants and warehouses. The wide Fraser River is crossed on the high arch of the Port Mann Bridge, and then the four-lane races through the increasingly agricultural Fraser Valley. The road aims southeastward nearly to the US border, and then northeast past Abbotsford and Chilliwack, cities that with their surrounding sprawl form urban islands amid extensive farm fields.

Somewhere beyond Chilliwack, the pastures, hay meadows, cornfields and barns are replaced by forest as the freeway arrows into the Coast Mountains. At this point, traffic thins. The bumper-to-bumper mass of vehicles clogging both eastbound lanes is reduced to stretches of empty asphalt traversed by an occasional vehicle or small clusters interspersed with tractor-trailers—many of the latter with Alberta or prairie licence plates.

In later years I would feel a physical release when, past Chilliwack, the highway at last enters an evergreen wood. Fir, spruce, cedar and hemlock, zipping past on either side, enough resemble the Interior Wet Belt forests of the West Kootenay to offer a reassuring image of home.

At Hope, the Trans-Canada swings north to enter the Fraser Canyon. And Highway 3 begins, its Hope–Princeton stretch mainly two-lane. The mountains grow higher as the road winds through Manning Park. At the Park's height of land, Allison Pass at 1,300 metres, the air noticeably changes—from moisture-laden on the western side to much drier as the highway descends the eastern slope.

Indeed, just before Princeton, the landscape transforms to sparse pine forest and rolling ranch land. Some fields are irrigated where water can be pumped up from a river. Then, near Keremeos, hayfields are replaced by the orchards of the south Okanagan Valley: cherries, peaches, plums, apples. The terrain remains primarily semi-arid hillsides all the way to Osoyoos, though in the 2000s many of these slopes were converted to vineyards. Osoyoos touts itself as existing in Canada's only desert.

Leaving Osoyoos, eastbound Highway 3 switchbacks steeply up the sheer face of a mountain—presenting, as the road ascends, ever-more-stunning views. After the Anarchist Mountain summit at 1,100 metres, empty tableland, broken up by pine and larch groves, extends on both sides of the road toward distant blue mountains. These are the southern Monashee Mountains, a range that forms the West Kootenay's western border. A drop nearly as precipitous as the climb up from Osoyoos lowers the highway down to the hamlet of Rock Creek. Soon the route leads again through densely forested country.

Loaded logging trucks begin to be frequent amid the traffic, sometimes hauling cedar trunks of impressive dimensions but mostly wooded down with spindly fir, pine, spruce or hemlock trunks bound for what are known as "spaghetti mills." This mocking designation for sawmills is a recognition that in the days before BC's forests were high-graded, these mills would have scorned to process such small-diameter logs. The looming bulk of chip trucks also appear: a tractor towing two huge semi-trailers. Their cargoes of wood chips are being transported to pulp mills on both sides of the us border, which through this region is never far from the highway and its settlements.

The day Bea and I travelled in convoy, I had enjoyed as ever the fascinating run across half the southern portion of the province. Yet, with Grand Forks in the truck's rear-view mirror, my worrying about all that could go wrong without a reverse gear absorbed more of my thoughts than any appreciation of the landscape.

Another worry was the thickening light as Highway 3 bored ever-deeper now into the Selkirk Mountains. Once Christina Lake was behind me, traffic became scant as the twisty road lifted toward Paulson Pass. I peered ahead, hyper-alert: at dusk the deer move to water. The threat of a deer's sudden emergence onto the pavement markedly increases as night approaches.

In the dark, the reflectors of a deer's eyes will pick up and return the light from headlamps: where coins of light bob along the shoulder or in roadside ditches, danger is evident. But at dusk, as human eyes' cones give way to rods as the primary source of vision, the brown shapes of deer are hard to spot. Even deer observed standing motionless on the shoulder constitute risk. Deer poised beside the asphalt are as likely to spring into traffic as to bound back into the safety of the woods.

Almost everyone who drives in the West Kootenay sooner or later hits a deer. A common sight is one of the animals lying dead on the shoulder. The experience of slamming into one is awful, as years later I was to learn first-hand. The animal's size and weight approximate a person's, and the sickening thump of contact evokes every driver's deep-rooted fear of destroying a human being. Plus, the damage to a vehicle from colliding with a deer can be catastrophic. Also horrible are accounts of deer injured but not killed by an encounter with a car or truck. The Mounties stress that you're not responsible for putting the wounded animal out of its pain.

Nevertheless, stories abound of people attempting to do just that rather than phone the cops or the Conservation officers, neither of whom respond quickly to such calls, if at all.

So as I piloted the Ryder truck through the dimming light, I drove with eyes obsessively scanning the edges of the road for a doe or buck dashing out to her or his death. Such tension was layered on top of my gnawing concern about the truck's missing gear. What if I happened on an accident or other obstacle such that I needed to reverse in order to manoeuvre around it? What if, nearing my destination in the dark, I made an error in judgment steering from the highway onto the back road where my new house was located and needed to back up to properly make the turn? Similarly, would I be able to negotiate the 90-degree turn from the back road onto the driveway to my new place without reversing?

We reached Castlegar and then, 15 minutes later, Playmor Junction, where Highway 6 joins the Castlegar–Nelson route. I left the truck on the shoulder just before the junction and rode with Bea in the Corolla the short distance ahead to the Dam Inn. A few minutes later, I felt some of the tightness drain from my arms and shoulders as I sat sipping a beer. I stretched my legs out under the table with a sense of temporary relief.

The roadhouse is named for the series of five large dams built along the Kootenay River from just west of Nelson to Castlegar. Four of these five were constructed by West Kootenay Power, a Cominco subsidiary, to generate electricity for that company's giant lead-zinc smelter south of Castlegar at Trail, as well as for the area mines that originally supplied ore for the smelter. Eventually hydroelectric power was sold to residential and business customers throughout the region, and as far west as the Okanagan.

The fifth dam, closest to Nelson, was built in 1907 and continues to generate power for the city-owned electrical utility, Nelson Hydro. Opposite the roadhouse, the river's flow had been twinned in the 1970s by BC Hydro's construction of the Kootenay Canal. This channel, before returning the water to the river, leads to penstocks and yet another power-generating station, which began to produce electricity in 1976.

All this history was far from my mind as Bea and I wolfed down a plate of sandwiches kindly provided by the Dam Inn's barman, even though the kitchen had stopped serving supper. As we ate, I sketched out on a napkin a scheme I'd concocted for the last push to the house.

I wasn't confident I could find my new place if we turned off Highway 6 where a convenience store and restaurant marked "downtown" Winlaw. Winlaw is the unincorporated area where my new house was located: about 300 people living along both sides of the Slocan River for several kilometres. During the process of purchasing the house, I had always travelled five minutes or so past Winlaw's commercial enterprises to where the back road along the other side of the river crosses over to rejoin the highway. I remembered how at that junction a porch light always burns at the Threads Guild building, a former one-room schoolhouse taken over by a group of weavers and dyers that Bea had been part of when I had taught in Nelson between 1980 and 1982 at David Thompson University Centre, a consortium of the University of Victoria and the local community college. I was reasonably confident I could spot that light in the total darkness of the valley night and know where to turn.

If I missed the light, without reverse gear I'd have to drive another 10 minutes to the village of Slocan before I'd be able to steer the truck around a block to head back. Yet, assuming the best, Bea would pull ahead of me once I was on the back road in order to scout out the new house's driveway.

We decided that I would park as soon as I pulled into the drive and postpone until the next day figuring out how we could position the truck to unload up at the house without employing reverse gear. Bea, who had accompanied me for two of my three excursions to look at the house, was more certain than I of our ability to find the right driveway in the dark.

I was enormously grateful for her presence. Despite this move representing an unravelling of a decade and a half of our living together, she had volunteered to take a week off from her job at a Vancouver antique store to help me. I had promised her that the week wouldn't be all driving and unpacking, that we'd do some hiking and try out the new canoe. But we had each moved enough in the past to be aware how much effort is involved in transplanting a household: all the unpacking and sorting and deciding what goes where, even if, while she was here, the dwelling only had to become operational enough that we could cook meals and sleep.

The previous week had been far from pleasant for either of us, as I packed my life into boxes and temporarily stockpiled them in the basement and garage of our small rented house in East Vancouver. Because I was the only one leaving, that house remained functional, although increasingly bare as evidence of my presence began to be packed away. Mostly I felt numb as I loaded the truck and car in a day and a half. My time-worn possessions were melded with new purchases I'd made from a list of all I could anticipate requiring in the country: garden hoses, tablecloths, lawnmower, washing machine, towels, kitchen utensils.

My intent was to quickly unload the day after we arrived and return the truck to a Ryder office in Castlegar. Then we could at least make a dent in what we knew would be a surrealistic pile of boxes and bags and packages and suitcases and cross-country skis and snowshoes and everything else currently stacked, wedged, propped up or lashed to the walls in the truck box and squeezed into the trunk and back seat of the Corolla.

As I settled our bill at the Dam Inn, suddenly weary to the core from worry and the long day on the road, I wondered if I could have driven an inch farther if I was making this trip without Bea. Her confidence that we would have no trouble locating the driveway to the new house provided the impetus I needed to go on. I swung up one more time into the truck's cab, made the turn onto Highway 6, and headed up the Slocan Valley through the blackness.

By night the highway, like any country road, was only a tunnel my headlamps created of pavement and roadside vegetation. Off in the distance to right or left an occasional set of house lights or a farmstead yard light drifted past. Infrequently the blinding twin rays of an oncoming vehicle flared into view, dimmed and vanished.

After 20 long minutes in the dark, we approached the lights of Winlaw's store and café. The highway passed a volunteer fire department hall, a directional sign for the Winlaw community hall, and once more we were driving into night. My anxiety increased as I stared through the windshield searching for the lamp on the Threads Guild building. I found myself driving slower and slower.

Then, unmistakably, the light I sought gleamed through the trees. I made the turn, and in front of the Threads Guild building pulled onto the shoulder to let Bea scoot around me and take the lead.

Just west of the Threads Guild, we crossed a single-lane Bailey bridge over the Slocan River and followed the back road as it angled sharply left then wound through woods as it climbed. My lights picked out the occasional start of gravel driveways leading to left and right. At the bottom of some of these, a sign in my headlights momentarily proclaimed four numbers. The real estate agent had explained to me that these numerals were "fire numbers" and not addresses. Apparently the numbers had been mandated some years before to ensure the volunteer fire department could locate specific houses once enough newcomers had moved to the valley that fire department members no longer could identify each house by who lived there. Referring to the numbers as "addresses," I was told, was regarded as a city thing.

The numbers visible in my headlights descended in value as the road twisted south, although I could glimpse the signs only intermittently. Suddenly Bea's right turn indicator started to flash, and she vanished up a steep earthen driveway. I yanked the wheel sharply to the right, drove a short distance off the pavement following her tail-lights, and killed the engine. For a moment, I just sat in the stillness.

Through my open window, the warm August night reverberated with the rhythmical call of insects. Across the valley sounded the occasional muted hum of a vehicle headed down the portion of highway we had recently covered. Otherwise, all was silence.

I saw a flashlight bobbing down the drive. As I climbed out of the cab, I was amazed to see overhead a million stars. Then Bea was alongside, and together we gingerly opened one of the truck box's rear doors, careful in case any of the load had shifted. We extracted sleeping bags and air mattresses we had packed last, along with a suitcase each. Thus burdened, we laboured up the drive to where Bea had parked the Corolla alongside the house.

At the parking area, we crossed through an open wooden fence gate onto a lawn south of the house's large deck. The people I had bought the house from had constructed ornamental fencing that edged the lawns around the building, using 4 × 4 posts and 1 × 4 rails. We trudged up the lawn to the deck's western end, where stairs led up to it.

Carrying our gear, we struggled along the deck to the front door. I put down my luggage, dug out the unfamiliar key, and fumbled at the lock in the wavering illumination of Bea's flashlight. The door opened, and we stepped in.

We moved from room to room, snapping on lights. I was eager to see what I had bought: I knew, from decades of renting, that viewing a dwelling when somebody else is living in it is very different than experiencing it empty for the first time.

I was pleased with what I saw. The entire length of the southern wall of the house, spanning kitchen, dining nook, and living room, was panelled with finished cedar boards, providing a warm feel to the interior I hadn't been conscious of when I had toured the place before. On the sill of the big east-facing window in the kitchen, the former owners had left us a vase full of flowers by way of welcome. And on the kitchen counter were manuals for the appliances of theirs I had bought along with the house: stove, refrigerator, dishwasher.

The only surprise came in the basement. Because of the slope of the lot, the basement is buried at the western end of the house but emerges to ground level at the eastern end. The northeast corner of the basement, the times I had visited, had been a child's bedroom, with windows looking north and east. Now that everything had been removed from that room, I realized it was simply a corner of the basement. The floor, previously covered with rugs, was bare concrete. The room's walls, which had been obscured by posters and chests of drawers and other furniture, were revealed as unpainted wallboard, its joins not even taped. The ceiling, which I really hadn't noticed before, was the same as the rest of the basement's: joists through which passed electrical wiring and copper water pipes.

On the main floor again, we opened some of the big screened windows that in the daytime filled the place with light. As the night air flooded in, Bea and I unrolled our sleeping bags on the thick living-room carpet. For more ventilation, we slid open a glass door that provided access to the deck through a sliding screen. We could see the stars shining down above the giant evergreens to the west and south. With a breeze now filling the house, lying in our sleeping bags on the rug felt like we were camping outside.

I lay awake a long time as my body slowly released the strain of the day's drive while my mind repeatedly considered and rejected various ways I might bring the truck up to the stairs at the west end of the deck to unload. Obviously, waiting for daylight to decide on a procedure that didn't require reverse gear made the most sense. But I flogged my memory to provide an accurate picture of the grounds.

Could I pass through a bigger gate onto the south lawn down at the spot where the drive took a sharp curve up toward the house? From that gate I could steer up the lawn past the house, stop, and roll backwards toward the deck stairs. Or, could I drive to the deck stairs, unload, then drive forward around the north and east sides of the house before descending the drive? Yet was the gate in the fence north of the house wide enough for the truck to pass through?

Exhaustion finally won out over evaluating and re-evaluating plans that depended on surveying the situation in daylight. I had almost drifted off when a piercing cry of agony somewhere close outside crashed into the living room.

I bolted upright in my sleeping bag, gaping toward the darkness beyond the deck. The howl of pain was repeated, the horrifying wail of a person suffering physical torment, or anguished over the death of loved one. I thought the sound originated below the driveway on the road.

I wasn't sure if Bea was asleep or awake, but I hoped the latter. I tried a tentative whisper: "Did you hear that?"

"Yeah," she replied out of the dark, to my relief.

"What do you think it is?

"Don't know."

Another crescendo of wails resounded.

"Could it be an animal?" Bea asked.

"Maybe one of the neighbours is into s&m," I tried to joke.

"I'm not sure it's human," Bea said as the latest burst of misery trailed away.

I struggled out of my sleeping bag, slid the screen aside, and stepped naked onto the deck. The night was completely silent once more. Bea joined me at the deck railing, and we peered into the blackness.

Abruptly the terrifying howls and screeches resumed, rising in waves and then fading away. They seemed to originate to the south, down the road.

"We'll have to ask somebody about it tomorrow," Bea said in a low voice as the country quiet resumed.

"What if everyone around here pretends not to notice?" I babbled, attempting to offset the disturbing sounds with lame humour. "'Howls at night? I never heard no howls at night. You hear anything like that, Maudie? Nope, she never heard nothing like that, neither.'"

"Maybe. But we've got to find out," Bea said.

The now-still-again August dark kept its secret. After we went back inside, I lay in my sleeping bag tensely anticipating the resumption of the unearthly screeches. The thought struck me that it would be prudent to close and lock the sliding glass door that led to the deck. The fresh air wafting in was welcome, however, and I concentrated on not fretting about the open door.

Later I thought I heard the yells of acute distress coming from a greater distance. I must have fallen asleep and dreamed the sound, because when I lifted my head to listen, all I heard was Bea's regular breathing beside me. The room was distinctly lighter, though: I could distinguish our suitcases where we had shoved them against one wall. I rolled over, and when I next knew anything, the room was ablaze with morning sunshine.

Chapter Two

ADVICE FROM A CLOUD

T HE PROPERTY I HAD BOUGHT IS JUST SHY OF 9 ACRES: IT
extends about 80 metres wide along the back road, and half a kilometre up a forested ridge. That landform is Perry Ridge, which for
25 kilometres forms the western wall of the Slocan Valley before
the latter bends eastward from a north–south orientation about
15 kilometres south of my place. At its highest, Perry Ridge rises to
2,100 metres, and at its broadest is 9 kilometres across.

The ridge's namesake is the civil engineer who surveyed the
Canadian Pacific Railway up the east side of the valley, Charles
Edward Perry (1843–1906). For the first four years after I moved here,
about twice a week a train chugged up the valley at slow speed to
pick up lumber from the sawmill in the village of Slocan, at the
southern end of Slocan Lake. The last train to Slocan ambled up
the tracks in September 1993, and within a few years the rail line,
including ties and rails, was gone.

The absent railway still has a presence, however. My property had been part of 1907 grant by the railway of 1,500 acres along
both sides of the river to Andrew Nelson Winlaw. He was the son
of John Brown Winlaw (1855–1939). At the turn of the century, the
latter operated a sawmill where a small elementary school now sits

beside a short road from downtown Winlaw to the modern-if-modest Winlaw Bridge. This construction, like the World War II-era Bailey bridge by the Threads Guild, spans the river to the back road. For the 1907 land grant, the lumberman's son paid $3,385, the equivalent of about $89,000 in today's (2024) dollars. Due to the terms of the railway's land grant, the deed to my acreage still has a rider on it that states the railway owns any trees on the property other than those the occupier of the land needs for "fuel, fencing and buildings." If more timber is cut by the owner than for those purposes, a schedule of fees owed the railway is helpfully provided.

I've never heard of the CPR attempting to ding any locals for removing trees on their land. Indeed, several years after I moved in, my then-neighbour to the south clear-cut about a dozen acres of his property above his house, and I'm sure the railroad didn't get a penny. Since the railroad abandoned its line in the valley, and knowing how contrarian and feisty many of my neighbours are, I doubt the railroad would ever attempt to collect from the present landowners.

The back road winds more or less north–south along the base of Perry Ridge. Most houses on the road are modest, sitting amid cleared fields either now unused or on which cows or horses graze. Stretches of woodland interrupt the series of homes. An occasional unpaved loop road wanders from the back road toward the ridge and returns, or else swings closer to the river before reconnecting with the back road. For most of the latter's extent it's called Slocan River Road, except that about a half kilometre south of my place, the name changes to Perry's Back Road.

Climbing up from the road, the lower 3 acres or so of my property holds lawns, garden, meadow and a 1,000-square-foot house—one storey and a basement—built nine years before I bought it. The house was the product of a divorce. Bob and Lynn Lidstone had arrived in the valley during the area's Vietnam War-era flood of US draft resisters and back-to-the-landers. The Lidstones bought 20 acres, on which Bob built a house in 1978. When the marriage came apart, the couple subdivided the property, and in 1980 Bob built a second house—the one I came to occupy—on what had been the southern portion of their property. Because the couple had two kids, the idea was that co-parenting would be easier if the parents lived next door to one another. That arrangement was short-lived: Bob soon sold the place and constructed another house closer to downtown Winlaw.

But Bob had meant the second house to be his to live in: it was not a spec house. As a result, the structure is exceptionally well constructed. Every contractor I've hired for modifications has pronounced it, admiringly, "over-built." Any errors or shortcoming in design or fabrication Bob made in erecting the house next door he corrected when he worked on the second dwelling.

The couple who bought from Bob, and from whom I purchased the property, were both hospital administrators. One had been working to the south in Trail, an hour and a quarter's drive from here, where the hospital is now the main regional one. The other was employed about 40 minutes' drive north in the village of New Denver, on Slocan Lake. The house originally had three bedrooms in a row on the main floor: a master bedroom at the house's east end and one for each of Bob's kids when they stayed over. The subsequent owners knocked out a wall of the westernmost bedroom, thereby enlarging the living room into a light-filled L-shaped space.

My buying such a solid house was strictly an accident, however. I had never purchased a home before. Despite having taken a Vancouver School Board multi-week night-class in house-buying when I lived in the city, I definitely didn't know what I was doing. Especially not when it came to purchasing a house in the country.

My plan in any case had been to rent for a year in Nelson while I tried to sort out what I wanted to do about my life in Vancouver: about my relationship with Bea that I seemed unable to improve or withdraw from, and also about my involvement in a small radical labour organization I believed in, but which involved a treadmill of chores for me without much lasting impact. When I finally drove up in June 1989 to see what I might rent, staying at a motel about 6 miles from town, I discovered a near-zero rental vacancy rate in the area. Nelson had very few apartment buildings, and instead of houses being available for rent, the local real estate market had cratered so properties were being offered for very little.

The town and region had not yet recovered economically from the shutdown of three major Nelson employers earlier in the decade. In the summer of 1982, the Kootenay Forest Products sawmill and plywood plant on the Nelson waterfront had closed. KFP and its feeder businesses had been an economic mainstay: subsequently, friends who had been students at David Thompson University Centre were able to buy a house while they were on Unemployment Insurance: $5,000 down and a very low mortgage payment. Then, on May 1, 1984, DTUC was shut down by the BC government. This meant the absence not only of faculty and their families, but the financial loss to the town of the spending of hundreds of students. Also in 1984, CPR's large diesel-engine repair facility in Nelson closed.

Although I had left DTUC in 1982 to go back to Vancouver, I became involved in the fight against DTUC's closure. When I first returned to the Coast, I spent the fall on UI, and in the spring term served as writer-in-residence at Simon Fraser University. For fall 1983, I taught English and writing at Kwantlen College in Surrey. That autumn was particularly inspiring because I was part of the province's public sector general strike, called in response to a provincial budget featuring draconian cuts to public services accompanied by a wage freeze for public sector employees in defiance of collective bargaining. These budget provisions were resisted by Operation Solidarity, a unified trade union response to the budget that included the faculty association at Kwantlen, and the Solidarity Coalition, an assembly of citizens' groups and organized labour.

As I've written about elsewhere, a general strike pulls the veil away that usually cloaks who in society are actually the significant individuals: those whose daily employment is essential to how a community, province and nation—a society—functions. A general strike is in theory also a non-violent way to effect major social change.

The time was a heady one for me. During Operation Solidarity, in both private conversations and public meetings I attended, the subjects discussed matched those of a lot of my poetry: the centrality of daily work to most people's lives, and the effects of a person's employment on their existence both on and off the job. So much was being rethought publicly and privately—social hierarchies of all kinds, and the roles of government, unions, community, and more—that for some weeks a new society seemed trembling on the verge of being born.

As sector after sector of the public service went out on strike in a planned sequence, the BC Federation of Labour leadership panicked at what they had inaugurated. At the height of the strike's success, with picket lines holding firm throughout the province and more sectors scheduled to go out the following week, the BC Fed executive capitulated to the government. No one on strike was given an opportunity to vote on the surrender terms.

In the weeks that followed the sellout of the general strike, the provincial government felt free to take revenge. Among the punitive measures the BC government announced was the closure of DTUC in May 1984, at the end of the current academic year. A government-appointed committee had in the fall approved the school's continuance for at least another five years. But West Kootenay residents had been particularly strong and vocal supporters of the strike.

In January 1984, as the fightback campaign against the closure got underway in Nelson, I was hired jointly by the faculty and student associations to come up for six weeks to establish a media centre connected to the campaign and instruct students to staff it. Among my teaching duties when I taught at DTUC had been an introduction to journalism course, so the fightback organizers thought I was the right person to develop media relations to assist the struggle to keep DTUC open. Enraged by the sellout and fired up by the promise of a better world that seemed realizable during the general strike, I was willing to resign from Kwantlen College and take up this new, if temporary, post. I soon had the media centre operational.

Ultimately the government didn't budge. When I returned to Nelson to look for rental accommodation five years after DTUC was shuttered, the local economy—including real estate—still was reeling from the series of economic setbacks, each with its multiplier effect. During my June 1989 visit, I narrowed my search to three different houses I could buy. One was in Nelson itself, and one on Nelson's North Shore—a stretch of closely packed houses extending 30 kilometres along the West Arm of Kootenay Lake. The third was the Winlaw property, which I found on a day's exploration of the Slocan Valley, rarely visited by me during my previous time in the region.

All three houses were about the same price, and each had some aspect that appealed to me. My decision in the end came down to whether renovations or other time-consuming work would be required before I could resume writing. Since I left DTUC in 1982, three more collections of my poems had been published—one with McClelland and Stewart (1983) and two with Harbour Publishing (1986 and 1989). Harbour had also published in 1983 a book of my essays about work-based literature, *Inside Job: Essays on the New Work Writing*.

At the moment of house-hunting I was assembling, with my friend and fellow author Calvin Wharton, an anthology of poems by writers living in East Vancouver. The collection would appear later in 1989 as *East of Main*, from Pulp Press. And I was engaged in crafting the poems that would appear five years later from Polestar Press as *The Astonishing Weight of the Dead*.

Being able to get back to my desk, set up my computer and dot-matrix printer, and resume literary work as quickly as possible was paramount in my choice of which property to buy. I was entitled to a year's UI from the Kwantlen job and planned to use the time to concentrate on writing. When I considered my shortlist of dwellings, the Nelson house badly needed repainting inside, plus some other repairs before I could designate one bedroom as a study. And the place up the West Arm, attractive because waterfront property, really was more of a cottage than a house. It would require proper insulation if I was going to spend a winter in comfort. In contrast to the other two houses, the Winlaw place looked like I could simply move in, unpack, and be back writing without having a menu of substantial household improvements to undertake and pay for.

The price for the Winlaw property was $65,000 for the nine-year-old house and its acreage: about $234,000 in today's (2024) dollars. Certainly inexpensive, although as with any major purchase I've ever made, the amount was more than I expected. I had budgeted $50,000 due to preliminary research that had informed me that many houses in Nelson and the region were on sale for that amount. My parents agreed to loan me the difference, interest free. So, once Bea had flown up and endorsed my selection of a house, I signed the papers to take possession after August 1.

My choice of where to relocate also hinged on an evaluation of positives and negatives: the West Kootenay wasn't the only destination I initially considered. Despite Edmonton's bitterly cold winters, I had enjoyed living in the same city as my only sibling, my brother, when I served as the University of Alberta's writer-in-residence in 1978–79 and stayed in the city an extra year so Bea could finish a master's degree. Literary friends I made during our stay contributed to that city's appeal for me. During the previous decade

I had also been writer-in-residence at the University of Windsor in 1975–76, and the following year taught English and writing across the river in Detroit at Wayne State University. Not only had I made friends with people from those cities, but during my time based in Windsor I had frequently visited Toronto, where my parents lived. I had become friends with several people in the Toronto literary world. As well, CBC Radio in Toronto had hired me in the summer of 1976 to interview authors, editors and publishers for the summer replacement of the national "Gzowski on FM" show, and I had formed friendships with some members of that program's crew. Spending a year in what in those days was Canada's literary and cultural capital was another attractive possibility.

However, recent experiences in the West Kootenay helped me decide where to relocate. The two previous Junes, I had spent a week on the property of long-time Vancouver friends of mine who had moved to the Slocan Lake area several years before. These visits for me were a welcome break from what had become obsessive pondering about what to do to straighten out my life. My friends Phil and Emma lived about 30 minutes' drive north on Highway 6 from Winlaw. Given the remoteness of their acreage, between the highway and Slocan Lake south of the hamlet of Silverton, they had been able to buy sufficient land that only one neighbour's place was distantly visible through some trees across a field.

Forest crowds in on three sides of their lawns, and the great peaks of the Selkirks tower close around them. The live in a former Doukhobor farmhouse, beautifully converted into one large room with a loft by a California couple who had returned to the States. The clearing in which the house sits is alive with flowers in summer, since Emma is a gifted gardener.

I had first met Phil at the University of BC. After dropping out, he had enrolled at Simon Fraser University, where he had been active in protesting the firing of some popular instructors and also in organizations envisioning a new kind of educational institution. After dropping out of sfu, he become a commercial pilot, and courted Emma when she worked in the two-person office of a small freight airline at the Vancouver airport. She was originally from a dairy farm east of Regina and had moved to Vancouver after taking secretarial training.

My friendship with the couple had been forged when we were all active in protests against the Vietnam War and in various labour and left-wing organizations. The marches, meetings, sit-ins, meetings, picket lines, and more meetings we participated in had continued well into the 1970s. Emma had helped form a new union whose organizing efforts were directed at mostly female-staffed workplaces; the organization struggled to achieve the first union certification in Canada of bank tellers. By the end of the decade the couple were burned out. Much to their friends' surprise, including mine, they moved to a geographic region that felt to me at the time enormously distant from the Vancouver urban activist milieu.

On their property are a number of outbuildings: a chicken house, storage shed, and small log cabin. The latter, situated about 15 metres across the lawn from the main house, was where I would stay when I visited.

I loved living in that cabin. Each week I spent there contrasted hugely with my hectic life in Vancouver, where I juggled my duties as a teacher, my volunteer commitments to the small radical union, and my literary activities, including giving and helping to organize public author readings, and writing and submitting pieces for publication. To open the door to the cabin and step inside was to enter a much calmer world. Here I was hidden from the ceaseless ringing of my phone. With Bea hundreds of kilometres away, I could forget the nagging voice inside my head that for years had been ordering me to stop stalling and *do* something about the situation between Bea and myself: improve it or end it. Each time I occupied the cabin,

I hoped to gain some perspective on my personal situation. Failing that, my goal was to just enjoy the temporary reprieve from trying to figure out what to do about my life.

Electrical power had been strung to the cabin, so I had access to a refrigerator, two-burner hotplate, coffee pot and portable heater. These and the building's lights were all on one circuit, so caution had to be exercised so as not to overload the system. Rather than the current being routed through circuit breakers, it passed through an old-fashioned fuse box. Making a meal was always a balancing act between having heat, light, coffee, and a burner for cooking. I soon learned to pick up spare fuses at the Silverton grocery store when I drove into town to stock up on supplies.

My sense of the cabin was that it fundamentally was a friendly and welcoming place, although it took mischievous delight in plunging its interior into darkness when I was in the midst of cooking spaghetti for supper some evening.

"I keep telling you: pay attention to what you're doing," the cabin would chuckle as it watched me fumble to locate my flashlight in order to change a blown fuse after I had absent-mindedly turned on the heater while stirring the pasta sauce. "Apply this maxim to every facet of your life, and you will be rewarded. Fail to do so, and, more than metaphorically, you'll find yourself in the dark, hungry and cold."

I was tempted to respond, as I struggled with the fuse box: *Don't give yourself airs. You're just a shack in the middle of nowhere, not some guru.* But I kept such thoughts to myself. Experience had taught me that if the cabin decided my reaction to one of its "jokes" was insulting, it was capable of blowing two fuses in a row.

A faucet over a sink brought cold running water into the structure. If I wanted hot water, I had to heat it in a pan. An outhouse stood under some trees a few steps from a small front porch. A table and chair, a bed, and a small rag rug on the floor were all the space had room for besides the kitchen area, except for two floor-to-ceiling bookcases. Phil likes to read when he's home from the airline, and the cabin bookcase shelves were crammed with novels, travel tales, biography, twentieth-century history. Books were stored here to make room for new volumes over in the main house.

I seldom dipped into the cabin's literary offerings, though. The jumble of titles and cover designs radiated an energy that seemed too unpleasantly similar to my jangled life in Vancouver. I loved instead to listen to the cabin's mellower moods: the hum of its elderly refrigerator, the wind rummaging at the plastic sheeting stapled over the north window for extra insulation, rain falling on the wooden shakes of the roof as I lay in bed in the dark, a squirrel chittering in the closest fir tree as I woke to first light.

My routine during my visits was to go to bed not long after supper, and after breakfast and washing up, enjoy a coffee on the porch in the new morning. Then I'd tackle various writing tasks at the cabin table: drafts of new poems in longhand, reading proofs I had brought along of some soon-to-be-published material, or reworking old poems on my portable typewriter. After lunch, I'd report to the main house to volunteer for chores: lawn-mowing, bringing in firewood, helping dig out a new section of waterline. Occasionally, I'd take Emma and Phil's large, energetic, but stupid German shepherd, Dumbo, for a walk through the woods.

Dumbo's preoccupation was squirrels. On a walk with me, he'd charge off after hearing some squirrel I'd been unaware of. He failed to react at all if a deer and fawn stepped into sunlight on the trail ahead of us. If I saw fresh bear flop on the ground, I'd call Dumbo back from some anti-squirrel foray in the underbrush and retrace my steps. If the dog encountered a bear on one of his chases after squirrels, I was confident he'd lead it straight back to me to see what I might like to do with it.

My days at the cabin drifted by in a haze of heightened perceptions: the June air freshened by the wind off the glaciers, the gritty feel of the earth between my fingers as I weeded in Emma's garden, the intense chill of a cup of cold water before bed. Or a morning spent bundled in a cozy sweater, writing at the table while drinking coffee as, outside, rain hammered down.

One occurrence during my first spell in the cabin ultimately influenced me to relocate to the area. My writing had gone well all morning while Dumbo slept on the floor beside me. I made sandwiches for lunch and ate them outside on the porch, blinking when I first stepped through the door into bright sunlight after the relative dimness of the interior. When my meal was over, I returned inside to brew one last cup of coffee to drink before heading over to the main house to see what today's chores were to be. Once the water boiled, I took my coffee outside and sat on the lawn between the cabin and the house.

A couple of metres away, butterflies and bees swooped and hovered amid the multi-coloured mass of one of Emma's flower beds. A hummingbird paused mid-flight before a red geranium blossom. Robins bobbed along on the grass trying their luck for worms, while above, a raven travelled wing-stroke by wing-stroke from a hemlock behind the storage shed over the house toward another part of the forest. The sky this noon-hour was pure blue, and the tops of the distant peaks were still white with winter snow. A breeze that brushed the skin of my arms and face where I was seated registered as now hot, now deliciously cool, as swirls of air arrived from different directions.

A feeling swept over me like a rush of goosebumps, and I shivered. The sensation's effect in the noon sunshine was simultaneously pleasant and unsettling, strange and yet vaguely familiar. As the feeling lingered, my conviction increased that I had known this emotion sometime and somewhere before, if I could only identify it. I considered the matter over and over in my mind. Finally the answer surfaced: the feeling I was struggling to name was *happiness*. Not the kind of adult happiness that is linked to achievement, to fulfillment of some pre-established hope. On that Kootenay lawn,

I was suffused with the happiness I had known as a child now and then: pure enjoyment just of being alive.

Once I realized what the sensation was, shock set in. I was stunned that such contentment was so foreign to how I was living that I had to strive mentally for some minutes to identify it once it appeared. I felt sad about how many years of my life had slipped past since I was so completely happy.

A subsequent experience at Phil and Emma's also swayed my decision where to move. When I arrived the following June, Phil proudly showed me a trailer holding a new 16-foot runabout with a 10-horsepower outboard. He suggested we go fishing on Slocan Lake in a couple of days, when Emma would be at work. She had obtained a part-time job as a lawyer's secretary in Nakusp, about a 40-minute drive further north.

On the appointed day, I found Phil in the kitchen preparing some gourmet sandwiches for us to take along. Phil is a large, burly man, who very much enjoys his food and over the years has become an inventive chef. Any dinner he cooks is always a delicious and creative blend of ethnic and original recipes. Emma, on the other hand, regards food preparation as a bothersome chore. When Phil is away working—he stays with a mutual friend in Vancouver during the weeks he's flying—she subsists on raw garden vegetables, cheese and bread. She'll brew tea from time to time but prefers not to even have to boil water.

Part of Phil's delight at cooking and eating arises from his continual ingestion of marijuana whenever he's not at work. I was amazed at his ability to over-indulge at home while practising strict temperance on the job. Yet I had also previously met through my union activities tugboat crewmen who were teetotal during their 30-day stint at sea and complete alcoholics while ashore waiting to ship out again.

Decades of ingesting large quantities of marijuana smoke, however, had resulted in certain synapses in Phil's brain becoming clogged with resin, like an old hash pipe. Thus, he had been forced to purchase stronger and stronger grass in order to obtain the effect of which he had grown fond. Luckily for him, his desire for more powerful product grew in lockstep with the local marijuana industry. The weed available to him in the West Kootenay was orders of magnitude stronger than that available to us in Vancouver in the 1960s, when use of the herb was a mainstay of the city's counterculture.

Because of previous sampling by me of Phil's current existence-enhancer, I was cautious when he, after loading into a small knapsack the food we were to bring with us on our fishing expedition, suggested we smoke a joint before setting sail. Still, when Phil handed me a lit joint before we left the house to hitch up the boat trailer, I wasn't prepared to argue. Phil's years of command in the air have given him an aura of authority he can evoke at will. Frequently his authoritarian manner is tempered with humour, but his conduct is also influenced by the knowledge that his imposing bulk has in the past been able to physically reinforce his orders. His round, beefy face sported sideburns, giving him the appearance of a Victorian gentleman—a ranking officer in a Guards regiment, say, or a Dickensian factory owner—accustomed to his commands being obeyed without question.

I practised my usual wariness by taking only a few tentative hits from Phil's joint. He meanwhile put four more in a small tin box to sustain him during our hours on the water. Soon, despite some ineptitude on our part at backing the boat trailer down the ramp of Silverton's boat launch, we were properly underway, headed across the lake, with the motor sounding its loud single note and the beach receding behind us.

Once we were clear of land, Phil, sitting in the stern steering the boat, fired up another joint. I shook my head as he offered me more, feeling bubbles already rising in my brain.

The lake was flat calm, and we were crossing to its west shore in the midst of a perfect Kootenay early summer day. Slocan Lake is bounded to the west by the Selkirks' Valhalla ranges, mountains high enough to show bare granite above treeline. The immense peaks' rugged magnificence are truly suggestive of the Nordic deities after whom they are named. In this morning's sunshine, snow clung to many of the summits, and horizontal bands of white still striated rock cliffs that reared out of the higher regions of thickly forested slopes.

Yet the mountainsides were marked as well by wandering vertical ribbons of a lighter emerald than the conifers' deep green. These brighter tones revealed where deciduous trees followed an invisible creek bed or former avalanche chute.

We were nearing the middle of the lake. When I looked back toward the shrinking Silverton shore, I saw an osprey with its distinctive W-shaped wings gliding majestic as an eagle in the sunshine. The unvarying sound of the outboard and our apparent slow pace across the lake were mesmerizing. As my gaze caught Phil's eye where he sat with one hand on the motor's steering handle, he gave me a thumbs-up sign with the other hand. I gave him back the same *ain't-this-grand* signal, then rotated to peer ahead to try to spot the creek on the farther shore at whose mouth Phil had said we'd be fishing. I stuck my fingers in the icy water alongside for a moment to remind myself that this experience was real.

I noticed that to my right, a squadron of huge puffy white clouds had appeared in the distance above the north end of the lake. The aerial constructions seemed anchored in the sky, and I began to trip out on them, thinking how their fluffy massiveness constituted the essence of beauty on this gorgeous day. I sat captivated by how glorious a cloud-mountain can be.

Then I distinctly heard a voice: "Look up." The words seemed to be inside my head—while audible, they certainly weren't yelled by Phil over the loud drone of the engine.

"Look up," the voice demanded again a moment later. This time I thought I also detected in how the words were spoken a trace of light-heartedness, as though the command involved a joke.

Even so, a chill rose along the back of my neck. I knew I shouldn't be hearing voices. The boat bounced a little as we crossed the wake of a small runabout that had passed in front of us moments before. Phil had twisted to bend forward a little over the stern to study something on the lower part of the motor.

"Look *up*," the voice insisted a third time.

Instead, I kept my eyes fixed determinedly on the approaching shoreline. My hands gripped the gunwales as I tried to think how to deal with this disturbing situation.

After a few minutes during which nothing further happened, curiosity began to win out over my fear. Centimetre by centimetre I tilted my face upward.

"*WOW.*" The word sprang out of my throat before I could stop myself. A gigantic puff of white floated just over the boat, seeming only a couple of metres higher than our heads. The enormous white mass, every bit as lovely as the ones up the lake, was laughing at me.

"Beauty doesn't have to be admired only from afar," the cloud chortled. The voice was the one I had heard urging me to glance toward it. "Beauty is near, always. You only have to look."

I sensed a benevolence radiating from the luminous towering whiteness, mixed with a sense of fun. The planet loved me, and wanted me to delight in my life on it.

I had to share this discovery. Turning toward the steersman, I yelled, "Hey, Phil," pointing straight up.

His face tilted aloft for a second as he glanced at the cloud. "It won't rain," he shouted toward me.

"No, no," I yelled back over the noise of the outboard. "It's. Wonderful. Friendly!"

Phil's appeared puzzled for a moment—either he couldn't hear or thought maybe he'd misheard. He throttled the engine back, as the shore loomed nearer. "Pass me my tackle box, will you?" he said as we coasted toward a creek mouth on the waves of our own wake.

When I returned to Vancouver, I weighed and re-weighed alternative destinations. "Where have you been happy lately?" I asked myself. I recalled, too, the advice given me by Phil and Emma's cabin, and that of the cloud on Slocan Lake. Beauty might be everywhere, as the cloud had advised. But when, as the cabin insisted, I paid attention to my experiences in the West Kootenay, the area definitely emerged as the best choice for me.

How many places want you to live better? I thought. *Want to show you how to find beauty?* Even if, I reminded myself, to receive that guidance from the Kootenay sky, I had to be totally stoned.

Chapter Three

GARDENS AND A GRAVE

MY FIRST WEEK IN MY NEWLY ACQUIRED HOUSE, BEFORE
Bea had to return to her Vancouver job, felt as stuffed full as the box
of the rental truck when the morning after our arrival we swung its
doors wide to begin unpacking. Once we had gotten up that day, we
had retrieved from the Corolla a cooler, box of food and some pots,
fry-pan, cutlery and plates. We made breakfast, which we ate picnic-
style on the deck in the hot morning sunshine. After boiling water
on the stove for instant coffee, with mug in hand I checked out the
lawns around the house, trying to determine how best to position
the truck with no reverse gear so it could be unloaded.

I decided I could drive up the lawn to where it levelled off by the
deck stairs. By stopping close to the forest's edge, I judged I would
have enough room to swing the wheel sharply and let gravity roll
the truck backwards in a U-shaped path until the truck was pointed
more or less down the lawn, its back end facing the house. From
there we could haul the truck's contents to the deck stairs and into
the house. Since the truck would be aimed approximately downhill,
once the box was unloaded I could steer back to the driveway without needing reverse.

When I fired up the vehicle a few minutes later, however, I couldn't stop myself checking the gears one more time. Miraculously, unbelievably, reverse gear had been restored. Jubilant—although shaking my head at the capriciousness of machines—I piloted the truck through the open gate at the bottom of the south lawn and up to the house.

The next few hours were a blur of sweat as, with the help of a dolly we'd brought, we trundled, heaved and staggered under the weight of my boxes, bundles, washing machine, canoe, and more. Eventually a cleared space on the floor of the truck appeared, and little by little expanded. Toward noon we shifted to emptying the Corolla, then drove to eat lunch in the restaurant across the highway from the Winlaw convenience store. After the meal, we resumed unloading the truck. At last I stood in the slightly echoing empty truck box, sweeping the scuffed wooden floor boards with the new broom I had bought for the house.

That chore finished, Bea and I drove off in convoy for the Ryder office in Castlegar. We did a big grocery shopping at the Castlegar Safeway, and then I climbed behind the wheel of my car. For a few minutes, driving this low to the ground seemed abnormal, and the Toyota incredibly manoeuvrable.

The next days sped by with us picking our way between the slowly diminishing piles of boxes and gear strewn throughout the house. IKEA beds and tables got reassembled, and the kitchen made operational with sufficient household utensils and dishes unpacked to enable me to cook. Computer, a table and filing cabinet were arranged in the short part of the L-shaped living room, where I could anticipate returning to my writing.

Big windows in that nook looked west to lawn and forest, and north to lawn and a garden shed. Beyond the shed and past the closest neighbour's house—originally that of the couple whose divorce precipitated the building of my place—I could glimpse white horses grazing in a pasture. If, sitting in a chair at my keyboard,

I stared south across the living room and out the windows and slid-ing glass door, I observed at the bottom of the lawn seven immense trees clustered together. These giants on the southern edge of my property—spruce, fir, pine, and a trembling aspen—were easily twice as tall as their companions on either side, mainly cedar. I guessed that the seven were the size of trees here before the area was cleared by the first homesteaders. I dubbed the exceptional grove the Seven Sisters.

Green mountains, though, were the most striking feature out the windows in every direction but west. The master bedroom's large window was like an enormous viewing screen showing the valley's eastern ridges a couple of kilometres away. At the kitchen sink, I gazed south at more summits and ranges.

I soon became aware that the appearance of these slopes changed depending on different combinations of light and weather. Bluffs and gullies invisible under one set of atmospheric condi-tions stood out when different conditions prevailed. Time of day, cloud cover, or—as I was to discover—the seasonal disappearance of the deciduous trees' leaves and the larches' needles all affected the view.

Through the windows looking west, the ridge's evergreens over-looking the lawn were impressive in height, even if not as towering as the Seven Sisters. I was aware from maps that my woods in this direction merged seamlessly with Crown land higher up.

During our first days here, Bea noted that the row of south-fac-ing windows spanning kitchen and living room were all different sizes. Each window was framed with identical mouldings, and that detail, plus how their tops were the same distance from the ceil-ing, gave the illusion of regularity. "He must have built the house around the windows," Bea observed. I wouldn't learn until winter that this expanse of double-paned glass along the south wall, catch-ing the arc of the sun's daily travel, makes the house solar-passive, helping keep the interior toasty on sunny winter days.

Not that Bea and I spent all that week in the house. Besides indoor chores, we explored on foot the loop road that descends from the back road to run parallel to the river below my place. Strolling around the route took an hour or so—a pleasant afternoon break from unpacking and arranging. As on the back road, between the houses hayfields or untended meadows alternated with patches of forest. A spectrum of dwellings was evident, from small hand-made cottages to mobile homes to landscaped suburban-style two-storey houses. Fences confined horses, cows, chickens, geese, and/or goats, while other yards and fields held junked cars and pickups, or logging trucks, excavators, or skidders. Vegetable gardens were extensive. Driveways could be two ruts nearly hidden amid tall grass, or paved and lined with tidy flower beds. Vehicles in the driveways generally matched in appearance the level of maintenance of the house and grounds.

An astonishing number of wild apple trees grew along the gravel shoulders, the trees' fruit reddening in the August sun as Bea and I ambled by. Roadside bushes that Bea identified as saskatoons bore sweet black berries that we occasionally grazed on.

Bea and I also ventured farther afield. Twice we hoisted my new canoe onto the Corolla's roof racks and paddled once on the Slocan River and once on Slocan Lake. At the east end of the Bailey bridge near the Threads Guild, we found a short path leading down to a small river beach. A couple of women in bathing suits were keeping an eye on some five- and six-year-olds playing in the water as we carried the canoe down from the road and clambered aboard. The current was stronger than it looked from shore. But with both of us paddling hard, we slowly worked our way upstream. Around a bend of the river some distance from the bridge, the mouth of an oxbow opened to our left. A few more minutes of determined paddling took us out of the current. We drifted between two reedy banks.

After the exertion of our upstream voyage, to laze along the oxbow was bliss. Only an occasional stroke was required to keep us headed away from land. The water was alive with mallard ducks, and we spotted an eagle high on a cottonwood snag before it launched itself into air and flapped away upriver.

A deer and fawn materialized at the edge of the wooded island the oxbow had formed. The pair stared at us for a moment, then retreated into the undergrowth. To the west, a couple of house roofs were visible through the trees beyond the river bank, and in a field closer to the water, a herd of Black Angus cows stood motionless. We drifted nearer and saw where they had broken a muddy trail down to the oxbow's edge to drink. Farther north around the island, sheep were grazing in a fenced pasture. Swallows and pine siskins darted along the banks. All was silent except for bird calls, the lap of water against the canoe when we paddled a few strokes, and the occasional distant truck engine or motorcycle passing on the invisible highway to the east. A flicker briefly hammered at a dead cottonwood.

We swung toward the bank and climbed out of the canoe to sit and enjoy a snack of apple juice and trail mix we had brought. The bucolic scene seemed idyllic as we soaked up the sunshine in the peaceful afternoon.

To launch the craft on the lake, we drove north to the village of Slocan. The hum and clang of Slocan's large sawmill dominated the waterfront. Alongside the mill yard, however, a public sandy beach featured a log breakwater protecting a swimming area. The breakwater was anchored by tall clusters of pilings, from which kids leapt with excited shouts into the lake. A boat launch ramp was busy farther east, past an open extent of sand perfect for loading our gear into the canoe and pushing off.

I steered us north, paddling across where the Slocan River flows out of the lake, then keeping close to the west shore. This side of the lake, for much of its 40-kilometre length, is a provincial park. The current here was much less pronounced than on the river, and stroke by stroke we slowly passed by a shoreline of boulders intermixed with cedar, aspen, birch or cottonwood. The terrain reminded me of the forested edge of Lake Superior in Ontario, except that on both sides of Slocan Lake, mountains lift steeply. We could observe 3 kilometres away to the east a tiny vehicle following the highway high above the lake.

As we paddled, the clanking of the mill gradually diminished. After a half hour, I could hear, besides the occasional splash of our paddling, only the drone of a power boat speeding along, and several minutes later the waves of its wake striking the rocky shore beside us. An occasional creek burbled out of the wall of foliage to our left, often heard but not seen until we were directly opposite it.

Once when we were coasting above some huge rocks visible through the clear water, I was startled to hear voices nearby. We watched two hikers break out of the woods and cross a moss-covered promontory before vanishing into the trees again. I later learned that a trail winds from Slocan along the west shore of the lake for 8 kilometres. This day we didn't travel that far: an hour from Slocan, Bea and I pulled in at a pebbly beach to rest, eat lunch and enjoy the vista before paddling back again.

One morning we drove the 70 kilometres into Nelson. We did some shopping, ate lunch at a restaurant, and noted which stores along the main commercial thoroughfare, Baker Street, remained of the ones we remembered from when we had lived here seven years before. Baker Street storefronts were mostly occupied, but many commercial spaces along the side streets were empty, with "For Rent" or "For Lease" signs in their display windows.

During Bea's visit, however, we mostly were on the property—if not making the house operational, then out on the grounds discussing what I might do with them. Bea had infinitely more extensive knowledge concerning flower and vegetable growing than I did. In the years after we returned to Vancouver from Nelson in 1982, she had taken the course offered by the city's VanDusen Botanical Garden in order to become a certified master gardener. She had developed a flourishing West Coast garden in the backyard of our house in East Van, with vats of manure tea steeping to ensure that watering also fertilized the plants.

The garden there had always been her preserve, with me only assisting when asked. But I realized that since I was going to be in the country, I really should take up gardening. Bea answered dozens of questions I had for her. She had also brought along spare copies of gardening books that she left for me. Among the most useful was *Harrowsmith* magazine's *The Northern Gardener* by Jennifer Bennett. It proved to be the agricultural equivalent of my kitchen's *The Joy of Cooking*. Both volumes contained needed basic information—in the former case, what, when and where to plant and harvest, rather than how to prepare French toast or the correct way to stuff and roast a chicken.

On one of my viewings of the property before I bought it, the wife of the couple who owned it explained that her husband had spent the previous year improving the gardens. He had a new hospital administration job lined up on Vancouver Island—which was why they were selling—but had decided to take a year's break before assuming his new duties. The administrator had planted a small rose garden on the far side of the narrow lawn east of the house. Beside it, what looked like an unfinished artificial pond project had left a 2-foot-deep depression about 9 feet by 4 feet, carpeted with flattish stones. To the southeast, below the parking area, a concrete bird bath on the lawn was surrounded by a circular herb garden offering oregano, thyme, parsley and chives. Not far away, a bed bristled with drooping green stalks that Bea identified as peonies.

The administrator's skill as a gardener became evident the following May. A row of three ornamental broom shrubs he had planted along the west side of the upper portion of the driveway bloomed in sequence: the one farthest from the house bloomed first, followed in succession by the others. Each bush had different-coloured flowers, too: the first to bloom were pink, then the next bush produced yellow blossoms, and finally the third was covered in whitish-yellow flowers. Another delightful surprise for me that spring occurred when a stream of red tulips opened across the entire length of the raised-bed garden spanning the east end of the house.

This garden was one of three waist-high raised flower beds supported by 4 × 4 cribbing; the others were on either side of the door into the basement. Bea explained how such beds reduce the amount of stooping that tending a garden can require.

As we inspected the grounds, at Bea's suggestion I began to envision adding to what the administrator had started. For example, beside the gate that led from the parking area to the lawn south of the deck, a levelled area of gravelly soil could be transformed into— and years later was—a bed bursting each summer with annuals: petunias, nasturtiums, alyssums.

On the north boundary of the property, Bea and I discovered a row of seven fruit trees—apple, plum and pear—that ran from close to the house down almost to the road. A plum tree and cherry tree grew farther south near the road, and the former, along with another plum on the lawn east of the house, still bore tasty prune plums. One apple tree on the boundary and two other apple trees east of the house were heavily laden.

I was aware that the West Kootenay had been an important fruit-growing area before World War II, with jam canneries functioning throughout the region. After the war, improved refrigerated transport by rail and truck led to the demise of the local fruit industry. Orchardists in the Okanagan, Washington and California were able to benefit from having a larger population of customers nearby and more available land than is found in the comparatively narrow Kootenay valleys. I had never imagined, though, that I would have such a bounty of fresh fruit mere steps from my front door.

A shaggy meadow extended eastward from the eastern lawn to a dilapidated barbed-wire fence along the road. Near the northern edge of this meadow, a square of exposed soil about 6 metres by 6 metres had been a vegetable garden, now full of weeds. The wife of the selling couple had explained apologetically to me that because they knew they'd be moving, they had not planted vegetables this year. She rattled off the crops they'd enjoyed other years. A row of raspberry bushes supported on wires alongside the former garden was loaded with berries.

Bea offered a list of veggies that she felt a neophyte gardener like myself should be able to grow successfully: peas, lettuces, onions, sweet corn, potatoes, squash, carrots. The following spring, those were the seeds I carefully placed in the soil, according to the advice on each seed packet, checked against the vegetable's listing in *The Northern Gardener*.

The eastern lawn sloped gently down from the unfinished water feature toward where the meadow started. At the southern end of the lawn was a mysterious cement-bordered rectangle measuring 5 feet by 14 feet. Rusted threaded bolts, hammered flat, protruded from the 5-inch-wide cement perimeter in a number of places. The bolts indicated that the structure once had been the foundation of a wooden-framed building, with the structure's bottom sills bolted to the cement.

Yet who would construct so elaborate a foundation for a building with such a small footprint? The space the concrete borders enclosed was small for even a chicken coop, and most such coops in the valley are rickety objects, hardly requiring so sturdy a foundation.

Whatever the rectangle's original purpose, the previous owners had adapted it to serve as a flower bed: a beautiful display of pansies, zinnias, snapdragons, gladioluses. What struck me as Bea and I stood admiring the flowers was that the space the borders encompass has the dimensions of a large grave. Now that the property was mine, I knew what was buried within. I designated the spot the Grave of Literary Ambition.

In an essay, "Sitting by the Grave of Literary Ambition," published in my 1993 collection of essays, *A Country Not Considered: Canada, Culture, Work*, I describe how part of my decision to remove myself from Vancouver had to do with feeling that my ambitions for writing and publishing had reached a dead end. Halfway through my forties, I had to admit that, unlike when I began to write, poetry had come to be regarded by most people as an insignificant and irrelevant art form. My recognition of the newly debased status of the art necessitated a reassessment of the expectations I had long held for my poems. A change of habitat to the Kootenays, I thought, would underline my need to reconceive what I believed my poetry could accomplish.

When I began to focus on studying and crafting poetry in the mid-1960s, poems were deemed vital cultural artifacts. In the US, where I went for graduate studies, poems featured in virtually every Sixties-era underground newspaper, whether the verses were well written, terminally strident or indifferent in quality. Publications of the anti-Vietnam War, anti-draft, and anti-imperialist movements, with which I became involved, also included poems as a mainstay, as did publications of the burgeoning feminist movement. In Canada, during the late 1960s and early 1970s Canadian nationalism was in the ascendant, and consequently the literary productions of the country's poets were considered important. The country, for an exhilarating period, acted as though determined to shake off its function as an economic and cultural colony of the US, as it shifted from its former status as an economic and cultural colony of England. New books by poets Earle Birney, Dorothy Livesay, Irving Layton, Gwendolyn MacEwan, F.R. Scott, and others were judged to be worth significant media coverage and even TV appearances.

As the years rolled on, however, and mass participation in protests and social change organizations declined with the end of the Vietnam War and the burn-out of anti-establishment activists, poetry became regarded as less and less important as a repository of significant social thought. As well, in Canada the powers-that-be decided to endorse "free trade"—what we now term "globalism"—instead of encouraging the development of self-reliant Canadian industries. Abruptly, Canadian nationalism, including the promotion of Canadian literature, was deemed a bad idea. The academy embraced a different role for poetry than nation-building.

By the time I purchased my property in the Slocan Valley, I had to acknowledge that poetry as an art form was no longer a valued part of struggles to improve our common daily existence or to develop a national culture. In the "Sitting by the Grave" essay I speak about how my literary ambitions had

> included the intent to help create a wider audience for poetry. I felt that clear speaking about everyday life, combined with humour, could regain an audience lost to poetry—lost because of the use of poetry as an instrument of torture in mass public education, and because of the accompanying academic attitude that regards the poet as a member of an artistic elite speaking to select individuals initiated into esoteric mysteries.

Since I view daily work as the central and governing experience of most people's lives, my intention was to help reinvigorate an audience for poetry by writing, and encouraging others to write, an accurate insider's poetic examination of the effects of our employment on our lives both at and away from the job. As I've described in various essays, the ways our daily work shapes our existence has long been a taboo subject in all the arts, despite how for the majority of Canadians our employment determines or strongly influences our standard of living, where we live, how much time and energy we have each day after work, who our friends are, our attitudes toward a vast array of fraught subjects, from ecology to immigration and much more. The arts may claim to tell humanity's story. But most anthologies of Canadian literature, to give one example, offer a portrait of a country in which nobody works.

In addition to the social goals I expected my writing to champion, I had relied on my poems to provide me with self-validation. My accomplishments as a writer meant that I had worth as a human being. Even if other aspects of my life—my intimate relationship, for one—were unresolved or in tatters, publication of individual poems and essays, as well as books, assured me I was functioning satisfactorily. Ambition for literary achievement—for instance, positive reviews, invitations to lecture or read, recognition as a person of cultural importance—could always be framed as providing a way to acquaint as large an audience as possible with my artistic and social ideas.

"Such ambitions for my writing," the essay on the Grave states, "were supposed to justify the behaviours I had adopted in order to realize these goals. The ends, then, were to justify the means." Yet after more than 20 years of intense effort, and lots of literary success, I had to accept that the social and personal ambitions for my writing were unlikely to be attained.

Naming the flower bed the Grave of Literary Ambition helped me internalize this reality. Within a couple of months, I found a suitable small rock for a tombstone and had an epitaph engraved into a plaque affixed to the stone: "R.I.P. Literary Ambition 1966–89." The first date was that of my enrollment in graduate school to study creative writing. The second date marked my purchase of the property.

I have kept the Grave as a flower bed. Yet, as I explain in the essay about it, "the burial of these ambitions in this place does not mean I have abandoned writing" nor my vision of poetry's potential social purpose. "Rather, I am trying now to pay attention to a more accurate sense of what my art can achieve."

At the Grave, or anywhere else Bea and I walked on the grounds, I noticed that almost all the lower portion of my acreage was visible from the road or from the house to the north. The Seven Sisters provided some concealment from the south. But between those trees and the road, nothing impeded anyone's view. I realized I desired a little more privacy.

My wish for grounds less open to viewing by neighbours or passers-by obviously had been shared in at least in one spot by the couple from whom I had bought the property. They had erected an 8-foot-high, 40-foot-long freestanding wooden wall north of the unfinished water feature and a nearby firepit and picnic table. My real estate agent had referred to the wooden construction as a "privacy fence." It blocked the line of sight from Lynn's porch, shielding any activities around the firepit.

I wasn't sure if my discomfort at feeling so visible had a psychological basis, in that I intended to wrestle with an important personal problem while I lived here. Or if my wish for more concealment had something to do with how I believe writing is private until it's been rewritten repeatedly into a state suitable to be shown to readers. Or possibly the trees remaining around the lower part of the property, and the forested ridge to the west, just brought back good memories of attending woodsy Boy Scout camps as a kid. I liked the idea of occupying a house in the forest, as if living at summer camp all year long.

When I commented to Bea about wishing the lower part of my acreage was screened by additional trees, she outlined to me the landscaping concept of "rooms." In this model, an open area is surrounded with "walls" of trees, so the middle of the "room" still receives lots of sunlight while the trees provide a sense of separation from the rest of the world.

I found the idea intriguing, and on a trip to Nelson, we stopped in at a large plant nursery, Georama, west of town. Two- and 3-foot-high firs, pines, and spruces were cheap, and I purchased five to launch the project of creating outdoor rooms. The first tree Bea and I planted was a slow-growing Colorado Spruce just north of the driveway. I spaced three of the other little trees along the northern edge of the property, since screening myself from the closest house seemed a priority. The fifth went alongside the driveway's south side. The tree-planting project continues to this day.

In digging holes to establish a home for the first baby evergreens, I learned the property is underlain by two different types of soil. If I was lucky, my shovel sank into sandy loam, and a hole the proper size to insert a small tree's root ball involved only a few minutes' effort. Alternatively, my shovel encountered ground consisting more of pebbles and rocks than earth. Many minutes of hard work yielded a hole only a few inches deep. Evacuating to a suitable depth was a slow process.

The two contrasting kinds of soil are unpredictable as to location and can exist mere inches from each other. Ten years after I began planting a dozen or so trees each spring, I learned why.

In 1999, a young geologist visited my property. He was employed by a roundtable initiated by the BC forests ministry, which brought together representatives of groups variously concerned about—or eager to begin—logging on Perry Ridge. The geologist was assessing slope stability to determine if logging high above our properties on Crown land might precipitate major landslips, flooding, or other disasters.

I had followed the formation of the roundtable with interest in the bi-weekly valley tabloid, the *Valley Voice*. The roundtable seated representatives of corporate and independent loggers, woodlot operators, valley-based businesses owners, environmentalists and water licence holders. The venture had also attracted some of the more reality-challenged Winlaw residents. One man had shown up to a roundtable meeting claiming to represent the ridge's bears. He pointed out that the bruins hitherto had not had a person at the table to speak on their behalf. The forests ministry official who chaired the meetings was unfazed, according to the *Valley Voice*'s account. The chairman said he would be glad for the roundtable to hear the bears' viewpoint, and that their spokesman would be welcome to participate as soon as he produced—as the others present had been required to provide—the minutes of a meeting of the group he represented that included a motion naming him their official delegate to the roundtable.

As I accompanied my young visitor up into my woods, he informed me the valley had been the location of a lake at the end of the previous Ice Age. The various benches—flattish areas—at descending levels on my property indicated successive lakeshores as the glacier-melt lake over time dwindled to become the Slocan River. He explained that the differing areas of sandy soil and pebbly soil on my property had been former beach and lake bottom, respectively.

The young geologist was also able to point to where in the forest small landslips had occurred on some steeper slopes leading from one bench down to the next. This discovery was a bit disconcerting, although in the end the instability of the terrain meant that no logging would occur above my property. The stretch between the creek to the south of me, Richards Creek, and to the north of me, Jerome Creek, was removed from consideration for being clear-cut.

The foot-long scrapes in the earth that ended with small piles of rocks and other debris were not the most alarming facet of the geologist's tour of my woods, however. When he appeared, he wore a backpack that contained a very young baby. He explained that he was on child-minding duty that day and hoped I wouldn't object if the baby accompanied us as we examined my land. The child tended to sleep while in the backpack, he assured me.

Once engaged in studying the soils and landforms up in the forest, the geologist would become transfixed by something on the ground: a species of mushroom, an animal track, or soil horizons that had been revealed where a giant fir had been blown over. Absorbed in what had caught his eye, the young man would abruptly bend far forward to study it more closely. Each time he did, the baby would be propelled by her father's motion nearly out of the backpack. I was terrified the child would be hurtled free of her carrier to land head-first on a log or a cluster of rocks we stood among. Again and again, the geologist would angle down to examine some object. And repeatedly, at the last possible second, he would straighten up and the baby would drop back to safety. Her father seemed unaware of how narrowly his child avoided death or serious injury.

Whenever the father said, "Hey, check this out," and started to lean forward, I would lunge toward him to try to intercept the human projectile. But after several of these manoeuvres by the geologist, I learned to restrain my impulse to save the baby. I was always uneasy, though, whenever the young man showed signs of being captivated by anything at his feet.

Whatever the geologic origins of soil composition on my property, 30 years after I learned about Bea's concept of "rooms," a double row of mixed evergreens now forms a high wall along the north boundary. Another line of evergreens stretches across the width of the property beside the road, and thick stands also line the south boundary.

A couple of clump birch already were growing east of the never-finished water feature. I planted a row of birch, incorporating the existing pair, that extends south–north across the property as an extra summertime screen between the road and house. The part of the property where I live and garden has the feel these days of a habitation enveloped on all sides by forest. As Bea predicted, the sun pours into the centre of a "room" no matter how dense the arboreal "walls" have become.

My annual spring tree-planting activities didn't go unnoticed. After six years, the wife of the older German couple, the Heinks, who lived across and a little way up the road from me, said: "No matter how many trees you plant, Tom, we know you're in there."

As the cost of trees for my annual planting session increased over the years, I tried transplanting ones from my woods. Yet upslope from the house the soil tends to be more uniformly stony and pebbly. Despite my best efforts to extract a big enough root ball from the mass of rocks and earth, only about 10 to 20 per cent of my transplanted trees ever survived, compared to 90 per cent or so of nursery-bought stock. At some juncture, I stopped trying to transplant.

Then a nursery opened only a few kilometres to the north up the back road, calling itself Trees Company. I was overjoyed to think I had a nearby source of trees to plant, and I was also pleased that Trees Company's prices were lower than Georama's.

I quickly learned, however, that the local enterprise's trees advertised for sale were a cover for mainly selling supplies for then-illegal marijuana cultivation. The staff at the business seemed to know little about the large field of trees—in pots or temporarily placed in the earth in rows—behind a building that offered lights, fertilizer, timers, and other paraphernalia useful to indoor and outdoor dope producers. When I stated my wish to buy a certain species, a Doug fir, say, whoever was behind the till would call for the one employee knowledgeable about where on the lot these trees might be found, and what the prices were.

Each year less and less effort was put into even pretending to sell trees, so I took home some real bargains. Then, one April, my inquiry at the till was met by a blank look from the salesperson. "Trees?" he asked.

I pointed silently to the name of the company on a plaque hanging nearby.

"Oh. Yeah. Trees. Uh, I don`t think we sell those anymore."

I returned to patronizing Georama, or another local nursery with trees for sale, Four Seasons Greenhouse, a few kilometres south of the Winlaw Bridge on the back road.

Besides planting evergreens and birches, I decided that no grave is complete without a nearby weeping willow. So I acquired a 4-foot one from Georama and planted it about 15 feet from the Grave of Literary Ambition. Enormous and weepy after three decades, the willow is the perfect complement to the Grave.

In April now, as soon as the deciduous trees on the property leaf out, my house can't be seen from the road. It's also hidden all year from an observer to the south, and the house to the north can scarcely be glimpsed through my trees. Within a few years, my house will be completely hidden in every season by the walls of Bea's rooms.

Growth creates its own problems, however. The double row of evergreens I planted along the north boundary grew to a height to shadow the neighbour's garden, so those trees must be topped every few years. The two rows have also shadowed out the line of original apple and plum trees between them. As the fruit trees died one by one from lack of light, I planted replacements across the lower lawn to develop a new orchard.

In the fall, the dim corridor between the two rows of spruce, fir, hemlock and pine provides a haven for bears. Where the line of conifers ends near the road, two original pear trees sag with fruit in late August and September. About that time, black bears begin roaming the valley floor in search of anything edible to fatten themselves up for winter hibernation. Most years one furry individual sets up camp by my pear trees and is frequently spotted between the rows of evergreens. A sign now proclaims the alley between those rows is "The Bearway." The name is a joke much of the year, but not so funny if I'm crossing the area in the blackness of a fall night while headed home from a visit to the neighbours.

As for names, Bea was the one who suggested the name for my property. Like me, she was raised on the stories and poems of A.A. Milne (1882–1956), the creator of Winnie the Pooh. She recalled that in Milne's collection of poems for children *Now We Are Six*, a poem entitled "The Knight Whose Armour Didn't Squeak" concerned a knight called Sir Thomas Tom. The poem relates how Sir Thomas's "castle (Castle Tom) was set / Conveniently upon a hill", just how my house is sited toward the bottom of the ridge looking down on the road, which is, in turn, above the river.

The poem begins: "Of all the Knights in Appledore / The wisest was Sir Thomas Tom." The portion of Winlaw where I live is, in fact, referred to as Apple*dale*. For example, the loop road below me between the back road and the river is called Appledale Lower Road. Thus, designating my place as Apple*dore*, as Bea suggested, seemed fitting—a nod both to a humorous poem from childhood and to the local name for where I was about to live. A few years later I installed, partway up the drive, a sign one of the professional signage companies in Nelson created for me: *Welcome to Appledore.* Afterwards, seeing the name each time I drove past helped make the designation feel official.

Chapter Four

TASK LISTS AND A BARBARIAN REFRIGERATOR

RELATIONS WITH BEA HAD BEEN SMOOTH ALL THROUGH the busyness of the move. Distracted by the discoveries and challenges of a new house in a new environment, I could mostly put off thinking about us being apart. But when, after our goodbye hugs and kisses, Bea walked through Security onto the plane at Castlegar, the challenge of my new life dropped onto me like a heavy backpack.

Alone back at the house for the first time, I was aware of the enormity of the shift I had enacted in my life, in our lives. Suddenly I would be living by myself after a decade and a half as part of a couple. I was far from my former daily routines in Vancouver, and my support systems of activities, friends, resources. Plus, I now lived in the country.

I knew that the one pressing task I had to confront was to assess the past and future of our relationship. Everywhere I looked at Appledore, though, I saw chores needing to be attended to. None were major, but they were numerous. I dove into these tasks, since they offered a diversion from having to sort through the jumble of my feelings. And from time, that in my new existence often seemed frighteningly empty.

My days had formerly been structured around Bea's activities and ideas, as well as my own. Now, with Bea in Vancouver, who cared how my waking hours were organized, what I did or didn't accomplish? When moments of doubt about the wisdom of my being alone at Appledore struck, I would sit down on one of my new kitchen chairs and force myself to review why I was here. Repeatedly in the weeks ahead, I followed this anxiety-reducing procedure.

For the rest of August, all of September, and into October, the balance of my day once I finished my morning's work at the computer keyboard was shaped by all that needed to be done to feel settled into my new place. Room by room I arranged possessions and hung pictures. The smaller of the two bedrooms became the temporary catch-all for unassigned boxes, stray items, and my tools until I was ready to tackle the basement. I named this cluttered bedroom the Blue Room, after its dark-blue walls and rug. When I at last carried the remaining objects and my tools down to the basement to join the pile of empty boxes and my camping gear already resting on the cement floor, I assembled an extra IKEA bed in the Blue Room and walked a somewhat-battered chest of drawers into it. I then declared it the guest room.

Each afternoon I worked at the minor repairs and adjustments any house requires before it satisfies a new occupier. Faucet washers needed replacement, and I wanted to change some light-switch covers so their colour matched that of the walls. In the bathroom, baseboards needed caulking, and in the kitchen and living room scuffed and stained wooden window ledges cried out to be sanded and restained.

I cleaned cupboards, shelves, and the refrigerator and stove. As I prepared meals, I saw where I needed to buy and install cup hooks, towel racks, and an under-the-cupboard light so I wasn't working in my own shadow at the kitchen counter. The master bedroom was missing the bifold door on its closet, which, like the new counter light, had to be bought in Nelson and installed.

My go-to source of advice in this flurry of work was Better Homes and Gardens' *Complete Guide to Home Repair, Maintenance and Improvement*, an inch-and-a-half thick manual I'd had the foresight to purchase before leaving Vancouver. The book divides how a house functions into its systems: electrical, plumbing, roof, and so on. In clear language and usually relevant illustrations, the guide shows the steps to unscrew, pry apart, examine, identify, replace, or repair just about every component of every system. For instance, I spent nearly four hours upside down under the kitchen sink one August Wednesday afternoon trying to tighten the faucet fixture, which shifted in place each time the taps were vigorously opened or closed. I used a recently purchased basin wrench—a tool unknown to me before studying the relevant pages in the *Complete Guide.*

My other source of vital information about "repair, maintenance and improvement" was a friend, David Everest, who lived with his family about 40 kilometres up Kootenay Lake from Nelson toward Kaslo. I had met David and his partner, Judy Wapp, in 1971, when they had travelled to BC from Toronto accompanied by Judy's two young kids from a previous marriage. They had been part of a hippie caravan looking for land on the West Coast and en route had passed through the West Kootenay. When David and Judy discovered that the sum they had saved to buy land was too small for coastal prices, they remembered they had liked the West Kootenay and retraced their steps to here.

Our connection was a mutual acquaintance, someone I had known in the anti-Vietnam War movement during my stint teaching at Colorado State University in 1968–69. This person had managed to get himself on the FBI's 10-Most-Wanted list, charged with sabotage because of some acts in Colorado in opposition to the war machine involving dynamite. He was currently hiding out in Toronto and had given David and Judy my co-ordinates for when they visited Vancouver. I met the couple in a downtown pub so they could pass on news of the fugitive. The three of us found we had a lot in common and have stayed friends ever since.

David can build and fix anything, as I learned during much interaction with him, Judy and their two kids during the two years Bea and I had lived near Nelson while I taught at David Thompson University Centre. A large, tall man, David is usually silent. When he does speak on a topic, he offers a well-considered response I always find astute. Whenever I phoned him regarding a problem with my new home, the line would go dead for several seconds while he weighed his answer. Next a series of questions would be posed, questions that themselves occasionally helped me determine a solution to my query without further input from him. Once he was sure he thoroughly grasped what I was inquiring about, he would tactfully suggest a way forward, most often using his own experiences as a point of reference.

The help was invaluable, and not just in my first months at Appledore. As just one example, several springs after moving in I had to change a defective gate valve on the irrigation system that served both my gardens and those of the property to the north. When the ex-husband built the house I bought, he had simply extended the existing irrigation line. As a result, the shut-off valve for my irrigation line was on the property next door. Every winter the system had to be closed down and drained, and each spring reactivated. Thus the shut-off valve received a lot of use and now would not open.

At the time of the repair, I knew no way of halting the water flow through the pipe that brought water to our properties from Jerome Creek, swollen with snowmelt as always in spring. Since the irrigation shut-off valve had failed to budge despite my best efforts, it would have to be removed and a new valve installed while a high-pressure cascade of water poured out of the pipe. The original occupant of the house to the north, the ex-wife, by this time had sold and moved away. The new owner was a single mom—also named Lynne, although with an "e"—unable to help with water line repairs. If we wanted to be able to irrigate our gardens that summer, I'd have to fix this myself. Local plumbers would solve water issues inside a dwelling, but nobody could be hired to deal with irrigation piping problems.

By now I was used to David's thoughtful series of questions and tried to anticipate what I'd need to do to successfully complete the repair. A considerable volume of water would be released once the jammed valve was removed. Consequently, although the irrigation line is buried about 4 feet down, I dug a fairly large pit around where the valve is located. That way the water would not quickly fill a smaller space in which I'd be standing while completing the repair. Extending the hole meant much extra work, but I could imagine the alternative: fumbling to attach the new valve while water poured over my boots and climbed my pant legs.

Experience had already taught me that I would need to apply heat to expand the PVC plastic water pipe. The heat would expand the pipe's diameter enough to allow the old valve to slip more easily out of, and the new valve to slip more easily into, the pipe. So I located my propane torch, remembered matches, and lined up hose clamps, screwdriver and crescent wrench. In case something went terribly wrong after I removed the old valve, I prepared a chunk of wood to hammer into the pipe-end that would be gushing water. Failure to stop that flow would mean water pressure in the houses would drop to zero, since a "Y" in the pipe just upstream of the dysfunctional valve directed water either into the irrigation line or to our homes.

When I phoned David the night before the repair, he listened to all my preparations. After a few moments digesting my description of what I intended to do, he cautioned me to be extra careful heating the poly pipe. If I burned a hole, I'd have to cut it out of the pipe, possibly making the gap between the pipe-ends, where the removed valve had been situated, too large for the replacement valve to bridge.

He also said: "Install the new valve in the open position." The latter wasn't something I'd thought of. In fact, my idea had been to first attach the valve in closed position so it would block the flow of water while I hooked up the downstream pipe-end to the valve. David's suggestion was to close the valve only after it was installed in the upstream pipe-end.

The value of his advice became clear during the frightening moment when I had wrestled the old valve off, and water was racing noisily out of the pipe into the hole around my feet more rapidly than I thought possible. I stood ankle-deep, then shin-deep, in ice-cold water as I desperately tried to jam the new valve into the just-heated pipe-end. Despite my efforts with the torch, the resistance of the pipe to accepting the new valve's metal flange was considerable. If at the same time as trying to push the valve into the pipe, I'd been pushing against the pressure of water battering against the valve's closed gate, I likely wouldn't have had the strength to wrestle the device into place.

As it was, I did manage to work the valve into the pipe, secure it with two hose clamps, and then close the valve, choking off the roaring flow. Suffused with adrenalin and with clothes completely sodden, I waded in the sudden silence to the edge of the hole I'd dug and sat perched on the lip for several minutes to catch my breath. I recognized that David's suggestion had averted what would likely have been a catastrophe.

This valve replacement was years in the future, however, as one by one I dealt with the settling-in chores. As I did, I was learning that undertaking such tasks in the country is different than starting on them in the city. If a screwdriver broke while I was installing a new lock for the basement door, I couldn't—as in my previous urban experience—just head out to the corner hardware store for another one. Instead, "screwdriver" got added to an already lengthy list where I had scribbled down every size of screw, plumbing part, or longer extension cord I needed to purchase on my next trip to town. Meanwhile, the basement lock replacement had to be put aside.

For the first time, I began to understand why so many country houses I had visited were unfinished: a boarded-up door on the side of a house below which stairs were intended to be built, or a row of studs inside instead of a gyprocked and painted wall. If a single component needed to accomplish a country task is mislaid, unavailable in town, or can't be borrowed from a neighbour, the entire project grinds to a halt. Sometimes indefinitely.

Country or city, though, the settling-in process requires a constant outflow of dollars to complete. Because this house was the first I had owned, I strove for perfection, aiming to correct every discernible blemish.

Some improvements defeated me. A wall-socket cover plate in the kitchen was missing one of three screws that secured it. When I tried to remedy this absence, I discovered that the hole in the socket receptacle below the cover plate would not accept the standard screw. I purchased a new socket receptacle and wired it in. All three screws now could be attached—except, once all three were in place, nothing plugged into the socket worked. Obviously the replacement socket receptacle was faulty; on my next trip to Nelson I bought another. Once it was installed, the same result occurred: a perfectly affixed cover plate but no electricity.

To test whether the fault lay in my wiring abilities, I reinstalled the original socket receptacle. Everything worked perfectly, except of course for the faulty screw hole. I stared at the thing for a long while, then left it as I had found it.

Meanwhile, the costs involved in steadily making small repairs and improvements began to be a worry. A children's story read to me when I was young centred on a magical hat: whenever the owner doffed his hat, a different one appeared underneath. And below that one would be yet another one. My list of tasks possessed an identical reproductive capacity. Unlike the owner of the magical hat, though, I had to pay and pay for what successively was revealed.

My monthly cheques to my parents for what I owed on the property were well within my UI stipend. And from my years as a renter, I had been conscious that establishing a new place to live is always more expensive than anticipated. So I had borrowed enough, I had thought, to cover unexpected costs. Yet my bank balance was rapidly draining away into the tills of the hardware stores and builders' supply yards in Nelson. A couple of writing grant applications I had made earlier had been rejected. And since any colleges in the BC Interior at which I might resume teaching wouldn't be advertising available positions until the spring, I was relieved when, well into October, the constant withdrawals from my bank account began to ease in frequency and amount.

Before then, however, I decided certain improvements were beyond my ability to attempt. For some plumbing matters, for instance, I forsook the *Complete Guide to Home Repair, Maintenance and Improvement* in favour of calling the valley's foremost plumber, Wolfgang Teiner. Despite my earlier adventures with the basin wrench, I resolved in October to replace the kitchen faucet due to multiple issues that afflicted it. I contacted Wolfgang even though the *Complete Guide* had detailed instructions how to remove the old device and install the new. I'd been intrigued by Wolfgang's irreverent company logo displayed in his ad in the *Valley Voice*: a naked person seated grinning on a toilet.

Wolfgang turned out to be an energetic giant of a man, with firm opinions on every subject, from the superiority of the German plumbing apprenticeship system over the BC one—right down to how many turns of white thread-seal tape is optimum—to the contradictory nature of certain Biblical passages. A mainstay of the Winlaw volunteer fire department, he had horrific tales of car wrecks, a consequence of the fire department's role as first responders to vehicle accidents. In the midst of replacing a frost-free outdoor faucet I'd noticed had begun dripping, he related in his slight German accent a harrowing account of the Winlaw fire volunteers struggling to extract a driver's body from the crushed cab of a pickup at the bottom of an embankment. On the road above, the dead man's girlfriend, alerted to the tragedy, had to be restrained as she shrieked and howled.

Plumbing mistakes committed by people who had built their own house were another focus of Wolfgang's conversation. He had strong ideas concerning health issues, too. Once, years after I had gotten to know him, I happened to mention while he was at work at my place that I had started following a low-fat diet to reduce my cholesterol count.

"Have you ever wondered why pigs don't have heart attacks?" Wolfgang asked, straightening up from installing a porcelain basement sink to replace the badly stained plastic one that had come with the house. He explained that in Germany pigs are fed a certain chemical which reduces the chance of clogged arteries while being intentionally fattened. He said he imported the substance and ate some each day.

When I asked why an obviously fit and active individual like him would worry about heart disease, to my astonishment he tore open his shirt and revealed a zipper scar extending from navel to sternum. He'd had a triple bypass, he said. A couple of times a week, he travelled to the public aquatic centre in Castlegar for a swim in order to stay in shape.

I phoned other experts as well to solve household problems I concluded I couldn't. I had vowed before I bought Appledore that if I ever purchased a house it would not have either permanently attached Christmas lights or a dishwasher. Both to me spoke of a stereotypical suburban existence. But my new house came not only with strings of the little coloured lights nailed all around the deck, but also a roll-out dishwasher.

The removal of the Christmas lights from the deck railings was high on my list of chores after moving in. I had briefly thought of refusing to accept the dishwasher when it was offered by the previous owners as part of the appliance package that included fridge and stove. But the asking price for the package was so low, I thought refusing the dishwasher would seem churlish, if not pretentious.

At Appledore, my preferred choice of washing dishes by hand proved especially agreeable since at the kitchen sink I could savour the view of my trees and lawns, and the ever-changing mountains. Yet since the dishwasher was present, why not use it occasionally? At my third attempt to turn it on, though, it refused to co-operate. I removed the back panel and gazed at the twisted maze of wires. Conceding defeat, I phoned a Nelson electrical repair shop that made house calls this far out of town.

By the time the repairman appeared, I had almost forgotten my request for help. Repairs in the valley by Nelson- or Castlegar-based firms occur at that unpredictable moment when the company decides enough valley business has been lined up to justify the dispatch of a truck this far out of town. Meanwhile, long hours of being on the place by myself had left me used to solitude. The sudden appearance of a van ascending my drive disconcerted me for a few seconds, until I realized who was finally showing up.

The repair guy, after declining coffee or a beer, unceremoniously tipped the dishwasher on its back to reveal the electric motor under the appliance. Even I could see that a wire leading to the motor had corroded and parted. An instant later the dishwasher was back in service. I felt foolish, because ever since taking mandatory electrical shop in Grade 7, I've been pretty good at stripping two wires and splicing them together. Eight months in 1973 employed as an assemblyman at Canadian Kenworth's Burnaby truck plant had involved, among other chores, installing headlights into fibreglass truck hood shells. I should have been able to return the dishwasher to service.

The refrigerator, at least, performed flawlessly at first. The appliance was in size somewhere between a bar fridge and a regular household fridge. Although I hadn't noticed its diminutive dimensions until I moved in, the fridge certainly proved large enough for my needs.

Later in the fall, however, the appliance underwent a personality change that involved delusions of grandeur. Perhaps it had been brooding for years about its short stature. Or more likely the fridge had peered over the former owners' shoulders as they watched a late-night TV presentation of the 1982 *Conan the Barbarian* movie starring Arnold Schwarzenegger. In any event, the appliance suddenly decided it was now Conan the Refrigerator.

I was alerted to this new incarnation of the appliance after being wakened one November night by clanging and banging from the kitchen: the sound of a sword repeatedly clashing against a shield in an attempt to intimidate an enemy. Subsequently I realized that whenever Conan shut himself off now, he liked to launch a demonstration of his anachronistic martial prowess. This warlike posing was faintly amusing in the daytime, but after being yanked from sleep once too often, I decided to have Conan's weapon taken away from him.

A second visit by the Nelson electrical repairman led to a new compressor being prescribed. The fridge was ancient enough that it took the Nelson firm a while to locate the proper compressor, but eventually Conan resumed his former identity as a well-behaved economy-size refrigerator. He kept his old name, however. And after his unexpected bout of what has come to be termed cosplay, I could never quite trust him not to again assume his former bellicose persona.

One problem I could not eradicate in the new house consisted of a swag hook infestation. An artifact from the era in which the dwelling was built, Appledore's swag hooks are devices designed to let people drape something artistically: the excess portion of a chain that suspends a lamp, say. Like many exotic species introduced into an environment, the hooks—found in various sizes—multiplied unexpectedly throughout home interiors, holding up not only festoons of lamp chain, but also planters, knick-knack shelving, and anything else that needed to be hung.

Viewed up close, a swag hook is stunning in its ugliness. The visible portion vaguely resembles an elephant's trunk curved upwards in a sort of salute to form the hook. The surface of the curved portion has a ribbed or corduroy surface extending laterally, and at either end an attempt at rococo detailing. Where the swag hook emerges from ceiling or wall, bulges and indentations vaguely resembling leaves create what would be the elephant's head, and a pathetic curlicue at the end of the trunk completes the gesture toward ornamentation.

What belief system could possibly have been behind such striving to debase the honest functionality of a simple hook? At Appledore, swag hooks had proliferated until they had established themselves in nearly every room, attaching themselves to walls as well as ceilings. As with knapweed, Eurasian milfoil, or other mistakenly or accidentally introduced invasive species, the swag hook has proven difficult to eliminate entirely. In my house, after a couple of attempts to dislodge the pests, each time involving subsequent application of Polyfilla to repair the damage to drywall, I admitted defeat.

Yet, despite the effort and expense that settling into Appledore involved, I remained charmed by the place. I loved working in the study I established in the short portion of the living room's "L." When I lifted my eyes from the desk or computer monitor, the views through the windows were enchanting. If the sliding glass door to the deck was open, I could hear through the screen a squirrel chittering as it gathered hazelnuts from one of the nearby trees, or the patter of paws as it dashed across the deck on one of its ceaseless getting-ready-for-winter missions. A cheerful clinking sound originated from a wind chime the previous owner had left suspended from the deck's soffits.

Late on August and September afternoons, I'd return indoors either because I was suddenly weary from cutting grass or completing another garden chore, or because a rainstorm threatened. I'd stretch out on the living-room couch while fresh air eddied in the sliding door. Through the west window, I could watch the tops of the tall evergreens at the forest edge sway in a breeze, their limbs' motions deliberate and grave. I would drift into sleep, lulled by the wind chime or the soft thudding of a downpour falling on the roof.

Before heading for bed in the evenings, I fell into the practice of stepping onto the deck to say goodnight to the mountains and nearby woods. Darkness fell earlier and earlier as August shifted into September, which meant that, any clear night, innumerable stars high overhead spanned the valley from ridge to ridge. Amid the constellations, the Milky Way formed a river of tiny celestial lights flowing from the southwest to northeast above me.

When I woke deep in the night, I often climbed out of bed and wandered through the house, gazing out my windows into the blackness. Looking east from the kitchen, I saw only a few scattered lights visible below the looming bulk of the mountains. Sometimes, late in September, a glowing moon illuminated a river of autumn mist that formed along the valley bottom atop the river of water. Once in October I caught a full Kootenay moon just appearing over the eastern valley wall. Trees along the top of that ridge were silhouetted for a few moments against the blazing white light of the lifting moon.

At night, a sense of deep well-being, similar to that I'd experienced in the cabin at Phil and Emma's, filled me. I believed I had even more to be thankful for than in those blessed days. By moving to Appledore, I told myself, I had taken the first step toward freeing myself from the uncertainties of my relationship, from my old life in Vancouver.

Staring out at the night, I imagined myself the sole occupant of a dirigible, riding high above a valley of profound peace. I felt the buoyant serenity and power of solitude: *I am living here, by myself, in a place of beauty. One by one, I am solving the difficulties that arise. Tonight, all is well with me, with my house, and my world.* I knew I had come to live here because of problems in my life, problems I had yet to successfully tackle. Though I was conscious that I still had to meet these challenges, they seemed issues of the day. The night was filled with joy.

Chapter Five

PANORAMA

AS LUCK WOULD HAVE IT, THE WINTER BEFORE I MOVED TO a valley nestled amid the Selkirk Mountains, I had been invited to participate in a July conference on mountain writing. Three weeks before I took possession of my new property, I was at the Castlegar airport to meet a friend and fellow poet, David Zieroth, who was also scheduled to speak at the conference. He and I had arranged to travel on together to the Panorama ski resort in the East Kootenay, the conference location. Panorama is near the town of Invermere in the Purcell Mountains, which form the west wall of the Rocky Mountain Trench.

Now that I was about to move to the mountains—and be a mountain writer, I guessed—I was excited to learn first-hand more about that role. My invitation had been to read and talk about poems by various other people describing aspects of their employment in mountain regions. The poems were from the anthologies I had compiled of contemporary Canadian and US poetry by people about their daily work, including *Going for Coffee*, published in 1981.

That collection included poems by David, who currently made his home in Vancouver with his wife and their two daughters. He had been asked to read his poems about living in Invermere for several years while working as a naturalist in nearby Kootenay National Park. Originally, he and I had planned to travel from Vancouver to the conference together. But since when July rolled around, I was staying with my friends David Everest and Judy Wapp up Kootenay Lake while I closed the deal on my new place, Zieroth and I hurriedly revisited our plan. Now, besides driving to Panorama together from Castlegar, the region's main air travel hub, after the conference I would drive him back to the Coast, where I would begin to pack for my new life in the country.

David to this day has a boyish bespectacled face and an intense curiosity about the world around him: the men and women, as well as the birds, rocks, animals, rivers and landscapes both natural and human-made. He has a careful way of speaking, sometimes suddenly posing a question like a journalist interviewing a subject: "What would you say was the high point of your winter?" Or: "What is the best book you've read in the past six months?"

I had known him since the early 1970s. Our poems started to appear in the same anthologies around that time, and our first books of poems were both published in 1973. One of David's poems from *Clearing*, his first collection, had special resonance for me now that I had purchased Appledore. In "The Mountains Have Not Yet Entered," he writes:

> The mountains have not yet entered
> my dreams and become familiar as the cities
> and the old places where the land
> is flat and the shadows are my own.

The conference we were about to attend was named after the title of another book of poems published in 1973: *Headwaters*, by the Alberta author Sid Marty. Sid, a friend of David's as well as mine, was scheduled to read from his writing the first evening of the gathering.

In 1978, Sid's memoir, *Men for the Mountains*, had appeared, about working as a park warden in Canada's Rocky Mountain national parks: Jasper, Yoho, Kootenay and Banff. Sid weaves the history of the mountain warden service into an account of his own adventures and misadventures in campground and wilderness. When I read *Men for the Mountains*, I felt this was the best book of prose ever written by a Canadian, a judgment that I've had no cause to alter. Unless maybe its equal is Sid's *The Black Grizzly of Whiskey Creek*, about the bungled official response in 1980 to attacks on people by a grizzly near the Banff townsite. Sid achieves the near-impossible by writing portions of the incident from the bear's point of view without a trace of anthropomorphism.

Sid's work as a warden has provided him with considerable experience dealing with bears. I remember asking him, a year or two after acquiring Appledore, for his advice on how I should behave when face-to-face with a bear. By that time I had learned that bear encounters on my property are common in every season but winter. I explained to Sid that some experts I had read claimed that in a bear confrontation you should climb a tree. Others decreed you should lie down on the ground and play dead. Still others said to back away slowly while talking to the animal. Which tactic, based on his many years working not only in the national parks but later in the Alberta provincial parks, did he recommend?

"It's up to the bear," Sid replied.

As my trusty Corolla with David and I aboard left Castlegar that hot July morning, our conversation dwelt on Sid and other Headwaters speakers we knew who had been featured in the conference brochure. From the airport, Highway 3 eastbound climbs a ridge as spectacular as the sheer face the highway ascends east of Osoyoos. Unlike above Osoyoos, however, no switchbacks and hairpin turns occur leaving Castlegar. So the view from a vehicle during the steep rise duplicates almost exactly the view from one of the Dash-8 prop planes that are the West Kootenay's chief aerial link with the world beyond the mountains. These aircraft have to lift rather steeply from Castlegar to clear the surrounding peaks.

Around us as my car sped ever higher through the cloudless day, the Selkirks' summits still displayed a topping of snow. To the northwest, the Kootenay River curved through mesa-like bluffs to join the Columbia.

On that river's western shore, the houses and businesses of Castlegar appeared smaller and smaller as we ascended. Directly below us was the unincorporated Castlegar suburb known as Ootischenia, a transliteration of the Russian word for consolation. Scattered amid its fields, modest homes and roads were pairs of the square, brick, two-storey former Doukhobor communal houses. Another pair across the Castlegar–Nelson highway from the airport serves as a museum of Doukhobor settlement.

The Doukhobors are a Russian Christian pacifist sect dating back to the seventeenth century, much oppressed by the Czarist government and denounced as heretics by the Russian Orthodox Church. Persecution of the Doukhobors spiked after they refused conscription in 1895 and burned all their weapons in three huge bonfires. Queen Victoria and Count Leo Tolstoy, among others, helped 7,500 adherents immigrate to Saskatchewan in 1899. In the early 1900s, the government withheld legal title to prairie farmsteads the Doukhobors had laboriously created. The group's religious dogma forbade swearing allegiance to royalty (a prerequisite for land ownership at the time). The BC government offered Doukhobors land ownership with no such requirement in the Castlegar region and also farther south near the US border at Grand Forks. Starting in 1908, the bulk of the sect migrated to the West Kootenay and established villages many places, including north of Winlaw.

Communal living mostly died out after the Second World War, but many of the distinctive communal dwellings still stand, now abandoned or converted to private homes or other uses. Doukhobor halls, cemeteries, Russian choirs, and religious and social gatherings abound in the West Kootenay. Hearing Russian spoken, or English spoken with a Russian accent, is not unusual. The group's enduring impact on the area includes an inclination, shared by many newer residents, toward organic food, world peace and a distrust of governments.

On the highway now far above Ootischenia, David and I watched the vista to the west disappear as, at the top of the valley rim, the road swung southeast into forest on a climb to the Bombi summit: 1,215 metres in elevation, 22 kilometres from Castlegar. An abrupt descent followed and, at a T-junction, Highway 3 turned east to bypass the village of Salmo and follow the Salmo River for a distance. Then the road began to lift toward Kootenay Pass, apex of the Salmo–Creston Skyway.

Topping out at 1,780 metres above sea level, Kootenay Pass is the highest point of any paved road in the entire Kootenay–Rocky Mountains region. My Corolla slowed on several long inclines rising toward Kootenay Pass, forcing me to downshift. The car still eased around scarcely crawling tractor-trailers, whose inch-by-inch forward progress made our plodding ascent seem zippy.

As we drove, David and I had plenty of time to catch up with each other's lives. Our chatter at first focused on anecdotes from our recently completed terms teaching at community colleges in the Vancouver suburbs. He had been instructing creative writing at Douglas College in New Westminster, and in May I had wrapped up my duties back teaching at Kwantlen College's Surrey campus. We knew a number of faculty colleagues in common, so had plenty of gossip and classroom shop talk to exchange.

Our conversation lapsed into silence as the highway skirted Moyie Lake, 25 kilometres south of Cranbrook. Then came one of David's interview-type questions: "So, why did you decide to move to the mountains?"

As I guided us around a curve, I thought for several seconds about how best to answer. As a guy talking to another guy, I couldn't mention my irresolution about my relationship with Bea. And I was aware that my motivating experiences at Phil and Emma's cabin and out on Slocan Lake could be interpreted as flaky. Instead, I explained to David my sense that relocating would help me adjust to the change in poetry's social and cultural standing. And I related how I had also started to find the texture of my life in Vancouver unfulfilling.

I briefly sketched my volunteer efforts as part of a small union dedicated to preserving within the labour movement an active commitment to major social change. Besides helping to draft leaflets and pamphlets, I had been participating in solidarity picketing, and in shutting down a storefront enterprise illegally charging people a fee while pretending to help them secure employment. I had been part of our bunch opening an unemployment and workers' rights advice centre on the city's Commercial Drive. In addition, I had edited a monthly newsletter for the union. While well received, the publication took a fair amount of my time to draft, see through the printing process, and help distribute.

I reviewed with David my involvement from 1984 to 1987 in the creation and operation of the Kootenay School of Writing, the attempt by former David Thompson University Centre writing faculty and mature students to launch an independent post-secondary creative writing institution in Vancouver. A residue of weariness from the endless amount of unpaid work KSW had required, I told him, probably influenced my growing lack of enthusiasm for my volunteer exertions on behalf of the union. In both cases, I had come to think I had done my share, and that the results of my frantic activity did not warrant the amount of time, imagination, sweat and money I had expended in these causes.

"Maybe I'm burnt out," I admitted. "But I feel like a hamster on a wheel. Moving to the Koots means I can step off the wheel for a while."

"Couldn't you do that and still live in the city?" he replied.

"I guess so, in theory," I said. "But I have too many entanglements there. Taking the geographic cure should give me time to figure out what I want to do and what I don't want to do."

David didn't comment. I went on: "This is maybe vaguer, but also I don't like what's happening to Vancouver."

My impression was that the city where I had lived more of my life than anywhere else was becoming meaner and uglier. Many people seemed infected now with the ethic that equated financial success with righteousness and societal approval. In the Howe Street financial district, I'd seen a slogan on a licence plate frame attached to a swanky sports car: *Ice in the veins means money in the bank.*

I had heard Vancouverites speak of having lifestyles, rather than lives. And everywhere across the city, old wooden houses, each with its own character—multi-coloured beer-bottle stucco siding, mossy roofs, and a dense surrounding foliage of evergreens, chestnuts, maples and flowering shrubs—were being torn down and their lots levelled. The unique dwellings' replacements consisted of "Vancouver Specials": identical rectangular, gable-roofed, two-storey boxes designed to cover the greatest legally permitted extent of a standard lot.

These structures, I ranted to David as the Cranbrook city limits sign approached, were only the low end of a real estate boom fuelled by offshore money—mainly from Hong Kong, as the rich from there became anxious to invest their loot somewhere else before the Chinese government were scheduled to take possession in 1997, only eight years away. The federal government welcomed this influx of money because the authorities claimed the result would be Canadian jobs. But such investment in real estate merely drove up house prices, forcing more and more children of those whose labour had built Vancouver to relocate to the suburbs if they wanted to purchase their own home.

My tirade was interrupted while I steered into the parking lot of a restaurant on Cranbrook's highway strip. David and I made small talk as, inside, we studied the menu. Once the waitress had taken our order, though, I explained that I was tired of feeling angry all the time about these developments. I hated hearing another friend report his rent had been raised beyond possibility of payment, or someone else I knew complain about trying to survive in an economy disconnected from the ever-rising cost of living.

"I bet you're sorry you asked why I wanted to move," I ventured as the waitress brought our food. "I apologize for going on and on. I just—"

"No, it's okay," David replied. He was silent a few seconds. Then he added: "You obviously don't like what's happening to the city. But I hope you're not expecting the country to always stay the same. Changes happen in the country, too, you know."

His comment startled me. I was aware of the big changes Nelson had experienced in 1984, but I had no idea whether or not the Slocan Valley had always been the way I'd seen it when I was looking to buy. David was raised on a farm in Manitoba and had lived in Invermere, a small mountain village. He certainly understood more about the rural than I did. His pronouncement would bear thinking about.

Lunch finished, I steered us north on Highway 93/95 through rangeland: open meadows and boggy areas between clusters of pine. The Rockies formed a high wall to our right. Back at Creston, at the south end of Kootenay Lake, we had left the Selkirks and wound through the Purcells, the range that since Cranbrook rose to our left. The first glimpse of the mighty Rockies had been, as always, a thrill. As Highway 3 rounded a curve in the forest just before Cranbrook, the gigantic peaks suddenly were visible. The scale of these mountains was breathtaking, reducing the southern Selkirks and the Purcells almost to hills in comparison.

Despite the austere magnificence of the mountains looming to our right, David and I chattered away the kilometres. Two hours beyond Cranbrook, we turned off the highway at Invermere. David, from memory, directed us to the road to the Panorama ski resort, 20 kilometres farther west into the Purcells and high above where the Columbia River meanders along the valley floor.

After we had checked in at the resort's lodge, we found a throng of people already filling the concourse where the conference registration table was situated. Book displays on tables lined one wall. We managed to catch the eyes of the conference organizers, Peter and Yvonne Christensen, to let them know we'd arrived.

Peter is a lean, tall outdoorsman with a laconic manner that registers delight in the ridiculous, whether met in the literary world, practised by bureaucracies, or manifest in the interactions of daily life. He and his wife, Yvonne, lived on a wooded acreage above the Radium Hot Springs golf course, 16 kilometres north of Invermere. David and Peter had become friends during David's years living in the area, and I had included some of Peter's wryly incisive poems in *Going for Coffee*. The same year *Coffee* appeared, Peter's book of poems about his previous employment in the oil patch, *Rig Talk*, had been published. Since then he had been working for a mountain guide service and as a seasonal park warden in East Kootenay provincial parks.

If the idea of a conference on mountain writing originated with Peter, Yvonne was the detail person who made it happen. Beautiful, wiry and tremendously energetic, in contrast to Peter's laid-back approach to life, Yvonne worked on Kootenay National Park's trail crew.

People who work in a landscape view it differently, in my experience, than those who encounter it as a tourist, or for aesthetic purposes, or with a singular goal in mind such as environmental protection. Peter's writing reflects his razor-sharp and multi-layered response to East Kootenay mountainsides and valleys where he made a living. His words often display an understated sense of humour.

Like everyone I've met whose occupation occurs in the weather, Peter acknowledges the dimensions to the natural world that can be felt despite humanity's persistent attempts to measure, control and transform the biosphere. In an introduction to a performance of his words involving singers, musicians and dancers staged in Alberta's Grotto Canyon on the eastern slope of the Rockies, Peter writes:

> When civilization reached the Americas it came to conquer, convert and exploit. The legacy of this conquistadorial arrogance remains and threatens the systems which support our lives.
>
> Dominion over the land, plants and animals means we have the greatest responsibility. To survive, we must respect the land which gives us our life and be thoughtful guardians. We must realize that the earth and all its inhabitants have a spirit, not the same as ours, but a spirit that in science and religion is dependent on our choices. There are no inanimates.
>
> The mythologies of the indigenous peoples have much to teach us. If we can combine the notion of a living earth with the will to survive, we will create a garden.

Peter was aware, too, of the natural world's function as solace. In a letter to me a couple of years after Headwaters, he reported that a grant application of his, to which I had contributed a letter of support, had been turned down. He acknowledged how these kinds of rejections, so frequent in any artist's life, can undermine self-confidence.

> I suppose all of us get to a point and do whatever we feel will rebuild the inner strength. I chose to climb a mountain. It was a peak that I had looked at for many years and not one I would have normally considered climbing alone. It was big and steep and had a lot of potential for trouble.

I scared myself in a big way by getting off route. I remember I had huddled up and eaten some strong dark chocolate. This stopped my shaking and regained my composure. I kept at the route piece by piece. That is, one piece of chocolate for every time I scared the heck out of me.

Finally I was on the summit. I sat for an hour looking out over the valley far below, looking out over the route down. At that point in time I believe there was no separation between my inner place and the physical space I was occupying. The internal dialogue, that constant questioning voice was stilled...There was only the stones and glaciers, the wind and sun and my being there. During that still and mystic hour, I was in a real way filled again with hope, with ability, with love of myself and with a purpose. Not the least of which was to get down in one unbroken piece.

Such rewards as an intimate encounter with a mountain can provide were the focus of a talk by Jon Whyte during a session on Headwaters' first day. Whyte, who was born in Banff in 1941 and died of cancer three years after Headwaters, was a Banff poet, book publisher, historian, and newspaper columnist. He curated the heritage house collection of Banff's Whyte Museum of the Canadian Rockies, formed from the historical artifacts and paintings by local artists gathered by the museum's founders, Peter and Catharine Whyte, Jon's uncle and aunt. Among his many literary activities, Jon helped found the Alberta Writers' Guild, which has named its annual essay prize in his honour.

Jon shared the same sense of humour as Peter, amused by much of the world's foibles and especially those of the inhabitants of, and visitors to, the Rockies. He wrote the text for *Rocky Mountain Madness*, a compendium published by Altitude Publishing in 1982 of occurrences and photographs depicting the madcap side to mountain settlement from the arrival of the CPR in 1883 forward.

I'd always liked Jon after witnessing his deft adaptation, a few years before Headwaters, of one of the ritualistic aspects of a public author reading. I'd been invited to present my poems as part of a reading series at the Whyte Museum. When we arrived at the building's auditorium on the appointed evening, a total of five people constituted the audience, a disappointing situation any author—and especially a poet—faces sooner or later. Undeterred, Jon stepped to the podium, welcomed everyone to the event, and announced he would now introduce the author.

"Tom," he said, looking at me where I sat in the front row, "this is Bob." Jon gestured toward one of the evening's attendees. "Beside him is his wife, Carol. Carol and Bob, this is Tom." In a similar vein, I was indeed introduced to the meagre crowd.

At Headwaters, Jon spoke on "The Literature of Alpinism," discussing accounts by climbers in the Yukon's St. Elias mountains, home of Mt. Logan, Canada's highest peak, at 5,959 metres, and Mt. St. Elias, the country's second highest, at 5,489. Whyte told the 60 Headwaters attendees that the writing of these mountaineers spoke to both what it is to be human amid a challenging environment and "what it is to be Canadian amid a landscape everywhere scarred by glaciers."

Writing by climbers, Whyte argued, especially defines and mythologizes the most obvious characteristics of mountains: their stark beauty, dangerous to humans who venture into them. "I do not overlook," he went on,

> ...the many other elements which help define mountain experience, activities like hunting, skiing, grazing cattle, making cheese, painting, logging, mining, developing hydro dams, studying glaciers or seeking Oreads [Greek mythological mountain nymphs], activities which more often than not can be more destructive to the mountains than tourism,

though in Banff we seem hell-bent on catching up to the Swiss in developing tourism's destructive capability.

Another Headwaters participant I knew, Caroline Woodward, offered a different slant on mountain living, her vocabulary rather different than Whyte's and other presenters' myriad mentions of ridges, passes, cols, moraines, arêtes, cornices, cirques and scree. Caroline and her husband, Jeff George, had been writing students at David Thompson University Centre when I taught there, and they hung on in Nelson after the school closed. Years later they operated a bookstore in New Denver. Caroline through the decades has written short fiction, crime fiction, children's books, and more recently a memoir of her and Jeff's post-Kootenay lives as lighthouse keepers on the BC coast.

At Headwaters, in the course of her presentation on "Rural Roots and Writing," she noted: "Mountain people are really valley people. We don't live on the mountain; we live in the valleys. Mountain living is rural living."

I was struck by Caroline's observation. The evident truth of it had escaped me until she uttered it. But like many a revelatory (at least to me) statement at Headwaters, Caroline's helped me make more sense of where I was moving to. And years later, I began to see what mountain dwellers and flatland rural people have in common: a physical and social landscape very different than that of the urban majority.

A further Headwaters speaker whose wisdom about being among mountains I found particularly informative was Alberta's Robert Sandford. At the time of Headwaters, Bob had lived in the Rockies for 20 years, 7 of them working for the national parks and 13 as "a student of the way visitors and locals alike perceive these mountains." His day job was as a tourism consultant. After Headwaters he went on to eventually become Global Water Futures chair at the United Nations University Institute for Water, Environment and Health, and the author of 30 books on the history and landscape of the Rockies and the West, and on water and its uses in various places around the globe.

Bob's talk at Headwaters picked up on Jon Whyte's comment about mountain tourism's "destructive capability." At first I couldn't grasp what tourism had to do with mountain writing. But when I reflected later, I decided that when we write about the mountains, our words in effect make tourists out of those readers—and this is the majority of readers—who don't live amid the geography we describe. Plus, both Jon and Bob spoke of the changes tourism can cause—which echoed David's comment on our drive to Headwaters about change occurring in the rural as well as the urban.

Bob traced the history of how tourism in the mountain parks refashioned itself when faced with changing clientele. People first travelled to the parks by train, then car. At one time park visitors were mostly Albertans and other Canadians, and then the Japanese arrived. In the face of such shifts, Bob stated, businesses determined to cash in on people's urge to visit the mountains will sacrifice locals' interests entirely.

Among other negative consequences, he warned, the ethic of short-term profit-taking by resort owners leads to a sameness in design: "You can go all around the world and stay in the same hotel room every night. You need a phonebook to know where you are."

The drive for profit also means prices continually rise, while "poor construction and ineffectual maintenance in time create resort slums. You see them everywhere: unpainted walls, torn carpets, chipped furniture."

These resorts and other tourist attractions find that the local inhabitants cannot supply enough seasonal staff, Sanford continued. "So the local culture changes. The enclaves of original residents become proportionally smaller and politically weaker. They complain about a loss of regional authenticity. The outside workers bitch that the townspeople will not recognize or accept them." Tourism, he stressed, can be just another polluting industry, eating up land and eating up people.

I was taken aback by his conclusion. In all that I'd read and heard, tourism had never been discussed as anything but a desirable alternative to BC resource extraction's impact on the landscape: vast hillside clear-cuts, huge log yards, extensive mine-tailings ponds, and valley-filling smoke from sawmill bee-hive burners, pulp mill stacks or smelter chimneys. While I was still digesting Sandford's startling-to-me categorization of tourism, he emphasized that *potentially* tourism could enhance instead of undercut local culture. The industry's planning must involve artists in the broadest sense, Bob insisted: "writers, painters, photographers, teachers, natural philosophers, wilderness visionaries." He explained that

[o]nly by mutual rapport with artists can business people prevent their community from becoming just one more modern slum in the great hungry maw of contemporary will-to-greed that is global tourism. Let's consider what Wallace Stegner [1902–1993; his *Wolf Willow* is about his Saskatchewan childhood] has done for southern Saskatchewan, Sid Marty has done for the Rockies, David Zieroth for the Columbia Valley. Artists are the only ones capable of reawakening people to their own capacity for wonder.

Though artists can *point* people toward the experience of wonder and awe the mountains can provide, Bob noted, only being in nature can *generate* these feelings in us. No screen can do it either, he emphasized. He was referring to television and movie screens, but his critique of a widespread immersion in technology was prescient. At a conference like Headwaters today, more than 30 years later, most of the audience would be unable to sit listening to a speaker for more than five minutes without furtively or openly checking their cellphones. The audience's addiction to these screens has rendered them desperate for news about any place except where they currently are, and about any person except who is in the room with them.

"What is wrong is that we have come to rely on technology to make us happy," Bob observed at Panorama,

> when, if we think about it, we must realize that it is we who must make us happy. Technology, if we rely on it for all our entertainment, all our inspiration, all our fulfillment, can only make us bored and bury our fascination.
>
> One of the most powerful influences in the destruction of human wonder is media over-stimulation. Media have replaced the world of personal exploration and self-development. People dream the mass dream and are powerfully hypnotized by media demands, fashion, and the need to keep ahead in their social milieu. With so many demands grabbing at one's conscious mind it's hard to find time to be yourself. It's hard to be alone enough to find out who you really are.

I was reminded of Bob's perceptive take on the deadening effect of technology when, in 2016, I listened to Vancouver ecologist J.B. MacKinnon's talk at Nelson's annual Elephant Mountain Literary Festival. MacKinnon, co-originator of the 100-mile diet, had a PowerPoint presentation based on his 2013 book on rewilding, *The Once and Future World*, a national bestseller that won the US Green Prize for Sustainable Literature.

One of the slides MacKinnon showed was a photo of a man sitting on the tailgate of a pickup at the Seattle waterfront. The seated figure is hunched over, staring at his smartphone. Behind him close to shore in the harbour, an eagle is lifting from a wave with a salmon clutched in its claws. "He is probably," MacKinnon said, indicating the seated man, "texting *Here I am on the waterfront. Maybe I'll see an eagle!*"

Despite the addictive lure of technology, Bob concluded at Headwaters, we retain within us that sense of wonder. The challenge is to unearth it, to incorporate it as part of our lives.

> Fifty years from now, 100 years from now, when the world is more crowded and more mobile, we will no longer be embarrassed by the emptiness of our wilderness. The wildness of Canada's mountains will be more valuable than we can even begin to imagine. Our mountains are important now, but they are not as important as they are going to be.

Reflecting on concepts like Bob's wasn't the only component of the conference that kept my mind in a whirl. At one of the first breaks, a woman attending the event approached me and introduced herself by her maiden name. She said she taught high-school English in Creston these days. I had first known her when we were classmates at the same Vancouver secondary school in the early 1960s. Until that moment at Headwaters, I hadn't seen her or heard anything about her after we graduated.

She had been an incredibly gorgeous, high-achieving student who I felt existed in a separate world than me and my friends, even though her family lived just a block over from mine. With a smile now, she said: "You got the English prize in Grade 12, and I've always believed I should have won it."

I was amazed that someone like her was not only present at Headwaters, but that she was actually talking to me. Her comment initiated a couple of days of intense conversation, off and on. Not male-female talk, and not about high school, either. More about what we had done with our lives since we shared our high school's halls and classrooms.

My brain was churning as we compared notes. This was someone who in high school I had admired remotely, impossibly, from afar. She was the daughter of a senior corporate executive. A genuine debutante, she had been expected—as she related at Panorama—to marry the right sort of upwardly mobile young man and become a wealthy West Vancouver wife and hostess.

Instead, she had joined the Canadian University Service Overseas, often known as Canada's Peace Corps, and twice served in Africa. She related how she married a man from the West Indies, with whom she had a child before they divorced. Currently she was married to a fellow teacher, helping to raise a blended family.

If I had thought of her after high school, I wouldn't have believed she'd ever be living near a rural place like Creston and teaching school. Yet, talking to her at Headwaters, I confronted a question about myself I had not even thought of before. How much of my sense of self with regard to women had been shaped by my years in high school when I was *totally* out of it socially? My two closest friends and I in those days had competed with each other for top marks on quizzes and exams, but we were completely clueless with regard to the opposite sex.

This appearance of my former high-school classmate at the very time when I was stepping back from my daily life with Bea, when I was determined to try to clarify my, our, emotional future, seemed to me another stroke of luck. Here at Panorama I had been given the opportunity to mull over the compensatory attitudes and behavioural patterns I had adopted in high school due to functioning as a social outcast—at least in terms of romance. Yet while I was grateful for this potential source of insight into my intimate behaviours, I felt a bit depressed. What other unexplored chapters in my life, I wondered, influenced without my being conscious of them how I functioned as an intimate partner?

After Headwaters' formal close on the Sunday afternoon, those participants who didn't have to depart immediately were invited back to Peter and Yvonne's for a celebration. With my head whirling with memories of old high school insecurities and gaucheries, and with new ideas about what my move to the mountains might mean for me and my writing, I was more than ready for a break and a beer.

The alcohol flowed freely, as did the conversation, although I kept my intake of the former to a minimum since I intended to drive back to the West Kootenay later that evening. Peter at one point circulated through the noisy crowd that filled his and Yvonne's living room and kitchen, offering slices from a platter of meats and cheeses. He insisted I try the meat, though he wouldn't identify the animal it came from. I assumed it was elk or deer. When several of us had eaten a slice, he announced it was bear. I had the nervous thought that now that I had chowed down on a bear, I could hardly object in the future if one of his or her relatives decided to reciprocate.

When I finally announced that David and I should depart, Peter seemed intrigued by the news that I was in the midst of finalizing the purchase of an acreage in the Slocan Valley. He had lots of questions. One inquiry had to do with how I planned to gather my winter firewood. I explained that I hadn't thought that far ahead but assumed that I'd buy it. Peter stressed that for the full Kootenay experience I needed to chainsaw my own wood supply.

On learning that not only did I not own a chainsaw, I had never operated one, Peter declared that I needed a lesson in its care and handling before I left the party. I countered that my friends Judy and David up Kootenay Lake had offered to host Zieroth for the night as well as myself, and I didn't want to arrive at their place too late in the evening. But Peter was not to be deterred. I followed him out of the house and across the yard to his woodshed, trailed by a few other conference-goers wishing to witness Peter's demonstration of the tool that he maintained was the backbone of country life.

As the sun sank toward the Purcells in the west and Peter's audience pulled solemnly on our bottles of Old Style, he showed us how to choke and start his Husqvarna, the implements necessary to sharpen its chain, and much more. In my case, this information entered a head already over-filled with all I had absorbed at Headwaters since Friday. As a result, not a lot of Peter's well-intentioned lesson was retained. But my farewell thanks to him and Yvonne for their work creating the conference were sincere. David and I clambered aboard my Corolla, and I glided down the bumpy dirt lane past the golf course to where, during a pause in highway traffic, I accelerated onto the asphalt and headed south.

Part 2

...IS THE JOURNEY

Chapter Six

THE SEASONS –
AUTUMN

DURING MY INITIAL AUGUST AND SEPTEMBER AT APPLE-
dore, I scarcely noticed the onset of a change in season. Yet every
year since, I'm alert to the first indications that summer's hours of
garden chores, vegetable and floral bounty, and hot-weather outdoor recreation are coming to an end. Probably the most dramatic
early sign is that by about August 15, the hummingbirds depart for
their long voyage to south of the Rio Grande.

Each May, suddenly hearing the high-pitched throbbing of
hummingbird wings as one of the tiny flyers swoops past me is as
much a cause for joy as first seeing in March a robin hunting for
worms on the greening grass between the piles of melting snow.
Watching the hummers' antics is a delight all summer as they fight
and fuss with each other around and between two feeders I hang
from the eaves above the deck.

In June, above the lawn stretching south from the deck toward
the Seven Sisters, the male hummingbirds put on their mating display. They fly a gigantic vertical ellipse in the warm air, shooting
upwards to an apex 5 or 6 metres above the grass, then whistling

straight down toward the lawn before arcing up again at the last possible second. The high-speed elliptical route is retraced two or three times before the little feathered particle of energy takes a break or retreats from the aggressive approach of a rival, perching atop the Japanese maple's spreading green canopy immediately south of the house.

All summer, the miniature flyers hover close above me while I sit at the table on the deck, taking an afternoon break from moving irrigation sprinklers or staking up a drooping columbine. Then, one day, the hummers are simply gone. Their bodies appear so minuscule they appear unable to travel as far south as downtown Winlaw, 6 kilometres away. At the height of August, however, they set out for Spanish-speaking climes, impossibly distant.

Another early indication that summer will eventually end is the first yellowing of the dogbane, a low shrub that occupies the edges of open spaces, proliferating along roadside ditches and marking the boundary where my lawns stop and the woods begin.

In spring, the emerald of the dogbane leaves is a vigorous participant in the symphony of deep greens, light greens, and yellow-greens, whose notes herald the return of new growth. Around mid-July, however, one morning I notice that a leaf or two of a dogbane bordering the lawn is turning pale.

For nearly two decades now, my attention usually is first drawn to this change by my neighbour to the north, Rod Currie. He was a long-time resident of the valley before he and his wife, Sharon Lang, purchased the property next door, the third set of owners since I bought Appledore. They moved in with their baby son, Evan, 16 years after I arrived.

Rod is a keen observer of the world about him. He possesses a photographer's eye: before digital cameras, he made a living selling stock photographs to a California company that in turn sold these to publishers wanting illustrations for book covers, calendars or greeting cards. Before his marriage, he was spending half the year in a more-or-less-renovated cabin on a friend's property just south of Winlaw and half the year in India.

When digital camera technology became the norm, Rod stepped back from photography as a livelihood. Since Evan's birth in 2004, Rod has worked where he can, like so many other West Kootenay residents scuffling a livelihood in order to stay in the area. Besides having considerable skills as a mechanic, after being raised on an acreage near Quesnel, Rod has all the necessary certificates to drive truck commercially. Many winters he travelled to find employment behind the wheel in the oil patch at Fort McMurray or Fort St. John.

Sharon eventually arranged for Rod and herself to be hired to maintain an extensive garden for an elderly Doukhobor matriarch. Sharon is a dynamo for work, up at dawn to plant and tend her home garden. She cans, freezes and otherwise puts up the harvest as it appears. She takes courses as a farrier and cuts horse's toe-nails and undertakes other equine tasks up and down the valley. For years she also laboured as a waitress—at the café in downtown Winlaw and later the Valley View Golf Course restaurant directly across the river from where we live. She home-schooled Evan until Grade 9, gives piano lessons to more than two dozen valley young-sters, and organizes and conducts the valley's volunteer choir.

In contrast, for Rod work is something you do if necessary, but otherwise avoid. He can speak so eloquently about the complete pleasure of lying on his couch, savouring the bliss of doing nothing, that I become sleepy just listening to him.

Nobody I've ever met does woebegone exhaustion better than Rod. He'll drop by my place and detail some chore he's just completed, like replacing the brakes on one of the family's cars or acquiring winter firewood. "You're looking at," he'll announce, "a total piece of hamburger. The brain-dead wreck of a former human being." And his gift for words doesn't stop at describing weariness. Most recently he completed a certification course to work as a security guard and is employed three nights a week working for a private firm contracted to patrol the local community college's student residence and classroom buildings in Nelson. When he took the job, Rod spelled out for me how little authority a security guard like him legally has: "All we are is a piece of meat in a uniform."

Given how busy Sharon is, Rod has done a lot of the parenting of Evan. Rod has encouraged Evan to apply intense visual attention to any situation. If the pair encountered odd winter animal tracks and markings in the snow, or an unusual disturbance of rocks and duff up in the woods, Rod would ask Evan: "What do you think happened here?" Together they would piece together the clues.

For Rod, parenting is enjoyable rather than work. And he has returned to photography, albeit cursing the necessity to master the myriad of choices available to tweak any digital photo. Despite relishing being horizontal, he's more than willing to sacrifice sleep to capture a shot he's after. For example, he'll forsake his bed in the very early morning to photograph the fog that, as the days cool toward the end of summer, shrouds the river and its banks at first light.

Not surprisingly then, sharp-eyed Rod usually notices the first yellowing dogbane before I do. Soon, though, I'll observe that amid the waist-high sea of green bracken that by July has filled my lower meadow, a few of the plants have turned brown. And on a mid-August afternoon, I'll see that the hazelnut trees around the property each now display a yellow leaf or three amid their green canopies.

In the weeks that follow, the resident squirrels busily harvest the nuts while the yellow leaves proliferate. Detached hazel leaves begin to lodge amid the ripening squash and cucumber in my garden plots, or between the rows of carrots and onions I'm now picking daily for salads.

Meanwhile, the clusters of mountain ash berries slowly complete their summertime alteration from pea-green to orange to full autumnal red. In September, the leaves around the berries begin to fade from deep green to tan.

By the middle of that month, on a drive into Nelson, I'm startled to see how golden the birch leaves along the route have become. The hamlet of Crescent Valley, right before Highway 6 joins the Nelson–Castlegar road at Playmor Junction, is at a slightly lower elevation than Winlaw. The change of season is as much as two weeks ahead of what occurs at Appledore.

For a few October weeks, the highway to town is breathtaking to travel. Pillars of gold shimmer in a still-warm breeze beside the asphalt, kilometre after kilometre. A roadside cottonwood that I've scarcely noticed all summer now is afire with spectacular gold flames.

On the mountainsides, the larch have transmuted to gold as well. In every direction, the slopes, which are a monotone deep green most of the year, suddenly are speckled with gold from valley bottom to summit ridge. Each fall I'm reminded how much of the local forest is comprised of larch. Also now evident on the ridges, the yellowed leaves of birch, aspen and other deciduous trees reveal the paths of invisible creeks as they follow clefts and gullies down toward the river on the valley floor.

A particularly stunning colour change occurs with my Japanese maples. I now have a few other ornamental maples, and oaks, around the grounds whose leaves decorate the autumn. But three large Japanese maples, south, east and west of the deck, respectively, outshine any other autumn tree on the property. The vivid reds and yellows of the Japanese maples can be overwhelming. Rod stops by with his camera several times during the three or four weeks these trees' leaves are in their glory. He claims the trees make the top of my driveway the most picturesque in Winlaw.

Out every window at Appledore in October, tree leaves waft downwards. The foliage of trees and bushes here and along the roads offers a pointillist masterwork that combines browns, reddish-browns, flaming reds, brownish-yellows, pure yellows and dazzling golds.

Intermittently the scene also swarms with birds. The hummers may have departed weeks before, but flocks of other flyers on their annual migration are active around the house for a few days and then vanish. Some I've learned to identify: cedar waxwings, evening grosbeaks. Others, despite me riffling through one of my many bird guidebooks, I never can name with confidence. Among these visitors, the robins keep bob-bob-bobbing from lawn to bird bath to tree branch. Until one day the robins, too, have departed.

Ruffed grouse are more noticeable in autumn, although I encounter these chicken-size birds in every season. Any month, but especially in the fall, I'll be walking somewhere on the grounds, thinking of something else, when one takes to the air right under-foot or from a nearby branch. They lift off in a heart-attack-causing explosion of wings.

Equally disconcerting is a grouse's occasional decision—most often in the autumn—to depart from a branch and fly full-tilt into the cedar siding of the house and break its stupid neck. Other birds during the year occasionally mistake the reflection of trees in my windows as a route through the forest. Despite various appliqués I've affixed to the glass, supposedly guaranteed to warn birds away, several birds a year bash into the windows with a startling bang. Frequently no ill effect results, but sometimes I have to pick up their bodies on a shovel blade and bury them in the woods. Yet a ruffed grouse will collide with the house far from any window. When I was growing up in the coastal town of Prince Rupert, we kids called these birds "fool hens." Watching one flap suicidally at speed toward a solid mass of wooden siding reinforces for me the accuracy of the nickname.

Besides the changes to foliage and to the local bird population, the onset of fall for me was indicated for many years by the appear-ance, in the week before Labour Day, of a large yellow school bus parked nose-out on a property across the road. The house there belonged to Wilf and Eva Heink—she being the one who eventually commented on my spring tree-planting efforts. In my first month at Appledore I'd noticed a small sign in front of the Heinks': *Organic Carrots*. Even before I met the couple, I could see a large field under cultivation on a gentle slope north of their house.

Despite being aware my first September that a bus had materialized at the Heinks', I was surprised when I was awakened before 7 a.m. on the Tuesday following Labour Day by a diesel engine starting. Early September still offers summer weather, so my bedroom window was wide open, with only a screen between me and the bird sounds and other morning noises: a distant rooster crowing, a dog barking somewhere on the lower road, clip-clop of a horse's hooves from somebody out on the road for an early ride. In the country quiet, the engine idling sounded awfully close.

I soon grew accustomed to Wilf warming up the school bus before heading out on his route. And if the bus engine firing up did wake me, I had the luxury, unlike Wilf, of rolling over and snoozing some more. Indeed, the sound became comforting after a couple of years. Having a neighbour be part of the beginning of another school year helped make me feel connected to the cycle of the seasons.

With autumn underway, I launch into the chores of tucking away the flower and vegetable beds for the winter. These tasks became increasingly time-consuming as I slowly expanded the area under cultivation. In spring 1990 I planted, following Bea's advice from the previous summer, a vegetable garden where one had existed in the lower meadow. By that July, I realized that tiredness or laziness while I was making supper discouraged me from traipsing from the house down to the garden to acquire a green onion or lettuce for my salad.

As a solution, the following spring I dug up a 4-by-12-foot portion of the lawn south of the deck for a raised-bed vegetable garden.

I reasoned that, once I was in for the night, I was more likely to dash out to this closer spot for a needed carrot or tomato than I was to head all the way to the lower garden. I subsequently added two more identical raised beds alongside the first to form collectively what I call the kitchen garden. And for added cultivation, in 2012 I installed, with help, a prefab 6-by-12-foot greenhouse in the lower meadow directly west of the big garden.

The number of flower beds also grew year by year. My first spring, not only was I astonished by the beauty of the hospital administrator's line of red tulips that appeared in the bed east of the house, I was also pleasantly amazed that June when peonies—as Bea had predicted the August before—rose white and pink from the steeply-slanted bank south of the parking area. Later, hollyhocks climbed into the summer air along a fence that marked the southern edge of where I parked.

After these inspirations, I subsequently inaugurated more flower beds here and there. In addition, I place pots of flowers on the deck. And tall marigolds, glads and other flowers crowd one large pot at the bottom of the driveway to welcome visitors to Appledore.

The amount of time and effort required to prepare the veggie and flower beds for winter makes me reluctant each September to launch into the job. As does how these hot early autumn days still *feel* like summer. Everywhere I look, colourful flowers still brighten the hours. Though the peas are long since eaten, and the bean patch has turned into a science project of curled brown leaves and slimy unpicked beans, I can still find plentiful cukes under the vine leaves, and my tomato plants remain loaded with their sugary red burdens. A few lettuces remain available for salads, even if most have bolted. Ripe ears of corn wait to be picked.

Unlike in high summer, however, the dimming of the light in late afternoon happens earlier and earlier: the sun sinks behind the west ridge at five o'clock, then 4:45, then sooner. Sometimes in late afternoon when I'm at work outside, I return to the house to pick up a long-sleeved shirt to ward off a sudden coolness in the air. The lower garden might be in bright sunshine another hour or more. But in parts of the grounds now already shadowed by the ridge, a colder season has started to insinuate itself.

One night, usually in late September, a touch of frost occurs. The leaves of squash and cucumber vines are shrivelled and brown next morning. Sometimes potato leaves are impacted. But since the potatoes already display a mix of green and yellowed leaves, indicating the tasty tubers are due for harvesting, I can tell myself that the changes to these leaves should be attributed to the maturing plants rather than the first appearance of Jack Frost.

And around the damaged greenery, the rest of the garden carries on in the sunlight. For weeks after a first small frost, warm days and temperate nights can give the impression that a harbinger of winter never happened, that summer will be endless.

Yet that initial frost often nudges me to take the first step in in putting the gardens away. On an afternoon not long afterwards, I'll dig up and repot the geraniums I've planted in various beds. Brought inside the house, confined to smaller containers, the flowers occupy window ledges until the following spring.

Glimpsing the empty space in the beds where the geraniums had blossomed initiates a melancholy mood in me that will accompany all my subsequent stripping of the gardens. Though I know the job is necessary, it marks the end of another growing season. A first hard frost that cripples everything in the beds can temper my feeling of sadness with one of urgency. Yet whether a severe frost occurs soon or not, once the geraniums are repotted, my clearing out of the gardens shifts into gear.

All vegetation remaining in a bed gets ripped out of the ground, piled into my wheelbarrow, and trundled away to the compost pile. The last carrots are picked, washed, and stored in bags in the fridge. Ditto tomatoes and cucumbers. Squash gourds are collected.

Any uneaten onions are laid out on newspapers on the basement's cement floor to dry.

As are dug-up potatoes. Digging a potato patch is a bit like opening Christmas presents. One hopes for pleasing gifts, or even exciting surprises. More frequently, the result is items that are merely useful. The number of large potatoes hoisted into the light on my garden fork is inevitably less than I'd like, despite generous fertilizing of the patch. Of course, two or three smaller spuds baked or boiled together provides the same nourishment as one commercial-size specimen, so I've learned to be satisfied with whatever the fork brings forth.

During an October afternoon most years, I'll stop work to photograph a basket filled with fall harvest: potatoes, beefsteak tomatoes, carrots, peppers. I have photos of my wheelbarrow transformed into a cornucopia of cukes and squash. Of course, since June, I've been eating lettuces: arugula, cilantro, romaine, leaf, butterhead. Radishes, peas and beans follow, then cherry tomatoes. All this produce provides me with a sense of self-reliance, even if only a portion of a meal originates in my garden. The first salad of the year entirely made of ingredients from the garden is a cause for celebration. And if I had the energy to can and freeze more of what I grow, as Sharon next door does with their garden's gifts, I could eat from my garden far longer than I do.

Be that as it may, after I completely empty a bed of vegetation it looks forlorn: a mere patch of brown earth that appears much smaller than when a profusion of green leaves and good things to eat filled it. Clearing beds can even feel like sacrilege. In the lower veggie garden, I took to planting a row of giant sunflowers that by late August lift their yellow-and-black blooms as high as 12 feet. Reluctantly, despite huge flowers still cheerily blooming well above my head, in October I chop down the plants' thick stalks and pry up their network of roots.

By then, glads, delphiniums, alyssums, petunias, and columbines will have finished blossoming. But marigolds, salvia, impatiens, and gazania can be flowering when I pull them up from beds and pots. Not for another six months will I be able to emerge from the house on a sunny early morning, scissors and basket in hand, on a mission to replace the contents of vases of fresh flowers in my kitchen and bedroom. The abundance of colours opening to the freshness of the morning won't return until crocus, daffodil, hyacinth, and tulip lift again from beds I've just reduced to an empty expanse of soil.

Spring bulbs, though, only produce flowers for a limited number of years. Thus, before I mulch flower beds in autumn, new bulbs have to be purchased in town and planted. I've replaced that wonderous row of red tulips spanning the raised bed at the foot of the eastern house wall three or four times.

Bea had explained to me how mulching beds, besides protecting against weeds becoming established at the start of the growing season, keeps the soil warmer than it would otherwise be. Warmer soil encourages spring bulbs to break dormancy earlier and start producing the shoots whose emergence through the soil announces spring.

Straw is my mulch of choice for the main vegetable garden in the lower meadow, and for roses anywhere on the grounds. Local plant nurseries, garden supply stores and hobby farmers offer heavy square bales of compressed straw for sale in spring and fall. Before I learned where to obtain it, luckily for me the previous owners had left three bales in a cold-frame construction down by the lower garden. A corrugated fibreglass top over a board-lined shallow excavation protects the stored straw from weather.

Prior to mulching the lower garden, I turn over the cleared soil with the fork. Cultivating this way is hard work—most of my neighbours use a power rototiller. But I consider the effort good exercise.

Despite the physical strain, like all afternoon outdoor chores this task is a welcome break from earlier hours spent sitting hunched at the computer.

Lower garden and roses aside, the bulk of the mulch I apply to my beds consists of fallen birch and maple leaves. The row of birch between the house and the lower meadow produces a thick carpet of golden leaves on the lawn. Shortly thereafter, the Japanese maples by the house drop *their* colourful leaves. For three or four weeks, I rake leaves into piles for at least an hour every afternoon.

The gathered leaves are either transported by wheelbarrow to be spread on whichever flower or vegetable bed I'm covering at the moment, or else I stuff a pile of leaves into large orange plastic bags, ready to be emptied onto the next bed that I strip. Bags to be stored are moved to my garden shed. These are light to lift if the leaves inside are dry, but surprisingly heavy if I've been raking on a rainy day.

I say "rainy day" but working outside my first autumn taught me that weather here rarely is consistent hour after hour. The stormiest afternoon has interludes when the rain ceases for an hour or two.

Also, Appledore frequently enjoys an Indian summer, even after an initial heavy frost. On such a warm day, the sweet odour of fallen birch leaves fills my nostrils as I bend to lift another double-handful into the wheelbarrow. A neighbour up or down the lane has already lit a wood fire in their furnace against the chill that will start in an hour when the sun drops behind the ridge. I savour the pungent scent of chimney smoke from burning fir or larch.

Before the last kitchen garden bed is mulched, I plant a couple of rows of garlic cloves. The herb will reappear as green shoots when I lift the mulch in early April, with the garlic bulbs ready to be harvested in July. Like burying flower bulbs, sticking garlic cloves into cold soil—the year's last vegetable planting—is in its own way a promise of spring.

Meanwhile, apples are ripening. Beginning in September, when I pass by an apple tree, I'll often pluck a likely looking specimen and bite into it to check if they are fit to eat yet.

Since my first autumn here, I've been able to gather several bushels of apples from two original, reliably producing trees. I store the apples in the basement, and much of the fall and early winter munch happily on them, as well as baking them into pies. By mid-January, though, any of the remaining fruit stockpiled in the basement has browned and decayed, needing to be carried through the snow to the compost pile.

If I constructed a cold cellar, my stored apples and root crops would stay edible longer. An alternative for apples, however, arose in 2017. Sharon, next door, mentioned that a relative who lived in Burton, along the Arrow Lakes south of Nakusp—a couple of hours drive from me—wanted to sell his homemade apple press. I was game, and Rod and I headed out in my pickup to purchase the equipment.

Ever since, at the end of September, most of my apple crop is turned into tasty apple juice, as are the apples from trees at Rod and Sharon's. What I purchased was an ingenious set-up. To mangle the fruit, an electric motor drives a rotating studded metal drum inside a wooden chute-like arrangement. The resultant mash drops into a plastic, somewhat-shortened 45-gallon barrel.

When the baskets and boxes of fruit to be pulped are empty, or the barrel of mash is nearly filled, the barrel is armstronged over to the press itself. The latter consists of a ring of wooden slats about a metre high, arranged vertically and bound together by thick metal bands. The ring of slats sits on a low wooden table, slightly angled downwards in one direction and edged by a 5-centimetre-high wooden rim broken on the low side of the table by a spout.

Rising from the centre of the table is a threaded metal pole taller than the ring of slats. After a perforated plastic lining is placed inside the ring, the mash is shovelled out of the barrel into this lining. A wooden cover is then placed over the mash; like the lining, the cover has a hole in its centre to allow it to slide down the metal pole. Wooden blocks are placed on the cover, and atop the blocks a heavy metal weight is positioned—it, too, has a hole in to allow it to slip down the pole. Finally, a metal crossbar with a threaded hole midway is connected to the top of the pole. As the ends of this bar are rotated, it presses down on everything below it, and out of the mash streams the delicious juice, to be caught below the spout by jars, jugs or pails.

Once processing the fruit begins, wasps are attracted to where Rod and I are working, darting in to land on tiny bits of apple sprayed out of the mangler's rotating drum, or attracted to the scent of the mash mounding up in the barrel. When the juice appears from the press, the wasps go crazy. Drunk from sipping the sugary fluid, the insects act entirely uninterested in bothering any of the humans busy around them. I can brush aside a cloud of wasps as I deftly remove a filled jar below the spout and replace that container with an empty one to catch more of the steady cascade of sweet juice.

While the apples are being pulped, I toss in a small number of pears from my three producing pear trees. The hint of pear, to my taste, slightly softens or mellows the juice. I'm not fond enough of pears to want to make pear juice, so blending a little into the apple juice means I'm making some use of the fruit.

Most of my pears are enjoyed by bears. Wasps aren't the only creature attracted to ripened fruit. In late August, bears begin to be a visible presence on the valley floor. The furry creatures are intent on fattening up for winter hibernation and are single-mindedly focused on packing on the calories. Rather than go around an obstacle like a fence, many bears will plough right through it. From my first month on the property, I was nailing up knocked-down 1 × 4 fence rails or replacing these boards if a bruin shattered the wood when it smashed through the fence.

As part of the animal's obsessive drive to gain weight, they also like to check out my compost pile southwest of the house, across the lawn. Their hope is to hoover down some appetizing garbage. The bears usually follow an identical pattern of movement at Appledore: up from the road to sample my pears, apples and any plums still not picked, then head for the compost. When they're finished rooting through that, they make a beeline for a huge apple tree on the lawn of the property to the south. When I first bought Appledore, that acreage was owned by Jim and Anita Warner.

By my third autumn I was tired of frequently replacing a particular board on a fence between my compost pile and the Warners' tree. That fence marks the southern edge of the lawn. While fall bears exhibited some individual behaviours, at least with regard to which other fences of mine required repair, every bear in strolling from my compost to Jim's apple tree knocked askew the same fence rail en route.

When I realized the pattern of bear misbehaviour, I stopped replacing that board. Above the gap thus left in the fence, I affixed a sign I ordered in Nelson: *Bear Gate*. Since then, no other boards along that fence have been broken or knocked aside. When I mentioned to Jim the success of my new sign, I told him I suspected bears could secretly read. Jim disagreed. He informed me that in order to stop the creatures breaking branches and damaging the bark with their claws as they blundered aloft into his giant apple tree, he had placed a ladder leading up into it with a sign: *Please use*. Yet many autumn mornings, Jim reported, trashed limbs were evident in and under the tree. He concluded that bears' reading comprehension, if it exists, is low.

Jim, raised in the valley and now nearing retirement, was very generous to me as a newcomer. An avid fisherman, he would bring me trout he caught after a weekend on local lakes. I later learned he and his wife had a developmentally delayed son, ordinarily institutionalized in Trail, whom the couple would bring home each summer. "He's my fishing buddy," Jim explained.

From time to time in conversation with Jim, I'd be reminded of how growing up in the area provided a different perspective than mine. He told me once he hated to go to Nelson. "I can't stand the traffic," he declared. I was dumbfounded: Nelson has a total of four traffic lights in its business district, plus two more on the highway that skirts downtown. When Nelsonites declare their municipality has a serious parking problem, you find on questioning them that they mean they've been unable to park directly in front of a store where they wish to shop.

Parking meter rates, too, remain incredibly low compared to Vancouver or Calgary. The fine for an expired meter in downtown Nelson is the cost of parking for less than one hour downtown in either metropolis. Still, Nelsonites can be as convinced as Jim that the automotive world is out of control. Nelson installed digital parking meters in the 1990s to replace the old manually operated ones. For months afterwards, someone under cover of darkness neatly beheaded digital meters at night and left the heads in a creek at the edge of town. The money in the meters was untouched.

Jim, as part of being a consistently good neighbour, was unfailingly diplomatic. During a conversation with him my first autumn at Appledore, he informed me that the bottom of my driveway had been built partially on his land, but that he didn't mind. Not knowing him very well at that point, I was dubious about his claim, although I didn't say anything to him at the time. Yet a few days later, inspecting the drive more carefully, I indeed found an iron survey marker, a property corner post, almost completely buried in the middle of the drive a couple of metres in from the road.

In 1995, after Jim retired and the Warners moved away, I was able to buy from the new owner of Jim's property a sliver of land to legally acquire all my driveway, plus the row of trees I'd planted along its southern edge. The purchaser of the Warners' property was subdividing 3½ lower acres and was willing to have me buy this portion.

Once I discovered Jim was right about the driveway, I was appreciative of how tactfully he had raised the issue. Autumn bears, too, can be diplomatic while stealing fruit. Some are discreet, tidy bears, whose attention to my orchard trees can only be detected by the sudden absence of apples or plums compared to the day before. Such bears leave behind a paltry few twigs and leaves on the ground around the trunk. In contrast, clumsy, destructive bears show up other years: klutzes who leave a tree with large limbs snapped off, other limbs torn and dangling, deeply scored bark, and a considerable detritus of broken branches and leaves strewn underneath the stripped tree.

Slocan Valley bears, who generally are no larger than a big dog, are mostly nocturnal. Usually, I am first aware of their arrival in the fall by spotting a large puddle of applesauce on the grass. Although I'm extra vigilant when working outside once fresh bear flop starts to appear nightly around the place, I know that the hairy weight-gainers are not interested in burning up any of the calories they are storing away by getting into a hassle with anybody.

During the 1990s when I was teaching in the Okanagan and home only on weekends, I was in a mad rush to tuck the gardens away whenever I had Saturday or Sunday hours free from marking or course prep. One Sunday afternoon while briskly clearing the herb and flower bed around the bird bath, some motion caught my peripheral vision. About 6 metres away, below me on the driveway where it makes a right angle turn as it descends toward the road, a small black bear stood peering up at me.

Ordinarily I would have backed off at the sight of the bear, wary of the muscles and claws of even a diminutive specimen like this one. But that day I was feeling pressured by the few hours I had left that weekend to make a dent in the autumn chores. "Get out of here. Go on! I don't have time for this," I yelled at him.

The little creature, probably only a couple of years old, obediently withdrew backwards out of my sight behind a bank of earth. I resumed my labours. A minute or so later, I glanced up to see that furry head peeking tentatively out around the bank, as if to check on how serious I was about asking him to leave.

"Go on. Git. Be gone," I hollered, waving my hands for emphasis. In an instant the bear's head retracted. Although I checked every few minutes for the next hour, the animal was seen no more.

Not all bears are so obliging. In fall 2000, for a couple of weeks, a much larger bear strolled onto my place every afternoon like clockwork around 3 p.m. Unlike few of its relatives since, it had a fondness for the red berries on my two mountain ash trees just east of the house.

After pulling down some branches and gorging on the goodies, the big bear would lie down, stretch itself out on my lawn and loll around, clearly in no hurry to leave. Its favourite location for taking its postprandial ease was below my bedroom window. I would lean out that window to yell at it to move along, and even heave shoes from my closet in its direction to encourage it to depart. All of which words and missiles it ignored.

I apparently represented no more of a threat than a squirrel chittering at it from a nearby tree. A friend named my visitor "Chutzpah." Despite all suggestions presented to it that it take a hike and never return, it would promptly reappear the next afternoon. Each day, when it felt sufficiently rested after its meal, it would get to its feet, amble around the north side of the house, then saunter down the lawn to check out the compost. If nothing interesting was discovered, it would mosey on toward the Bear Gate, step through, and disappear among the trees.

Eventually I grew weary of losing too many apples to the fur-coated transients. I began picking reddening apples from my best producing trees in late August. My picking would increase as I judged more of the fruit had ripened. But far too often I would head out to the tree one sunny September afternoon to find every remaining apple gone, whether ripe or not.

In the new century I at last purchased electric fencing to install around my productive fruit trees. The first rumours in August of bears being spotted in the neighbourhood have me erecting near one of the trees a wooden post holding the electrical controller. A widely spaced ring of five or six thin metal posts is arranged around each tree. The posts each have three plastic insulators spaced about a foot apart, and three strands of wire are rigged from insulator to insulator encircling the tree. A different wire connects the controller to one strand of each tree's fence, and another wire connects the controller to a buried metal plate that serves as a ground. Then the controller is plugged into an extension cord snaking out from an outlet on the side of the house.

Ever since, except for one year, my apples have been effectively protected. Once, however, my neighbour Rod had gone out onto his deck for a goodnight look at the autumn stars. Suddenly he heard an uproar from my property, sounding, he told me afterwards, like a bear was trying to break into my greenhouse. Rod claims the noise was shockingly loud, although I slept through it, despite my open bedroom window facing east toward the apple trees. Grabbing a flashlight, Rod left his deck and started to walk through the pitch-dark night across his lawn to learn what was causing the commotion.

As he neared The Bearway, a furry apparition burst out from between the trees and headed toward him on the run, trailing bits of wire. Rod said that at that moment he realized venturing out to investigate armed with nothing more than a flashlight probably hadn't been a great idea. For a second, he thought the bear was charging to attack him, or at the very least would bowl him over in a blind rush to escape from its electrical punishment. The bear, though, caught a glimpse of Rod, skidded to a stop, and promptly climbed one of the larger spruces along the northern row of The Bearway. Rod beat a retreat to the safety of his deck.

In the morning, the electric fence was a mess of twisted wire and bent metal fence poles. Rod said he figured the bear had gotten entangled in the wire and was repeatedly shocked. The animal's thrashing about in a desperate attempt to free itself eventually broke enough wires that it could flee.

Most fall days, though, are tranquil, with my ongoing effort to ready the gardens for winter suffused with that wistful sadness I've referred to. One autumn phenomenon that to me embodies that emotion is the morning mist. A thick fog forms during the night along the river. Then, as daylight arrives, the fog often expands, rising upward and flowing outward. As I eat breakfast, the mountains disappear and the view from my kitchen windows shrinks to the nearest lawns and trees. Wisps of diffuse fog above the grass and in the trees, and the opaque whiteness beyond that, mark the borders of the world. My dwelling has been transported to a mythical place, reduced in size but hauntingly beautiful.

Within a half hour, the warming air resumes its transparency. In the afternoon, though, with summer tourists gone and the local children in school, the valley can become totally silent, as though wrapped in a spell. As I rake leaves or clear another bed, not even distant sounds of highway traffic from across the river are audible. The profound autumn quiet seems an interlude magical in its utter stillness.

When the last garden bed is readied for winter, I haul outdoor furniture to the shed for storage or cover it with a tarp. I coil irrigation hoses and wheelbarrow them and the sprinklers to the shed. I bring snow scoop and snow shovel from the shed and lean them against the house wall on the deck, ready for use in the months ahead.

Then one afternoon everything is done. If I can't find some fiddly chore to complete under the sky—trimming back the summer's shoots of hazel, or maybe conducting another burn in my firepit of accumulated windfall branches and twigs—I'll go for a walk around the loop road below me. I note changes to dwellings and acreages since I last strolled by and enjoy the autumnal vistas across the valley.

In the early fall of 2011, I bought a mountain bike with hybrid tires suitable for riding on the dirt, gravel and sand surface of a route through the valley that follows the former railway line. The Slocan Valley rail trail was created in 2002 after the CPR abandoned its route to Slocan. Since I obtained the bike, I try to be out on the rail trail every second day once the rush to put away Appledore's grounds is over. Because fresh bear poop is everywhere along the trail, I carry bear spray in one of the bike's panniers, and sing as I pedal, so as not to startle any bruins. I also purchased and installed a loud bell to ring when navigating sections of the trail that wind through dense brush or around blind corners.

The volunteer committee that maintains the trail helpfully puts up signs when a bear has been observed repeatedly on a particular stretch. In all my years of riding the trail, I've never encountered a bear close up. I'm vigilant, though, if a warning notice has been posted. A couple of times, in the southern part of the valley, I've seen something black far ahead on the trail, moving slowly across it. Each time I've braked to a halt and squinted forward. Is the black shape a dog? Possibly not, so I've done a 180 and headed in the opposite direction.

A few times a deer has crashed out of the yellowed undergrowth and dashed across the trail close in front of me as I've pedalled. The sudden noise and abrupt appearance of the animal give me a rush of adrenalin as I jam on the brakes, sliding to a halt.

The only time so far that I've encountered an autumn bear in close proximity on the rail trail, I was on foot. My brother had been visiting from Edmonton, and on a crisp October morning we decided to hike the trail from the Lemon Creek trailhead north toward Slocan. Given that this was a weekday, we had the trail to ourselves. We strode along talking, with the ground under our shoes littered with yellow leaves and the trailside bushes mostly bereft of foliage. The river was intermittently visible to our left between the stands of evergreens and semi-denuded deciduous groves. All the bear flop along our route that morning looked like it was days old.

After a couple of hours, we reached an oversize bench looking out at the river, one of several such constructions a volunteer has built along the 50-kilometre length of the trail. Sitting on these benches makes you feel like a kid again, perched on adult-size furniture: you have to clamber up onto them, and your feet swing freely once you've seated yourself.

The big benches are sited at spots with especially interesting views. The one we sat on faces a wildfowl refuge, although few of the river's usual ducks, Canada geese and eagles were in evidence that day. We dug water bottles and trail mix from our haversacks. I'd tossed in my bear spray as well, just in case. My brother, who has hiked extensively in grizzly-ridden Waterton Lakes National Park in southwestern Alberta, keeps bear spray in his backpack at all times.

The two of us were enjoying our snack and the scene from the bench. Some sixth sense caused me to glance back up the trail where we'd just walked. A large black bear was proceeding toward us at a leisurely pace. The beast's head was down and swaying from side to side as it sauntered along, clearly thinking of something other than bumping into people.

"B-b-bear," I alerted my brother, pointing. "Let's get out of here."

I slid toward the north end of the bench, farthest away from our visitor. "This way." I started to climb down. In the surreal moment of the creature's appearance, I had forgotten entirely that I had brought bear spray with me. "Come on. Let's go," I urged my brother again.

Bear spray wasn't on my brother's mind, either. "Where's my camera? Where's my camera?" he exclaimed, busily pawing through his pack.

Clutching the camera, he leaped off the south end of the bench toward the bear. The animal had halted a few metres away and lifted its face upon hearing us. Without ceremony, it turned to its right, plunged through the underbrush away from the trail, and vanished. My brother wasn't far behind, although he stopped at the trail's edge, camera lifted.

No matter how expected, the arrival of snow can be just as surprising as the sudden appearance of that bear. On the valley bottom, afternoons and nights grow progressively cooler. Yet the first appearance of snow on the high peaks is always a shock. Every year, during a drive north toward New Denver to visit friends, I'm astounded to see the topmost summits of the Valhalla Ranges across Slocan Lake glistening white, which they weren't a few weeks before when I travelled this way. Or, headed toward Nelson, I notice that certain distant peaks of the Selkirks are now snow-covered, unlike three days previously.

On a chilly evening around this time, I'll head down to the basement to light the first fire of the autumn. Wood to start the blaze is removed from the 2-metre-high stack of firewood I wheelbarrowed into the basement on hot June afternoons that seem eons ago now. As the house warms, the sweet smell of the burning wood permeates the rooms. The heat and scent provide me with a feeling of cozy comfort that contrasts with the cold now present beyond my walls, out in the fall dark.

After a couple of years at Appledore, I decided a predicted overnight temperature of four degrees or lower is when I'll first build a fire in the furnace. Four degrees during the day is for me the start of sweater weather. If an obligation takes me to town some morning when my thermometer shows that temperature or chillier, for the initial time that fall I extract a sweater from the chest of drawers where it was bundled away the previous April. By noon I might have peeled the sweater off and even rolled up my shirt sleeves in warm October sunshine. But the first sweater day remains another marker of a change in season.

Then, after a rainy autumn night, I look out my bedroom window to see that the top of the valley's eastern ridge has whitened. The snow aloft on the valley wall may be gone a few hours later, but its appearance marks winter's first claim of sovereignty over the valley. Most years that first snow atop the ridges doesn't manifest until well into October, although one year snow high up appeared on the last day of August.

As the days and weeks pass, the snow on the summit ridges becomes a fixture. Some weeks later, after another cold rain overnight, the valley walls are white almost down to the highway, the river, and our acreages. By afternoon the mountainsides are again green, flecked with golden splashes of larch. Soon enough, however, the ridges stay white nearly to the valley floor day after day. This condition can last weeks. I work on the grounds, bike the rail trail, or drive the roads with the sense that something foreboding looms not far above me. Winter has established itself in the forest only a few metres higher than where I live.

Finally, one dark November afternoon, the air in the valley fills with flakes slowly descending. The lawns at Appledore turn greyish-green, then even paler, then pure white. The deck and driveway, too, transform to a mottled pale appearance, then white. The empty boughs of birches and aspens, and the branches of evergreens, also gradually whiten under the next season's first snow.

Chapter Seven

THE ELEMENTS–
LOW WATER

I HAD ONLY BEEN IN THE HOUSE A MONTH WHEN, ON A Sunday morning, I went to use the kitchen sink and nothing came out of the taps. I was baffled. Maybe there was a problem with the kitchen pipes? Yet no water was forthcoming in the bathroom, either. The basement sink faucet produced the feeblest of trickles.

I sat on the living-room couch to try to figure out what to do. Anxiety gripped me. When I began looking at real estate in the West Kootenay, I didn't think about water. On the one hand, I knew better than to believe the walls of a dwelling are full of water, and you just stick a faucet into the gyprock someplace and have hot and cold running water. During the Vancouver School Board evening class I took on buying a house, the lecturer covered sequentially the various systems of a house—structural, electrical, heating, plumbing.

But I had always lived where a municipal department employed people to ensure a supply of clean water. As a long-time renter, if I had ever had a problem with the water supply, I would have regarded the issue as the landlord's responsibility. When I was buying Appledore, the saleswoman may have mentioned that the house was on a gravity-fed water system. But if she did, the words and their implications didn't mean anything to me.

Now, I had no water. For the first time, I realized that a house without water is a beached ship. Functions for which a dwelling is designed—cooking, keeping clean, using the john—cannot occur. I felt sick with worry.

Since I had no idea where the house's water came from, I was clueless about how to rectify the problem. And did the trouble affect just me, or were other people along the road also suddenly without water? If so, who? At this juncture I had only briefly met my closest neighbour to the north, Lynn, the divorced wife of the man who had built my house. She and I had spoken a couple of times when I happened to be along the north edge of my land and she came over to speak to me. She didn't seem very friendly. I knew from observation that she had a couple of kids, and a boyfriend who visited on a noisy motorcycle. Whenever he stayed over, he left her place early in the morning. With my window wide open to the summer air, I would be wakened by his motorcycle blasting into life at 6:30 as he, I presumed, headed off for work. Now, I wondered if I should walk over to her place and ask if she had water and if she knew why I didn't have water.

From time to time I'd stand up from the couch and open the kitchen faucets again, in case the absence of water was a momentary blip. Nothing continued to emerge from the taps. Would I have to sell the house and look for one with a reliable water supply? Could a house without water be sold?

I was distracted from my obsessive worrying by the sound of a pickup gunning up my driveway. Spinning tires tossed dirt behind as the truck sped toward the house and jolted to a halt outside the basement door. Since I didn't know anybody who drove a pickup, I headed downstairs to learn who my visitor was.

The driver, a middle-aged guy in jeans, dark green T-shirt and a well-worn ball cap sporting the Midas Muffler logo, was climbing out of the cab as I emerged from the house. He slammed the truck door shut. His face was one big scowl.

"Listen, buddy," he said without preliminaries, striding in my direction with one finger pointed at me. "No matter what you and Lynn say, no *way* am I using too much water. That's bullshit." He stopped a couple of feet from me. "Pressure is down at my place, too. I don't have as much as one sprinkler on, so it's complete crap that—"

"Wait, wait, whoa," I protested, frightened by his vehemence. I held up my hands, palms out. "I'm new here. I haven't talked to anyone about not having water. You don't have any either?"

His eyes narrowed suspiciously. "Lynn told me you were mad because I was using more than my share of water."

"I didn't say that," I stressed again. "I'm not mad at anybody. I haven't talked to anybody today. I've only spoken to Lynn maybe three times since I moved in., Your water stopped, too?"

"What a bitch, eh?" His face relaxed. "Yeah, something's wrong with the system." He held out a hand. "Ed Jacobson. The wife and I are your neighbours. North of Lynn's."

I introduced myself and we shook hands. I was trying to think why the woman next door would claim I blamed this guy for my lack of water. Was she trying to triangle me into some dispute with him? My mind whirled at having gotten in trouble with a local through no fault of my own. I asked Ed if he knew why we didn't have water.

"I was already up to the distribution box and everybody but us had plenty in their compartment," my visitor said. "So there's no shortage of water from the creek. I'm first on our line, and if all three houses on it—yours, Lynn's and mine—don't have water, there has to be a problem on the line between my place and the distribution box. I was going to go check. Want to come?"

I had no idea what he meant by "distribution box" or "compartment." Or what creek he was referring to, or where the line was that he intended to check. But a chance to help restore my water supply while learning about the system sounded like a good idea. I scrambled up into the pickup. As Ed backed down my drive, in response to my series of questions he began to explain something of how water ordinarily came to flow out of Appledore's taps.

The gravity-fed system dated to the early 1960s, he said. Nobody was employed or was otherwise responsible for maintaining it, except we users. We did have to pay the BC government for annual water licences. Each property is allotted a set amount of water according to a domestic-use licence and an irrigation licence. I admitted to Ed that I had seen these documents in the pile of papers given me when I purchased the property. But I had only glanced at them. They had seemed just a formality.

We headed up his driveway and parked. Ed, who I'd discovered by now was a skidder and backhoe operator for a logging company, showed me approximately where the buried water line to our houses entered his property on its northern boundary. He announced that we'd look for a leak in the line by walking northwards from this spot in the direction of the distribution box, following where he figured the line went. Almost 30 years after the underground pipes had been laid, he said, nobody knew exactly where they ran.

We'd be on Ellen Bazaroff's land, Ed added, gesturing at the overgrown meadow that stretched north of us, its width extending from the road to where the ridge's woods began off to our left. He said he'd phoned Mrs. Bazaroff before he'd driven over to my place. She was on a different water line than ours, although on the same system. He had her permission to cross her property to search for a leak.

I still had no clue what a "distribution box" was, but after he located a couple of shovels, we squeezed between the strands of a barbed-wire fence and started through the thigh-high grass and weeds. Ed said a leak usually revealed itself by a damp spot on otherwise dry ground. Sometimes a break in the line produced a miniature fountain, but only if we were lucky. The piping, parts of which had been replaced over the decades, now was mostly plastic, rather than the wooden pipes bound with wire that had been used for some of the original conduits. A stone positioned against plastic, he said, could be moved by the freezing and thawing of the ground to eventually rub a hole in the pipe. If the hole faced downward, a leak could be difficult to locate. However, a leak big enough to lower the pressure on the line as much as had happened that morning would be fairly large, and we should be able to readily find where it was.

Clutching our shovels, we paced slowly, eyes scrutinizing the jumble of vegetation at our feet. Ed said to watch for a linear depression in the ground or other indication that might confirm the location of the pipe as it crossed Bazaroff's field. One of us would pause occasionally to bend over and check with a palm a patch that looked damp.

Twenty minutes later, our combing of an area that might not even be near the route of the water pipe began to seem futile to me. I wondered to myself if an alternative technique for finding a leak might exist. Yet Ed seemed never to tire of our present approach, so I continued to scan the ground parallel and to the right of where he stepped along, carefully assessing the terrain.

As more minutes passed, I was increasingly certain our effort was pointless. Then abruptly Ed announced, "Over here." A puddle about 6 inches in diameter had formed in the grass. No rain had fallen for a few days. But at this location, not far from a drooping, half-collapsed barbed-wire fence marking where the forest began to the west, the meadow was shaded by overhanging aspen branches. I asked if the moisture could be water that hadn't evaporated yet from the most recent rain.

"The puddle *is* pretty small," Ed agreed. "Maybe there's more than one leak. This one will need to be fixed even if it's not the main culprit." He drove his shovel into the ground beside the puddle. "Let's have a look-see."

We began to dig. The soil was crammed with roots, small rocks, and the occasional large stone, making deepening the hole slow going at first. With two of us alternately lifting out a shovelful, however, after a few minutes we seemed to have gotten below the tangled upper layer of the ground, and the excavation grew at a quicker pace.

I was sweating, and stopped to wipe my glasses. "How far down is—"

"Most of the old water line easements specify 18 inches deep," Ed said. I waited for him to swing his laden shovel clear of the hole and then jabbed my own shovel in. "After all these years, no telling how deep it actually is," he continued. "Ground is getting wetter as we dig, though. Which is a good sign. But you're right: we'll have to start taking care not to stick a shovel into the pipe."

I asked what an easement was. He said I should have gotten copies of those, too, when I bought my place: legal agreements whereby a landowner grants permission for a water line or a driveway to cross his or her property. I promised to go through my file when I got home, and, if the easements were there, read them.

"Should be four for your property to do with the water line," Ed said, as in turn we hoisted out more dirt. "Mrs. Paquette's, where the distribution box is. Then Bazaroff's, then mine, and then Lynn's place."

The earth by now was sodden, close to mud as we scooped it out. The opening in the earth we were making was nearly 3 feet deep when Ed's shovel scraped the side of a black plastic pipe 2 inches in diameter. Ed cautiously cleared earth away from the other side of the pipe and beneath it, leaving half a foot of it exposed. His shovel suddenly bared a slit in the bottom of the pipe from which water gushed forcefully straight down into what speedily became a small pool at the bottom of the excavation.

"That's her," Ed pronounced. He rested on his shovel handle a moment. "I'm going back to the house and fetch something to fix this. See if while I'm gone you can clear a space all around the leak where we'll be able to work while we patch it."

By the time he returned I had extended the hole surrounding the break, although the water cascading out spread immediately across whatever new space I created. My running shoes were soaked. I saw Ed had changed into rubber boots.

He squatted beside the pipe and wrapped the end of what looked like an old inner tube around a dry portion of pipe upstream of the leak. Positioning two hose clamps to secure the rubber, he tightened the clamps with a screwdriver. He then wrapped the repair material snugly around the pipe over the leak. Water sprayed up toward him as the flow from the break was briefly redirected while he pulled the rubber hard against the pipe. He issued a volley of curses. But having brought a towel with the repair items, once he attached two more hose clamps to hold the patch in place, he dried his face.

"We'll just wait a bit to see if this holds," Ed said. He sloshed to the edge of the small pit, whose water level was already diminishing, and climbed out. "This fix is kind of mickey mouse," he said. "The proper way would be to cut the pipe where the leak is and install a plastic join. I don't have any of those at my place, unfortunately. It's Sunday, which means we'd have to leave the hole open until I picked one up in town tomorrow. We'd have to shut the water off up at the water box, too. There's no valve, so you have to jam a board down to cover the outlet at the bottom of our compartment. Not the easiest thing to do. Then we'd have to hang tough until all the water in the line between there and here drains."

I still had no concept of what he meant by "our compartment." And was the "water box" Ed mentioned the same as the "distribution box" he'd referred to earlier?

"How far are we from the, uh, box?" I asked. "Also, since what you did stopped the leak, isn't that good enough?"

Ed stepped back down into the excavation and applied the towel to dry the repaired pipe. With his fingers, he tested the edges of the rubber wrapping upstream and downstream of the clamps securing it. He retightened the clamps.

"Let's give it a few more minutes." he said. "Seems to be holding. It's a temporary job at best, though."

When Ed was satisfied his repair was effective, he said we should fill in the hole to prevent an animal wandering into it in the night. He added that if we didn't get back to properly deal with the leak before winter, any exposed portion of the line would be vulnerable to freezing. As I shovelled dirt back into the now-mostly-dry hole, Ed manoeuvred himself between the nearby fence wires and returned from the woods a few minutes later with the straight portion of a branch about three feet long. When we'd finished covering the pipe, he stuck the branch into the restored surface of the meadow.

"I'll tell Mrs. Bazaroff we've marked where the leak is, in case she wonders why there's a pole sticking up in her field," Ed said.

At his place again, he turned on an outside faucet and we were both glad to see water leaping out. "Okay, buddy, we're done," Ed declared. "We'll have to get back there and do it right later on. But for now, we're aces."

Ed and his wife sold their house and moved away the following spring. In all the decades since, our temporary solution to that leak has never been revisited.

The loss of Appledore's water had shaken me, however. On my next visit to town, I purchased at the Nelson Farmers Supply store several of the grey plastic pipe joins Ed had referred to, for various dimensions of pipe. Plus a bag of a dozen pipe clamps of different sizes, to also have on hand in case they were needed for any future repair.

I mulled over my new sense of vulnerability concerning my water supply. After a couple of weeks, I decided to explore putting in a well as a backup to the gravity-fed line. The well-drilling companies listed in the phone book were all located in the East Kootenay, in Cranbrook, about a two-and-a-half-hour drive from Nelson. I phoned one of them, Owen's Drilling, at the recommendation of my friends David and Judy, for whom Owen had drilled a well in the 1970s. The person I spoke to at Owen's proved very helpful, outlining what putting in a well would involve. The cost of drilling was based on how many feet down they had to go to find water, she said. They would be drilling in my area the following month and could accommodate me then.

While I was told the driller would likely find water—the person I was talking to assured me others along the Winlaw back road had wells—no guarantee was offered. I learned, too, the drilling company didn't install the well pump and connect the well to the house. A separate outfit, West Kootenay Pump, did that after the well was dug—again, assuming it reached water.

I had recently received a $5,000 bequest from the estate of my aunt Beryl Lowry, one of my mother's sisters. Given that this unexpected financial windfall could cover the cost, I told Owen's I wanted to go ahead. The expense, I reasoned, represented insurance that my purchase of a house with a less-than-reliable water source wasn't a financial disaster.

Later in September my parents visited from Toronto. I think they were relieved when they experienced how comfortable the house at Appledore was—saw for themselves that I hadn't bought a cabin in the wilderness. My mother happily pottered in the garden. Since I had mentioned to my father that the well drillers would be charging by the foot, he noted that the lawn south of the house sloped down toward the Seven Sisters. He suggested I locate the well at the foot of the lawn, since the lower elevation meant I'd save in drilling costs.

Owen himself showed up in October, in advance of his crew, to determine where the drilling equipment would be set up. I explained my father's idea to him as we toured the area near the house, and he listened intently. We ambled down to look at the site my father had indicated, then returned to stand beside the house. After a minute or two of rumination, Owen announced, "I think we'll put the well here, close to the house." He indicated a location on the lawn a few feet beyond the west end of the deck.

When I reported my progress toward obtaining a well to my friends David and Judy, David said that when they had their well dug, they had first hired a water witcher. The witcher eventually declared an underground stream transected a corner of their property. When Owen arrived, he had listened to David's account of what the witcher had said, and David and Owen inspected the designated area. When they returned to the front door, Owen had said, "I think we'll put the well here, close to the house."

Several weeks later, I understood the wisdom behind Owen's declaration. When the well was dug, the well installer, Kim Wik, arrived. He explained a trench had to be created from the wellhead to the house. The pipe from the well would enter the basement about 4 feet below ground level, due to the basement being mostly underground at the house's west end. That meant the 20-foot-long passage from wellhead to house would have to be about 4 feet deep.

Given my ever-diminishing bank account, due both to settling into the house and—despite Aunt Beryl's bequest—to well expenses, I decided I would dig the trench from well to house myself rather than hire someone with a backhoe. Unfortunately, of Appledore's two types of soil, the ground west of the house is mainly a shovel-resistant mix of rocks, pebbles, stones, and roots. Prior to starting the project, I invested in a pick, and soon developed a technique of loosening the next lower couple of inches of ground with the pick, then clearing the loosened material away by shovel. Then pick again. Then shovel again. After the first 45 minutes, I was very grateful that the location of the well wasn't an inch farther from the house than it was.

Much of a week of afternoons was spent at this labour. I have a photo a friend took of myself up to my chest in the trench, grinning feebly. Kim, the installer, had also asked for an open area around the top of the well shaft where he could work, and I took pride in clearing a space large enough that anybody would be comfortable using tools without feeling crowded by the trench walls. When the installer returned, I asked him what he thought of my efforts. Kim carefully examined the trench. He thought for a moment while I waited for his verdict. "You're hired," he said.

He was kidding, of course. But I looked at my calloused and blistered palms and politely declined.

Before the passage between well and house needed to be dug, though, I had to live through the drilling of the well. Late one October morning, after I had been advised by telephone the day before that the drill crew would show up the next day, I heard the roar of a heavy truck ponderously climbing up the drive. A crane-like structure rested horizontally on the huge truck's deck: the drilling rig. The drill truck passed through the lower gate onto the lawn where only two months before I had driven the rent-a-van that had just regained reverse gear. Like my van, the truck rose up the lawn and stopped on the grass west of the house. Two men emerged, and after some discussion the truck was moved forward a short distance to position it more precisely.

Meanwhile, a second large truck, laden with lengths of drill pipe and towing a pickup, ascended the driveway. Before the pipe truck passed through the gate, a man exited the cab and unhooked the pickup, parking it down at the bottom of the drive. The pipe truck started up the lawn, and then, in a series of back-and-forth manoeuvres, turned itself around. The vehicle proceeded in reverse the rest of the way and stopped at the rear of the drill truck.

One of the guys from the drill truck stood at an impressive bank of hydraulic control levers on the vehicle's side, unfolding stabilizing jacks. He then raised and extended the drilling structure, which soon towered above the house. Another of the crew attached a drill bit. Almost at once, drilling started, the bit's rotation powered by an incredibly loud engine on the truck deck.

With my ears battered by the racket, from where I stood on the deck watching I could feel the deck planks shake as the bit chewed into the earth. Periodically, the drilling stopped while a cable from the rig lifted a length of piping from the back of the pipe truck. The pipe was coupled both to the pipe already connected to the bit, and to the rotating mechanism driving the drilling. The hours passed. The ear-splitting cacophony of the onboard engine notched up and down in volume, and the vibration of the house died away and resumed while the shaft descended ever lower toward what I hoped was water.

Owen had told me that wells along the base of Perry Ridge generally hit water at 125 feet. I'd been informed by him again, however, that they couldn't offer any guarantee. I had expressed surprise that successful wells locally were that deep. Grade-school textbook explanations of the water table I remembered featured illustrations that showed underground water at the same level as a river surface. Given that Appledore is only about 50 feet in elevation above the Slocan River, I had assumed this would be the well depth. Owen stated that underground water didn't work that way. He related an experience drilling a well next to a river in the East Kootenay, where the property owner had abandoned the project after the drilling had reached 400 feet with no water.

I hadn't found his story reassuring. As the drilling continued, I would leave the deck and try to write indoors at my computer, ignoring the thunderous din from outside and the trembling of the house as the drilling went on and on. Silence was restored for a half hour at lunch, and I went out to ask how things were going. The guys were noncommittal, having only reached 30 feet, and soon enough the clamour outside began again. Around 5 p.m., quiet descended. The drillers walked down the drive to the pickup and disappeared. I went out to gawk at close range at the motionless giant trucks and their gear.

The crew were back in the morning after eight, as I was washing the breakfast dishes. I inquired if they wanted a coffee, which a couple of them did. Soon, though, the house was quivering amid the now-familiar howl and clangour of engine and pipes as the drilling resumed.

I knew that the longer the noise persisted, the more the procedure was costing me. Remembering Owen's story about the deep well that had produced no water, I had reviewed my finances the evening before in an attempt to calculate at what depth beyond Owen's estimate of 125 feet I would tell them to quit. When I had taken out the coffee mugs on a tray with milk and sugar, I was informed that they had reached about 70 feet the previous day. All morning I kept expecting to hear the engine stop as the bit reached water.

I was out on the deck in a flash about noon when all went quiet. But the cessation of drilling was only for lunch. Gerry, the driller who seemed in charge, said they were passing through broken bedrock. I asked if that was any indication they were closer to striking water. He could see I was getting nervous about how deep, and hence how expensive, the shaft was becoming.

"Here's what I'd advise clients, if I were Owen," Gerry said, grinning. "Buy a bottle of Scotch, and sit out here on your deck. Start drinking when we start drilling. That way, the farther down the hole goes, the farther down the level of Scotch in your bottle will be. The longer we drill, the less you'll care whether we hit water."

Not long after lunch I was inside at my desk when I heard a change in the pitch of the engine. When I looked, what appeared to be a spray of water was pouring from a pipe. I dashed outside, but Gerry shook his head when he caught sight of me. From the deck I could see that what I had observed was a jet of very fine gravel, now heaping up on my lawn beside the trucks.

An hour after that the engine stopped, and while I was sure the crew were taking a break or tending to some piece of equipment, I walked out on the deck. Gerry was holding a hose from which water was streaming into a pail.

"A hundred and fifteen feet," he announced when he saw me. "Ten gallons a minute."

I felt enormous relief. "Wow, great," I enthused. "But, uh, how do you know for sure it's that much water?" I had imagined an operation this professional would have a flow meter of some scientific nature. "Isn't that pail smaller than 10 gallons?"

"I timed it. Water filled to the gallon mark in six seconds. A smart guy like you should be able to do the math."

"Oh. Yeah. Um, is 10 gallons a minute good?"

"What's your domestic licence allotment?"

I knew the answer, having reviewed my water licences after fixing the leak with Ed. "Five hundred gallons a day."

"That's about usual. Your well would give you your entire day's worth in just 50 minutes."

"Oh. Right."

"Believe me, five gallons a minute is plenty. Ten is better. Congratulations."

The crew reversed the drilling procedure, hauling the drilling pipe out of the hole, uncoupling it, and swinging it over to stack on the pipe truck. A couple of hours later they were ready to leave. I paid Gerry's invoice, and after the drill truck driver managed to slowly back the rig down the lawn, out the gate, and down the drive to the road, they were gone.

I was left with a foot of 6-inch-diameter steel casing sticking out of what had been lawn, with a flat square of metal tack-welded to the top so nothing would fall down it to contaminate my water. The Water Well Record form Gerry had filled out showed that the metal casing extended down 58 feet. On the surface, my grass was scarred and rutted with tire tracks, and covered with fans and piles of gravel and mud. But I had another source of water.

The following month, when I had finished the trench to the house, Kim of West Kootenay Pump began to make the well operational. The temporary cap on the shaft was cut off, and a plastic well liner 4½ inches in diameter was installed. A cylindrical pump was lowered into the water far below. The pump was suspended 9 feet off the bottom so that sediment or other impurities that might accrue over the years wouldn't clog the device.

Water was conveyed to the surface from the pump through inch-and-a-quarter plastic piping. This pipe passed through an opening cut in the steel well casing and then along the bottom of my magnificent trench. A hole drilled in the cement basement wall brought the pipe indoors. Electrical wiring to power the pump meantime ran inside its own protective plastic pipe from the pump to the basement via the trench and a second, smaller hole cut through the foundation. An electrical control box for the pump was attached to the inside basement wall above the two holes.

On the basement floor below the control box, Kim hooked up a pressurized tank about half the size of a 40-gallon hot-water tank. He set pressure to fluctuate between 30 and 60 pounds per square inch. The pressurized basement tank, he explained, meant the pump didn't have to turn on each time a toilet was flushed or water run to wash dishes. Instead, only when an amount of water from the tank was used sufficient to drop the pressure in the tank below 30 pounds would the pump down the well click on. The pump pushed water up and into the tank until the water within was pressurized to 60 pounds. At that point the pump automatically stopped. The process of refilling the tank took about a minute.

Kim incorporated a check valve into the system, so water from the tank couldn't flow back into the well, and he installed copper piping to tie the tank to the house plumbing. A simple shut-off valve downstream of the tank let me disconnect the well operation, just as a similar, already-in-place, shut-off valve elsewhere in the basement let me disconnect the gravity-fed system. By manipulating a couple of valves, then, I could alternate between my two water sources.

When Kim's bill was paid, the overall cost for the well system totalled $800 more than Aunt Beryl's bequest. Since by now I was used to paying more than I expected for most aspects of setting up the house, I scarcely blinked. Reducing my anxiety about further stoppages on the gravity-fed system was worth any amount of dough.

Ever since, I've been relieved to be able at the slightest sign of trouble on the water line to switch over to the well and continue daily life as before. Equally, when power goes out during a storm, I'm glad (if I happen to be connected to the well) to be able to switch over to the gravity-fed system.

Not that the well has been free of problems. Occasionally in the middle of the night I hear the well pump kick in. Or it starts during the day when no water is being used. Most often the cause is that I haven't completely turned off a faucet, and the resultant trickle eventually lowers the pressure in the tank enough to activate the pump. Yet to be lying in bed in the dark and suddenly hear the well pump start means I have to haul myself out from under the covers and begin to troubleshoot the plumbing. The well clicking on in the night is not my favourite sound.

Other glitches concerning the well system have occurred from time to time. Two and a half years after the well became operational, one spring day when I was connected to the well no water emerged if I opened a tap. I phoned Kim Wik. He was always busy, I knew, but all summer I kept phoning him to come out and see what was wrong. He repeatedly promised to show up, but only in October did he actually arrive. He diagnosed the issue as the pump being set too high in the well. In other words, the water level in the well had dropped, for whatever reason, below where the pump hung above the well bottom.

Kim lowered the pump and the problem seemed solved. However, the following January, once again no water appeared from the taps when the well was activated. I decided to try a different local well expert, Ken Jensen. As far as Ken could tell, when in snowy February he lowered a line down the well, no water was found where the pump was situated.

I worried about the well having gone dry. But in April when Ken returned, water was present. He decided the pump represented the problem, speculating that the intake might have become jammed with pebbles or other debris. The following month, he pulled and replaced the pump with what he said was a reconditioned model. This one worked fine.

I was miffed, though, at having the pump out of service again that year from January through May. So when, after nearly a decade and a half of trouble-free operation, a new problem appeared in the winter of 2008, instead of phoning Kim or Ken, I called Wolfgang the plumber. He now advertised expertise in pumps. My pump had been mysteriously turning on even though all faucets inside and outside the house were definitely shut.

Wolfgang thought perhaps the check valve Kim Wik had initially installed had become defective. The valve's close proximity to the pressure tank led him to test the latter once the valve was replaced. He found the tank had come to the end of its useful life. As soon as the new one was operational, everything functioned as intended.

But in chatting with Wolfgang about my adventures with the previous well experts Kim and Ken, I mentioned that the pump the latter had put in place would the following May have been in uninterrupted use for 15 years. Somewhere I'd heard or read that the expected life of the device was about that long.

I suggested to Wolfgang that in the summer we should pull the pump and have a look. Ken, after all, had told me that it was a reconditioned model, although I had never received promised paperwork for the device. Wolfgang was dubious about the need to lift it out, but said he would if I wanted to.

A contradiction exists between the concept of preventive maintenance and the proverbial saying, "If it ain't broke, don't fix it." I'm generally a fan of preventive maintenance. All things fail under stress, and if something can be examined and replaced if necessary before it completely fails, why not take such a step and avoid a catastrophe?

Thus, on a July day I accompanied Wolfgang to the well to watch him extract the pump. Everything about the system was working splendidly, but I intended to swap out the pump this time *before* it malfunctioned, if an inspection by Wolfgang revealed such a move looked warranted.

The pump and its attendant piping ordinarily are suspended from a device at the top of the shaft called a pitless adapter. Neither Kim Wik nor Wolfgang was clear about why the gadget is called "pitless," but it allows the pump with its down-the-well piping to be readily unhooked and hauled out via an attached cable.

Wolfgang removed the well cap that sealed the stub of 6-inch-diameter metal casing that protruded from the lawn. He duly unhooked the in-well gear, and, huffing and puffing, began to yard on the cable.

"I'm getting too old for this," he told me between yanks. "I can pull a pump up, but it's getting to be an effort."

Shortly, however, the pump refused to budge any farther, despite all Wolfgang's mighty exertions. We both hauled on the cable, to no effect. The pump seemed immovable. How this could happen was baffling: the pump was at the bottom of a shaft lined for nearly 60 feet with the steel casing, and below that, with the smaller diameter white plastic liner extending to where the shaft passed through bedrock. Nothing we could think of should have impeded the pump's ascent.

The stuck pump set in motion several days of attempts by Wolfgang to extract it. We tried angling the cable over a makeshift A-frame before securing the line to the front of Wolfgang's pickup. The plan was to back the truck up and thereby hoist the pump. We proceeded warily, though, and it became clear the cable would break before the pump would budge. Wolfgang even borrowed the Winlaw fire department's rescue truck in order to use that vehicle's powerful winch. The result of this initiative proved to be the same as our efforts with the pickup.

One theory Wolfgang began to favour was that, in hauling the pump up, it had become wedged against the bottom edge of the plastic liner. He speculated about how it might be jarred free.

A bill I had from Wolfgang about this time is for 25 hours labour, although he had spent far more hours than that at the well site, trying this and that, and, of course, pondering the situation at home on his own time. One hilarious incident saw Wolfgang ordering a rental mobile crane to lift out the pump. As he tells the story, he was having coffee in Winlaw's café when he spied out the window a gigantic crane truck lumber up the highway and signal to turn onto the Winlaw Bridge Road. He dashed out and flagged the enormous vehicle down.

"I'm Wolfgang," he told the driver. "This isn't the crane for me, is it?"

"Sure is," the driver told him.

"No, no, this is way too big," he informed the driver. "I told the company when I ordered it I just want to pull a well pump." The crane they sent, he said, had the capacity to lift the whole house.

Eventually Wolfgang suggested I call a well driller, in case they had encountered this problem before and had a solution. Because one Cranbrook well contractor, J.R. Drilling, advertised a Castlegar phone number, I wondered if they had a local guy who could maybe have a look at my well without me waiting until a crew was working in the area.

I phoned in early September. After I mentioned Wolfgang's theory, they said that they could probably lift out the plastic liner, in case the pump was snagged against the liner's bottom lip. If they couldn't extract the liner, they could drill it out, although the cost for that was estimated at $4,200—more than the well-drilling itself cost in 1989.

A month later, in early October, I again witnessed as I had in 1989 a huge drill rig slowly ascending my driveway, followed by a pipe truck. However, the autumn rains had begun. Although the weather was only cloudy on the day J.R. Drilling arrived, their heavy truck bogged down immediately after it passed through the lower gate and tried to climb the lawn to the well.

The drilling crew, Wolfgang and I spent hours trying to figure out how to get the rig up to the house. But the vehicle's spinning tires propelled grass and mud in all directions without any forward motion each time a fresh attempt was made. Deep ruts were gouged in what had been lawn. One effort involved squeezing Wolfgang's pickup past the floundering drill truck and attaching a rope to the latter so the pickup could provide extra assistance to help the rig get past the boggy lower part of the lawn. I was amazed that the drill truck, which I presumed frequently had to operate in rough terrain, wasn't equipped with four-wheel drive. But nobody else present seemed to think a lack of 4WD was odd.

This was the day that Wolfgang began referring to "the well from hell." The attempt to get the drill truck up the lawn was eventually abandoned. Not completely daunted, the J.R. Drilling crew subsequently looped a rope around the visible portion of the metal well casing, attached the rope to the hook of a small mobile crane, and used its boom to propel it up to the well. They managed to extract the old liner, although they noted that the well bottom appeared to be at 96 feet, rather than the original 115 feet. A new, slightly-smaller-in-diameter plastic liner was inserted. But the pump still wouldn't budge.

By this time Wolfgang began to suspect that what had happened was that the bedrock walls of the well had collapsed inward above where the pump was set. The well hadn't been lined all the way to the bottom because the original drillers had decided a liner wasn't needed below where the shaft toward the lower end passed through solid rock. Because the pump was totally functional until I decided to extract it, presumably the pipe bringing water to the surface hadn't been crimped by the collapsed shaft walls. If I hadn't tried to inspect the pump, I would still have had an operating well.

When we tried to lift the pump out, Wolfgang now reasoned, its ascent was blocked by the cave-in. This would explain, too, why the present crew found bottom at 96 feet—presumably the top of the collapsed section of shaft.

The J.R. Drilling guys agreed this was a likely scenario. The conversation turned to me: what did I want to do next?

Drilling down through the existing shaft was ruled out because it would have meant drilling through the existing pump. Apparently hitting the pump would damage the bit, plus leave mangled bits of metal in the well: a bad idea. My choices were either give up having a well after 19 years of service or drill a new well a few feet from the existing one.

I opted for the second choice. At least we knew where water was down below. The drill crew said they could drill next spring. But before they showed up again, they stipulated, the ground where their drill truck had lost traction would have to be completely dry. To be on the safe side, they suggested I spread a load of gravel at the bottom of the lawn. The latter area was now a morass of crisscrossing deep gouges and ruts, which, after everybody left, I raked into some semblance of order.

While spending another winter without a well, in February 2009 I phoned J.R. Drilling and was told they could drill in late May. So as the weather warmed that spring, I had a load of pit run dropped off by a local sand-and-gravel operator. To spread the gravel, I hired Mickey Shkuratoff and his trusty Bobcat, whom I had called a couple of times before over the years to clear my driveway after a particularly heavy snowfall.

I alerted J.R. Drilling once Mickey was finished, and in early June, up the driveway rose the drilling rig one more time. Wolfgang was standing by to lend a hand in case of any difficulties. But the drill truck and pipe truck rolled up the now-gravelly lower portion of the lawn like they were on pavement. The drill truck stopped beside the west wall of the house, intending to erect the rig about 6 feet south of the plugged well.

Unfortunately, J.R. Drilling's vehicle was longer than Owen's had been. Or maybe, in the 20 years since 1989, drill trucks had expanded in size the way pickup models each year swell larger and larger. With the nose of the drill truck flush against the treed earthen bank that marked the northern edge of the lawn, the business end of the big vehicle was several feet from the desired locale for the new well.

Wolfgang, unable to contain himself, let out a delighted guffaw when he saw the problem. "The well from hell, the well from hell," he proclaimed.

Once again Mickey trailered his Bobcat to my place. After he removed a portion of the offending bank, I smoothed the remainder into a gentle slope and planted grass and a couple of evergreens.

J.R. Drilling was having a busy summer, however, so were unable to return immediately after I notified them that the space beside the house had duly been expanded. Weeks came and went. In early September, just a month shy of a year after their trucks were mired in my lawn, J.R. Drilling said they felt bad about the continual postponement and were handing the job over to Owen's. When I expressed surprise that they would transfer work to a rival, I was told they all had plenty of work.

Owen's had a new owner, Harry Caldwell, who proved to be an exceptionally thoughtful guy. He had heard, I guess, about my situation, and he said that before me having to fork out the expense of an entire new well, he wanted to try something with a compressor. I wasn't sure I understood exactly what he had in mind, but I never received a bill when, in October, he showed up in a pickup towing a compressor and he and an employee spent some hours with compressed-air hoses snaked down the well. I think maybe the idea was that if he could dislodge the cave-in with compressed air, the pump would be freed and the well reactivated.

To no avail, however. After I spent a further winter without a well, in late April 2010 an Owen's drill rig was again noisily shaking the ground just past the end of my deck. This time the drill bit struck water at 129 feet, with the flow now 15 gallons a minute. Harry himself, along with his wife, showed up during the drilling. She and I talked pesto recipes after she saw a friend's posted on my kitchen fridge. I was glad to have something to take my mind off the drilling once the crew had passed the depth of the old well and hadn't hit water yet. The final 14 feet of the 2010 drill were long ones for me.

The new well had metal casing installed all the way to the bottom to ensure another cave-in never happens. The following month Wolfgang lowered a new pump and connected it to the existing system. I only had to dig out a space around the new and old wells so Wolfgang and a helper could work, since the existing piping into the house and the pressurized tank could be utilized. In the hole I excavated, Wolfgang cut off the top of old well casing below ground level and welded a plate atop it to prevent any contamination entering the aquifer.

I was elated to be shovelling the dirt back to fill the hole, once Wolfgang had completed rigging up the new well. And unless the pump that sits at the bottom of that shaft ceases to operate, I have no intention of even *thinking* about having it hauled up to check its condition.

Chapter Eight

NEGOTIATING BEHAVIOUR

Once my routines at Appledore were established, I felt I couldn't put off any longer attempting to resolve my relationship with Bea. I proceeded to purchase and devour relationship self-help books, one following another. I began this way because one of these sorts of books, or rather the announcement in spring 1988 of a University of BC community education course based on such a book, had helped motivate me to do something about my emotional situation.

The book that was the basis of the course had been published two years before: *The Fantasy Bond*, by a US psychologist, Robert Firestone, with a foreword by maverick Scots psychiatrist R.D. Laing. In the brochure that listed the university's forthcoming community ed offerings, the course description included a question that startled me: "Why are most intimate relationships unsatisfactory to those involved?" The adjective "most" was what set my mind reeling. I was certainly aware Bea and I had our problems. But could this really be true of *most* couples?

The two of us had been to a counsellor the previous fall. After we had described a little of our unhappiness at the state of our relationship, he asked what I thought was a penetrating question: "Do you want me to help you improve your relationship, or to help you break up?"

We both assured him we valued the relationship and wanted it to work. If the truth be told, though, I was in despair about ever making it better. Every time Bea said she wanted to talk about what was going on between us, I was both fearful of and resentful at having to reconsider the relationship one more time. I knew we should, but my preference was to drift along: our household ran smoothly with each of us doing our share of cooking, grocery shopping, cleaning and other household tasks. Growing up, I had been in Boy Scouts—as Wolf Cub, Boy Scout and Rover Scout—for 11 years, so I was no stranger to pulling my own weight domestically. We both had jobs, multiple interests outside the house, lots of friends, and each had problem family members to try to help.

Yet neither of us were satisfied with our emotional life. Bea wanted to start a family, and though I was certain she would be a wonderful mother—as the eldest of a large family, she had helped parent her younger brothers and sisters—I was evasive about making that decision. I had seen enough examples of couples who brought a child into a rocky relationship in the forlorn hope the latter would improve. Plus, I had been the main breadwinner for years. I felt financially responsible for Bea: when we had first gotten together, she had given up a good job in the public service to accompany me east when I was hired in 1975 as the University of Windsor writer-in-residence. She had never again found full-time work that was as challenging and enjoyable. Having a child would mean more obligations on me to keep us financially afloat. Above all, I wanted to protect my opportunity to write. I was aware from literary friends of how much a baby, toddler or child limited time and energy for work at the keyboard.

Not that I could plainly lay out these fears and worries when Bea and I talked about our relationship. My reservations concerning having a child appeared to me selfish, and uncaring about

Bea's needs. Since I wasn't forthright in describing my doubts about parenthood, Bea's frustrations with the impasse between us meant that when we tried to discuss what was going on between us, at a certain point she would break into tears. That would bring our conversation to a halt, since tears felt unanswerable to me. I never wanted to cause Bea grief, even if at the same time I stubbornly didn't want my life to change for what I judged would be the worse.

The counsellor correctly diagnosed our relationship as comfortable, but not satisfying. That formulation impressed me. But the counsellor had no real solution other than that we should take in a movie or do something else together by ourselves at least one night a week. Neither of us saw that as an answer, as we'd been to plenty of movies together already. We stopped making appointments with the counsellor and life continued as before.

Though I could grasp that we were in a stuck relationship, I greatly enjoyed talking about books and ideas with Bea, sampling her cooking—more adventurous than mine—and admiring how her gardening knowledge transformed the backyard of our East Vancouver rental house into an oasis of beauty. But when I saw the brochure's reference to *most* intimate relationships not working well, I wondered whether the book that the course was designed around held the information I—we—needed to move forward.

Though I couldn't imagine actually taking the course, I did drive out to the UBC bookstore and purchase a copy of *The Fantasy Bond*. What I took from my reading of it was that Firestone argues we begin life with a mother or other significant parent-figure whom we experience as responsive to our every need. Our mental image of how an intimate relationship *should* function remains for most of us that fantasy of the bond we had originally with our parent-figure, wherein we felt we were the recipient of another's total attention and care. Since that kind of bond is an illusion, especially between adults, relationships are bound to disappoint unless we re-examine our unspoken expectations of the link between ourselves and an intimate partner.

I thought there was much wisdom in this argument. Bea was loving toward me in dozens of ways, but her request—or, as I saw it, threatening demand—that my comfortable existence change to make room in our lives for a child definitely marred the fantasy of her being someone to whom my wishes and needs were central.

This insight, however, didn't provide any concrete advice as to how to extricate myself from a relationship I couldn't seem to make mutually fulfilling. But the step I took of actually buying and reading *The Fantasy Bond* provided an impetus for me to take another step toward resolving my—our—dilemma. That next step was removing myself to the Nelson area, audacious as such an act seemed to me. And now I had done it.

My hope was that even if *The Fantasy Bond* failed to indicate how to resolve the situation Bea and I found ourselves in, perhaps another relationship book would. At Appledore I devoured best-sellers such as *Men Who Can't Love; Cold Feet: Why Men Don't Commit;* and *Getting the Love You Want.* I also consumed some-what more technical books like *Between the Sexes,* by Judith and James Sellner, subtitled *A Self-Help Guide to Building a Successful Loving Relationship.*

I realized when I had read a few of these titles that each book provided me with a specific bit or bits of information useful in helping me understand my behaviour. Each book provided an opportunity for me to reflect on past interactions with Bea. Still elusive, though, was any indication of what I should do about my connection with her. Or rather, what I would feel justified and guilt-free in doing.

Instead, once I moved to Appledore, our relationship simply thinned. I visited her at our old home in Vancouver during the fall, and she drove up to spend Christmas with me. Though I visited her less thereafter, she had taken over contact with my father's brother,

Alex, his only sibling. *Alex's* fantasy, of a happy retirement with his Mexican wife in Mexico City, had evaporated when at 65 he stopped work on the potlines of Kitimat, BC's aluminum smelter and joined his wife in Mexico in the home she had bought with his money. His wife, on a long-ago visit to Kitimat, had judged the town too cold and remote, not to mention too un-Hispanic, to live with him there. Thus, during their marriage they only were together for the weeks of his annual vacation. Having him in the house all the time with no end in sight was another matter, and he subsequently relocated to Vancouver, where Bea and I had set him up in an apartment in East Van.

After a later futile trip to Mexico City to try to salvage something of his dream following the 1985 earthquake, he returned to BC suffering from cognitive issues. He said something about having been hit by a car, but the details were murky. His confusion increased as the months passed. He had refused our offer to re-establish him in an apartment and now lived in a downtown Single Room Occupancy hotel. With my removal to the West Kootenay, Bea kept a watchful eye on his condition, offering diligent and imaginative interventions to ease his situation. Some long-standing unexplained antipathy on my father's part toward my uncle, plus my father's geographic remoteness in Toronto, meant he was content to let first Bea and I, and then Bea, deal with my uncle's setbacks and decline.

Along with my reading about relationships and their discontents, I spent hours on the phone many evenings discussing my behaviours and attitudes with a former girlfriend from 1970 Vancouver, P'nina Shames, whom I had discovered was living in Nelson and working as a mental health social worker. I found her astute observations about human interactions, including mine, very helpful.

Meanwhile, I kept scouring self-help volumes for some revelation that would indicate the best path forward for me with regard to

Bea and grant me an easy conscience and relieved heart. I veered momentarily toward the Jungian with the US poet Robert Bly's prose volume *A Little Book on the Human Shadow*. I had met Bly when I was in grad school in California, and again when I held my first teaching job at Colorado State University. Bly is one of only two individuals I've ever encountered in whose presence I saw "another kind of mind there," as the Beatles describe the experience in "Got to Get You Into My Life." For me, the other extraordinary individual around whom I felt the same was the US poet Gary Snyder, whom I met when he also came to CSU to read. Both Bly and Snyder radiated a deep calmness, an energy at once profound and grounded, when you spoke with them or were near them.

After I returned to Canada from my stint in Colorado, for decades I enjoyed a desultory correspondence with Bly. He sensed something missing in my writing. "The poems are sometimes long and windy," he wrote me in June 1974, a few months before I was introduced to Bea by a mutual friend. "But the sufferings of others in them are so solid, and so carefully linked to their weight, that the poems are worth many light springy poems." On the other hand, he noted,

> [t]he outer world is too much in the poems for the long run
> of life—more "water," human intuitive possibilities lying at
> the back of your private brain need to come forward—be
> allowed to come forward, or up—to balance this marvel-
> lously developed sense of the solid world. You'll never lose
> your solid world. It will just be added to, by trees and some
> witches and talking animals.

I've certainly written lots of poems since about trees. Witches and talking animals, not so much. Bly's overall identification of my writing's shortcoming in his eyes was, however, evocative to me, as his own poems and translations are. But for all the interesting perspective on human behaviour in his *A Little Book on the Human Shadow*, it too failed to provide the key to escaping the emotional bind I felt I was in.

Two other self-help books I read and learned from that fall were Harriet Goldhor Lerner's *The Dance of Intimacy* and *The Dance of Anger*. In these I was introduced to a concept I hadn't considered before: how the acts of one intimate partner can induce a reaction in the other which in turn leads to a response—and so on. This idea was the dynamic writ large of what happened when Bea's and my discussions devolved into tears and I shut down. Relationships thus are seen not as a static situation—a problem to be solved—but as a fluid, ongoing back-and-forth process.

Another volume I found revelatory was Shad Helmstetter's *What to Say When You Talk to Yourself*. Besides admiring the great title, I liked how the author stressed the importance of not berating oneself after making a mistake of some sort: forgetting something or botching a task. When we call ourselves names, apparently the body has the same physiological reaction as if a stranger puts us down. Reading Helmstetter's book, I remembered a movement button from the 1960s that read: *Help the police. Beat yourself up.* I began to consciously praise myself to myself for even small successes that occurred in a day. And no longer would I denounce myself as idiotic, dumb or some other pejorative when I screwed up. Ending that behaviour included trying to stop putting myself down for not yet decisively acting to either cut ties with Bea or figure out a mutually beneficial way to reconnect.

My favourite two relationship books were jointly written by comedian John Cleese (one of BBC's zany Monty Python crew) and his therapist, Robin Skynner: *Families and How to Survive Them* (1983) and, after my concentrated reading of self-help volumes, *Life and How to Survive It* (1993). Both books are in the form of a dialogue between the two men. Skynner introduces concepts based on the then-latest research to do with families, marriage and

...Is the Journey

relationships. Cleese keeps the conversation light—and sometimes poignant—by his responses to the discoveries Skynner discusses.

According to Skynner, we're attracted to people who have the same relationship issues we do. He claims that if we walk into a room with 30 people in it, we're drawn to certain individuals—by body language, by how they speak, or other clues. They might on the surface seem to behave very differently than us—act as extroverts, say, while we think of ourselves as introverts. But if we get to know them better, Skynner says, they turn out to be affected by the same emotional shortcomings we have.

On a positive note, Skynner says that ideally an intimate relationship is where we can both go to be healed. Since the partners have the same fundamental behavioural issues, they can work on overcoming these together, supporting one another's efforts to surmount what has previously been an impediment to a fulfilling relationship. And even if this venture is not entirely successful, Skynner observes, at least such a relationship is good for a lifetime of conversation.

Despite the knowledge I was gaining from all this reading, and from my long late-night telephone conversations about relationship matters with my friend P'nina, I couldn't say my behaviour altered much. My connection with Bea in Vancouver became more tenuous over the next couple of years. Just as we'd previously drifted along together, we now drifted along apart. We no longer visited each other much, but neither did we definitively split up. We remained connected by phone and letter, often around Bea's care for my uncle, gossip about mutual friends, and our reactions to books we'd been reading.

Without much of a conscious decision on my part, I extended indefinitely my supposed time-out from the relationship with Bea. I liked my life at Appledore—appreciating my immersion in nature, and overcoming the challenges of country living. My friend the author, musician and educator John Lent arranged a job for me

150

for 1990–91 in Kelowna at Okanagan College, where he taught. This employment launched a pattern of working away in order to have the money to enjoy periodic uninterrupted years at Appledore.

Following a year back in Winlaw on Unemployment Insurance, I was hired for a three-year position starting fall 1992, again at Okanagan University College (as the institution was now called). Based in Vernon this time, I returned home each weekend (a four-hour drive). I began a relationship with Heather, an exceptionally bright single mother in Kelowna. With her, I re-established a distance relationship, in this case again both geographic and emotional. I wasn't going to give up Appledore, and Heather, with two daughters in school in Kelowna who had their own networks of friends, wasn't about to shift camp to Winlaw.

Plus, although Heather was aware of my tangled connection to Bea, the reverse was not true, which bothered Heather. She pushed me to clean up my act. I felt unable to do so, out of fear of the emotional storm a clean break might unleash, and maybe fear that with no impediments to a closer relationship with Heather, such a relationship would be demanded of me.

After a couple of years, Heather had had enough of my waffling. She suggested I talk to a counsellor who had recently moved from Kelowna to my area, Gerald Kennedy, whom she said had been helpful in her divorce from the father of her children. Although my previous experience with the counsellor in Vancouver hadn't been positive, and despite being nervous about approaching someone I didn't know to explore intimate matters, I was aware I had reproduced with Heather the exact same sort of distanced connection I had with Bea, despite all the reading I'd done. So I was willing to at least find out if Kennedy could help.

Kennedy and his wife, I learned at our first meeting, had wanted to retire early to a beautifully refurbished Victorian-era house in Silverton. But their plans to sell their Kelowna home and live off the proceeds had fallen through, so Kennedy had introduced himself to medical practitioners in the region and established a private counselling practice.

Sessions were held in the living room of his home. A fit individual in his late 50s, he approached work with me with energy and enthusiasm. His questions were more demanding than any the self-improvement books suggested I pose to myself. Our sessions churned up emotional turmoil in me regarding incidents in my boyhood or actions I had taken or not taken during past relationships, or due to his probing for motives for my behaviours. Back at Appledore after an hour with him, I frequently had to lie down for a nap.

He quickly showed me that one repeated behaviour of mine in intimate relationships was to establish an unwritten contract with the other person. This was a contract she had no idea existed. I would be supportive of her in every possible way I could, with the understanding—spelled out in the invisible contract—that in return for my help, she wouldn't ask me to be emotionally open. I began to grasp how frustrating this situation could be for the other person: "Here's someone who seems intensely interested in me and my well-being. But when I return the gesture and attempt to get closer to him, he withdraws."

Kennedy had amazing homework assignments. Early in our acquaintance, as the session neared the end, he stood up and beckoned me to accompany him through a door into the dining room. A piece of brown paper measuring about 6 feet by 6 feet was laid out flat on the hardwood floor. "Lie down and spread out your arms and legs," Kennedy said.

"Lie down?" I responded.

"On the paper."

I hesitantly complied, uneasy about where this was going. Kennedy picked up a blue felt marker, and carefully traced the outline of my body, producing one of those silhouettes that police are supposed to create on the ground or floor to indicate where a body has been discovered in a murder investigation.

"Okay, you can stand up now," Kennedy said.

He rolled up the paper with my outline on it. "Before we meet next time," he said, "I want you to write on this body map your feelings about each part of your body. How do you feel about your head? Your fingers? Your back? Maybe you have a memory of an event connected to how you regard your eyes, nose, knees. You can jot that down alongside your feelings."

He handed the paper to me. "Don't forget any organs."

I found completing the assignment a tremendously informative experience. After more than 45 years on the planet, how *did* I feel about my arms, stomach and, er, genitals?

At our next session I was eager to review in detail the discoveries that had bubbled up when I paid attention to my appendages and other parts of my body. To my surprise, as I began, he held up his hand to cut me off.

"What you learn is for you, not me," he said. "If the homework was useful, that's good. But what matters is what *you* gain from doing it."

I was a bit disappointed that I couldn't rattle on about what I now understood about myself as a result of this exercise. On reflection, though, I could see the wisdom of him not spending session time on such a review. He observed later that any knowledge about myself I had acquired would be revealed as we continued to meet. More importantly, such knowledge should affect my behaviours in a way that made my life less stressful or conflicted.

After a while I realized that my counselling homework assignments were usually designed to prod me to be more forthcoming about my feelings. Each session began to start with a summary of what I'd been up to since we last met. Kennedy would probe my emotional reactions to incidents I mentioned.

"How did you feel when she said that?"

"I can certainly understand why she might have reacted that way. If I try to see it from her point of view, I realize—"

"No, how did you feel?"

"She was certainly within her rights to say what she—"

"No. No. How did you feel?"

"When I thought about it afterwards, I had to agree that—"

"Not what you *thought*. How. Did. You. *Feel*?"

"I felt angry and resentful. I felt attacked."

"Whew. Now we're getting someplace."

Kennedy helped me understand I was stuffing away my emotional responses to people and events in my life. "Feelings are just information," he stressed. "It's when we don't pay attention to them that they become huge and powerful." He emphasized that we act more out of our gut than our brain, despite any conviction that we're doing the opposite. This source of motivation means, he said, that monitoring feelings is vital to understanding our behaviours and to changing them in a direction that makes us more comfortable with ourselves.

I learned to ask myself how I feel about bothersome situations and own up to those feelings, regardless of whether I judge the feelings to be shameful, petty or selfish. Confessing my emotional response to myself, no matter how awful that confession sounds to my ears, I find diminishes how large a disagreeable incident looms in my mind. Yet ignoring or trying to think away my feelings remains my initial impulse. "Your old tapes will always play," Kennedy assured me. "But once the old tapes come on and you recognize them for what they are, you can reach over and shut them off."

Not that I agreed with everything Kennedy said. When he pushed me to express feelings, his formula was: "Do you feel sad, mad, glad, or confused?" I maintained that his rubric omitted fear. Because of something I'd read and found accurate, at least for me,

I believe my feelings of anger arise out of fear. If I identify what I'm afraid of in a situation where I become enraged, I have a better handle on how to react. Kennedy, however, stuck to his "sad, mad, glad, or confused" spectrum of emotions. He appeared to regard fear as a subset of anger, whereas to me it is a *cause* of the emotion and hence worth exploring in its own right.

I went every two weeks to Kennedy for a couple of years. Eventually, at one of our sessions, he declared that our meeting together wasn't meant to be a lifetime procedure and that I should try functioning on my own. "Whatever way people behave, as long as they aren't hurting themselves or others, is okay," he said. "Naturally, they also have to be happy with how they're living. If you're not happy, that's when you need to seek help."

Kennedy said he touched base every few years with a counsellor he had worked with before, as a sort of emotional tune-up. Indeed, a year later, I did several months of more sessions with Kennedy.

Intrigued and grateful as I was by most of his techniques for helping me understand the roots of my default behaviours, other people I knew didn't share my excitement at his approach. They saw a focus on self-examination as self-indulgence, if not self-obsession.

I was explaining to my friends David and Judy that I had complained to Kennedy that my contact with Vancouver friends and acquaintances since I had relocated to the West Kootenay mainly consisted of them requesting me to do something for them. People from the literary world, for example, wanted letters of reference or advice or help about manuscripts, publishers, submissions to literary magazines, public reading venues or book promotion. They didn't express any interest in what might be happening in my life.

I reported that I had told Kennedy I wished they wouldn't keep asking me for favours. He had replied that people have the right to ask for anything they want. But that, equally, I have the right to say "no." I had been practising politely refusing requests or ignoring them if I really didn't wish to take the time and energy to provide what the askers wanted from me. Under such circumstances, I said to David and Judy, I no longer felt guilty if I didn't oblige them.

"Sounds like you're studying to be a prick," Judy commented.

Yet because of the insights I had gained from working with Kennedy, I felt I could now choose my response to certain situations and people rather than just react blindly. One of Kennedy's observations I thought devastatingly accurate was that a pattern of mine was to hang back at the edge of things rather than step forward into the centre of them. "Your writing life mainly involves poetry, which is a marginal art form, rather than fiction, which is mainstream," he said. "You've taught mostly at community colleges rather than for universities. And you certainly hold back from fully engaging in your relationships."

Kennedy speculated that my default position of keeping myself on the sidelines was due to having skipped a grade in elementary school in Prince Rupert: I had been allowed to bypass Grade 5. Such a procedure was common at the time, since educational authorities were convinced certain kids needed more of a challenge than coasting through a grade in which they would speedily master the course content and then be bored for the rest of the year. My brother had been accelerated *two* grades during his schooling.

Pushing pupils ahead of their peers like this, Kennedy declared, was a form of child abuse. I was amazed at his vehemence. He explained that because emotional development is age-based, skipping a grade has an adverse effect on a child's sense of who they are in relation to others. Reflecting back, I could confirm that, because I was always smaller physically than my classmates and because most of the Grade 6 class I was transferred into had been together since they started school, I frequently felt not only like a wimp, but also an outsider.

I assured him, though, that as the years passed, and especially when my family moved to Vancouver and I began Grade 10 there, I didn't feel so disconnected from my classmates, despite being smaller than most and behind in maturity. Also, I had realized that while I would forever be a klutz when it came to team sports, I could get top marks, or nearly, in academic courses.

Kennedy was unconvinced that my method of compensating for being pushed forward a grade—being a "brain"—was beneficial to me in the long run. Determining a balance between living in one's head versus paying attention to feelings was an issue on which we disagreed. I accepted that I needed to pay more attention to my feelings, but I maintained that rationally processing a problem or situation had often stood me in good stead.

I marvelled, though, at the accuracy of Kennedy's conclusion that I preferred the sidelines to being in the middle of things. Almost immediately, I had a chance to break this pattern.

After the provincial government's 1984 closure of David Thompson University Centre in Nelson, the former community-based DTUC Support Society was determined to restore university-level education to the city. In the end they concluded that a niche post-secondary institution might prosper. From their efforts emerged the Kootenay School of the Arts (1991–2020). The school's organizing committee managed to convince the city to back the idea and supply a building, making KSA a rare-for-Canada municipal educational initiative.

Since one of the new school's seven departments, or studios as they were called, was to be creative writing, in 1991–92 I taught one of KSA's first-ever courses, an all-genre writing workshop. In subsequent years, until the Writing Studio was axed by the school in 2002 as part of an ill-fated attempt to rebrand as a "craft" institution, I taught for KSA when I wasn't teaching on the Coast or in the Okanagan,

From the inception of KSA, I believed its faculty should be part of the provincial union of college teachers, called in those days the College-Institute Educators Association, or C-IEA (now known as FPSE, the Federation of Post-Secondary Educators). We

KSA faculty were working for about one-third the going rate of the province's college teachers, even if we enjoyed more freedom in curriculum design and implementation than our counterparts in the regular system.

I was acquainted with the then-president of C-IEA, Ed Lavalle, from our UBC student years. Ed ensured that I was provided with information about C-IEA and the working conditions of its constituent locals that I could pass around at our infrequent KSA faculty meetings. Interest in unionizing didn't pick up, however, until our founding executive director, David Lawson, stepped aside to chair the Clay Studio.

A saying in the union movement is, "The boss is the best organizer." That proved to be true at KSA as the school's new management threatened the autonomy that the studios believed we had earned through countless hours of non-academic volunteer labour, which included equipment and classroom furniture purchases, physical improvements to allotted teaching spaces, and janitorial duties. Yet the incident that sparked the signing up of the majority of KSA employees into our fledgling KSA Faculty and Staff Association was when management went to the home of one of the office secretaries after work one cold winter evening. Standing on her doorstep, the two management reps demanded her office keys and fired her, literally in front of her family.

Before working with Kennedy, I would have been content to leave leadership roles in the new union to others. But since so few faculty other than myself had any experience working in a unionized educational environment, and with Kennedy's words ringing in my ears about my habitual reluctance to step into the centre of things, I agreed to run for and was elected the founding president of our bargaining unit. I saw that, if I was ever to change my customary behaviour, this was a place to start.

Once the union certification vote passed, we began the task of trying to obtain a first collective agreement. C-IEA assigned us as staff rep and chief negotiator someone every bit as skilled as Kennedy at understanding relations between people and who indirectly also taught me much about my default behaviours and some better ways to function.

Our c-iea staff rep, David Piasta, a conventionally dressed individual in his late 40s, had instant rapport with our artistically inclined membership. He himself had a strong creative streak, building bows and musical instruments as a hobby. An inventive and knowledgeable chef, he could talk recipes for hours. As a release from the pressures of his job looking after several community college bargaining units besides ours, during his summer holidays he was an active participant in the bc Society for Creative Anachronism's annual medieval-themed camp-outs and war games.

When we entered collective bargaining, he began each day's negotiations with a canvass of our bargaining team: we each had to report on how we were feeling. He explained that if team members had missed breakfast or had a fight with their spouse before heading off to the morning's negotiating session, these events would affect his or her behaviour when we met with the administration's negotiating team. I recognized that Piasta's practice matched Kennedy's insistence that people are motivated to act more by their emotions than their head. Our union rep's perpetually cheerful demeanour and sincerity made people want to answer his morning question honestly.

Once we entered bargaining, Piasta would frequently ask two questions about a contract proposal, whether it originated with our team or management. Piasta would first ask, "What problem is this intended to solve?" Identifying the difficulty that a given proposal supposedly addressed often shifted the discussion from the merits or failings of a proposed solution to the nature and dimensions of the problem itself. With the shift in focus from the proposal to the problem, better solutions than the proposal on the table were mutually identified several times.

Piasta's second question regarding a proposal was posed once the problem was analyzed. He would inquire, "How would that work, then?" Having to detail how a proposal was going to demonstrably solve the issue in question often revealed to the proposer, as well as to others, shortcomings in the proposal and/or ways the proposal could be enhanced to better meet its goal.

Piasta viewed relations with people in every situation as a continual series of negotiations with his two questions in mind. I could see that these questions, like Kennedy's "How do you feel?", had applications beyond collective bargaining. And his deployment of the questions meant he often could head off trouble before it began. During one bargaining session, Piasta called for a break and pulled me out of the conference room into the hallway, literally by one ear. "Where are you going with that line of questioning, Tom?" he asked. I had been holding forth in reaction to some restrictive article management had proposed for the collective agreement.

"I want management to admit they're shallow and vindictive," I explained to Piasta.

He shook his head. "We can win things at bargaining," he said. "But nobody is going to admit they are shallow and vindictive." Of course he was right.

He related to me once how when one of his daughters had announced she was moving in with some guy, he assured her that he and his wife had no objections. But, he inquired, how did his daughter regard setting up house with this man? Did she view cohabiting as a prelude to marriage? A fling?

I understood that what he asked his daughter was a version of his negotiation questions. He reported that his daughter and the person she had decided to live with quickly married.

A third question Piasta sometimes asked our side I also found useful beyond the union milieu. At times our negotiating team would return to our break-out room incensed by some contract wording management had placed on the table, or by their dismissive response to contract language we had put forward. Piasta would let us blow off steam for a while, and then he would ask, "Is this a deal-breaker?" Most times the room would instantly calm as we weighed his question. Then, reluctantly, most of us agreed when polled that, although we found the matter at hand insulting, excessive or stupid, this wasn't a strike issue or, sometimes, even a major concern.

Ever after, I've found Piasta's third question a good one to consider when faced with behaviour or an opinion I find wrong or off-putting. I tend to be a judgmental person, but remembering Piasta's calm and, as always, cheerful question, "Is this a deal-breaker?" helps me sort out how important to me is some action or statement I find offensive. Is this really a hill to die on?

The wisdom of Piasta's approach to potentially abrasive dis-agreements wasn't lost on others in our bargaining sessions, either. His sunny and optimistic nature, plus his honest assessment of problems, led more than me to learn from his skill set. Besides his abilities with people, his thoroughgoing familiarity with models of academic governance due to his experience as a C-IEA staff rep impressed KSA's administration, too. By the end of negotiating our first agreement, they were listening as attentively as we did when in the midst of a session he outlined how this or that college had handled a governance issue. With his guidance, we obtained a contract that succeeded in preserving a considerable amount of studio independence compared with that permitted departments in mainstream colleges where I'd taught.

A fourth question Piasta asked I've also found useful ever since. In one break-out room session, our negotiating team had left the bargaining table livid about some new management proposal. Someone (not me) suggested an aggressive but unlikely counter. The suggestion, though far from serious or constructive, met with delighted approval all around. The ante was upped by proposed amendments that pushed our possible rebuttal into even more confrontational territory.

As usual, Piasta let our team vent for a time. Then, during a lull, he asked, "Well, do you want to be adults, or not?" As usual with him, this query was posed as a real question. He appeared willing to accept a childish response to management, if that's what we decided we wanted to bring back to the table.

As with so many of his questions, however, the atmosphere in the room shifted when he uttered it. People admitted they *did* want to behave like adults, despite the ridiculousness of the administration's latest idea. With Piasta's help, we crafted a less hostile and definitely more adult reply.

Many times in my life since, when I've been tempted in the heat of a moment to offer a bristly spoken, written or physical response to a situation or person, I hear Piasta's voice in my head asking: "Do you want to behave like an adult? Or indulge yourself?" Kennedy more than once had posed a related question. Like Piasta's, the counsellor's question probed whether the real goal in certain circumstances is to solve a problem or to express outrage and/or righteousness. Kennedy would ask, in the face of my stubborn insistence on the correctness of my reaction to some matter, "Do you want to be right, or happy?"

My answer was invariably: "Both." But Kennedy just shook his head and repeated the question. He and Piasta apparently agreed that on this planet, given how humans behave when challenged, achieving a happy outcome involves a more compromised position than that dictated by any one person's sense of rectitude, justice, fair play. A child will cling to her or his concept of a black-and-white morality. An adult, on the other hand, is aware that adhering to such a viewpoint does not bring the rewards it might appear to promise.

In 2018 I had this perspective reinforced when an annual New Denver literary weekend, on whose organizing committee I served, invited as a speaker the former chair of the environmental Suzuki Foundation, James Hoggan. The theme of our 2018 gathering was

"Keeping a Civil Tongue," that is, how to avoid the toxic discourse that so far characterizes the twenty-first century. A few years before his visit to New Denver, Hoggan had been asked by the Foundation's namesake, geneticist and broadcaster David Suzuki, to account for why, despite the best efforts of so many environmental scientists and lay environmental organizations, the majority of the population do not share the experts' and activists' sense of urgency regarding climate change.

Hoggan interviewed a host of world specialists in communication, from the University of California, Berkeley professor and political adviser George Lakoff to cognitive scientist and political gadfly Noam Chomsky to the Dalai Lama. The results were spelled out in Hoggan's 2016 collection of these interviews, *I'm Right and You're an Idiot: The Toxic State of Public Discourse and How to Clean It Up.*

The consensus of the book's interviewees, discussed in more detail by Hoggan during the New Denver weekend, is that invoking shame, blame and statistics to make your point—the current mainstays of the environmental and social justice movements—doesn't convince anybody who isn't already a true believer. Scolding, denouncing, and marshalling facts merely make the indulger in these activities feel righteous and moral. "Speak your truth, but not to punish" was one of Hoggan's alternative suggestions at New Denver, if one's aim really is to influence someone's opinion and not just to lash out at them. "Disagree without disrespect" is another of Hoggan's ideas. I thought of how many times in dozens of settings, whether at a political meeting, in the street during confrontations with authority, or in a bedroom, I'd tried to change somebody's mind by offering a combination of that unholy trio of shame, blame and statistics. In mentally reviewing these moments, I had to conclude that despite how *right* my position was, I never won anybody over to agree with my viewpoint. And I certainly didn't ever leave these arguments feeling glad about the outcome.

Eventually when I was working with Kennedy, I was able to draw a line with regard to my relationship with Bea that earned me a "*Mazel tov*" from the counsellor. That said, I've never yet achieved a relationship in which I exist daily in an intimate, loving environment. But the lessons gleaned from my interactions with Kennedy and Piasta mean I understand much more about why I behave as I do. And why other people behave as they do. I feel I can handle far more situations that once would have been threatening, disappointing or baffling,

Would I ever have gathered this practical, angst-reducing knowledge if I hadn't moved to the country? I'm aware that no one can predict with certainty the outcome of an alternative reality. I believe, however, that if I hadn't been able to take the tangible step—albeit a clumsy one in many ways—of moving to Appledore, my life would have continued to occur in a comfortable but ultimately unfulfilling milieu.

I may never succeed in achieving what I imagine is, ideally, the right way to live. Yet thanks to Kennedy and Piasta, I believe I have a pretty good sense of the reasons for my life choices and their consequences, of how to navigate with more equanimity through my days. Despite the inevitable difficulties and frustrations at Appledore, I feel happy here.

Chapter Nine

THE SEASONS–
WINTER

Even after the inaugural snowfall, winter doesn't behave as though it seriously intends to take up residence in the valley. For a couple of weeks, I can wake up to a skiff of snow covering the ground and tree limbs, but by noon everything outside is bare once more. The day has reverted to autumn, with occasional spells of drizzle or rain. Then, in the gloom of late afternoon, white tufts begin to waft downwards. The snowflakes melt as soon as they touch the lawn, the driveway, the deck. If I check just before bed, though, the snow has begun to stick. And in the morning, the world is white once more. By noon, however, winter has again abandoned the valley and the previous season has returned.

Appledore in fact is in a shoulder season: no longer fall, not yet full-on winter. But the nightly snow is a reminder winter will soon decisively arrive. Each evening during these weeks, I light a fire in the basement furnace. Kindling the first fire of autumn is always an event. When the wood catches, I like to walk out onto the deck and turn to watch the smoke lifting from my chimney. The sight is reassuring: the great ship of my house is steaming confidently through the new cold, ready to ride out the weather to come.

Air in a house warmed by a fire is mellower than air warmed by electric baseboards. A richly soft heat fills the rooms when the fire is chuckling to itself in the basement. Yet my electric baseboards, set to 10 or 15 degrees, keep the house from freezing if I'm absent— away for the day to town, or for a week to the Coast, or for the weeks between my weekends at home during the winters I taught on the Lower Mainland or in Calgary.

Winter truly takes possession of the valley on a day when snow descends hour after hour and remains thereafter. Snow can be the dominant feature of the valley from mid-December to mid-March, although more often, in this era of global warming, the season can be over, at least on the valley floor, at the end of February. At the height of winter, mid-January to early February, the accumulation of snow will be up to my thighs around the grounds at Appledore. I have photos of the deck supporting half a metre of snow after a single storm.

I love the winter world outdoors, with the air's icy purity invigorating my lungs with each breath. The mountains in every direction are the same unvarying colour, broken only where grey cliffs rise, streaked with white. On the valley floor, meadows and fields have become flat or rolling expanses of white, and the roof of every house, shed and barn is the identical shade. Other than the cliffs on the mountainsides, the only intrusions into the monochrome scenery are the unfrozen river and the highway's cleared asphalt.

I find something medieval in the starkness of the valley's winter landscape. The world seems reduced to the bare essentials of subsistence and their opposites: warmth/cold, fire/ice, daylight/ dark. How grateful I am to enter indoors into heat after too long a spell outside in the cold. How grateful for a bowl of hot soup on a freezing day. In the early dark, how glad for artificial light. In my imagination, such basic antitheses were the essence of human existence in that earlier time.

As then, the white countryside no longer provides food: sustenance preserved from a different season. Either you have made provision for this lack, or you are in peril. Winter travel through the cold and snow on foot or horseback was always difficult. Yet even automobile driving involves danger: one minute the pavement under you is as safe as in any other season; the next minute you can be steering on a slippery surface nearly blind amid the white curtains of a snow squall.

Yet the beauty of morning sunlight sparkling on a white pasture, the calming effect of watching a slow, hypnotic fall of flakes one afternoon, the wonder of standing outside awestruck below the shining tapestry of stars on a bone-chilling night are some of the rewards the season offers. And even though I treasure these gifts winter provides, surviving each day's cold and blackness is itself a gift I feel thankful to receive. I have a poem that speaks to this response, "Benediction":

> Each winter night last thing
> I bend to the bedroom window
>
> slid open a crack and inhale
> a taste of snow in the darkness,
>
> of wood smoke from my chimney
> if the wind is right,
>
> and of the silent white mountains
> that rise around me
>
> who launch from their summit ridges
> when the sky is clear

a myriad of stars toward the zenith
—those frosty pinpoints of light

shepherded by Orion
high over the trees to the southeast.

My mouth at the slight opening
between glass and frame

exhales gratitude for warmth, for
shelter, for the valley's stillness

and breathes in again a benediction
of icy air

that blesses my body,
my dwelling, my sleep.

In the black of night, I can wake to the sound of a snowplough passing along the back road. I know then that a significant snowfall must have occurred while I slept. Because school buses travel the road, it must be kept ploughed and sanded, ready for safe use in the early morning. I sleepily note to myself that I'll have to clear the driveway first thing, then drift again into slumber, cradled in the comfort of the bed's thick quilt and the house's fire-warmed air.

As the days grow shorter and I adjust to the new season's presence, I look forward to Christmas. Most cultures have a festival of light at the darkest time of year, and of all the holidays our neck of the planet celebrates, I most appreciate the Yuletide. After all, the view out every window at Appledore by the middle of December resembles the illustration on the majority of Christmas cards that have begun to arrive in my mail: snowy mountain terrain. I spend a few days at the start of the month writing cards myself. Some of the recipients I communicate with only once a year via these cards, so preparing the cards to send seems like renewing a network of old friendships. Card after card shows up for me in the Winlaw post office, and for weeks thereafter are perched on window-sills and crowded atop bookcases throughout the house. A few people send electronic greetings, but these feel more fleeting to me than the material connections with friends and relations I receive.

I take boxes of my Christmas gear down from a cupboard shelf. Soon Christmas-themed decorations—miniature trees, snow-men, reindeer—grace Appledore's kitchen and dining-room tables. Within a couple of years of acquiring my property, I planted a holly tree not far west of the deck. Clippings from this tree—now 15 feet high—embellish the table displays.

Outdoors, I'm busy with lights. The permanently affixed row of bulbs I left above the deck simply has to be switched on, and I festoon other lights along the deck railings and some fences. Strings of lights transform two evergreens east of the house.

A highlight of the holiday season for me is the acquisition of a Christmas tree. The first few years I would climb the ridge west of the house and ramble around in my forest until I found a recent fir or spruce blow-down whose upper 7 or 8 feet remained green. These tops could be spindly, but I was always proud to display them as a sourced-on-the-premises Appledore Christmas tree.

In 1994 my then-new neighbour to the south clear-cut most of his 20 wooded acres of the ridge, which led to a huge increase in the number of blown-down evergreens in the southern portion of my forest. For a while, this made finding a suitable blow-down somewhat easier. About 10 years ago, though, I discovered stands of small firs growing along the northern lip of one of two gullies that cut through my woods. Each December now, instead of searching out the latest blow-downs, I head straight for this cluster of firs.

Indoors, I mount my new acquisition on its stand in my living room and begin to adorn it with lights, ornaments and tinsel. I'm aware of the strangeness of bringing an evergreen into a house in winter and setting the tree upright. Even odder is to attach lights and small items to its branches. Yet once the tree is transformed, the object for me emanates a peaceful aura. I love to lie on the living-room couch, perhaps resting after a strenuous afternoon of clearing snow from the driveway, as the short winter day darkens. Across the room, lights on the glittering tree twinkle randomly. I recall family Christmases when I was a boy, with their exciting promise of gifts and culinary treats. I feel a deep contentment as I drift into sleep.

Another Yuletide highlight has become an annual concert by the valley's amateur choir. As I've noted, my neighbour Sharon directs this choir. But I'd attend anyway, given that I'm friends with some of the people who perform and many in the audience.

The concert takes place in the Vallican Whole. This community hall was conceived when 1960s Vietnam War resisters and back-to-the-landers who had moved to the West Kootenay saw the existing community and Doukhobor halls scattered throughout the valley and wanted a meeting place and performance space of their own. The building project began in 1971 in Passmore, an unincorporated area 8 kilometres south of Winlaw, and the structure was completed in 1975. The name of the hall arose out of local derision at how, despite some federal government funding for the mostly volunteer hippie effort, for a time only the basement was completed. This excavation was dubbed by nay-sayers "the Vallican Hole." "Vallican" is the designation of the telephone exchange that includes Winlaw and Passmore: the word is a shortening of "Valley of the Slocan."

When the building was at last completed, the extra letter was added to "Hole" by its supporters to reflect that the hall was the accomplishment of the whole counter-culture community. The Whole is a two-storey wooden construction, site of dances, community dinners, meetings, and musical and other entertainments. The hall is constantly being renovated, in part because of age or new building code requirements such as wheelchair access. Also because the building's designer, a local, conceived of highly imaginative but problematic dwellings.

One couple I know who lived in a house he had designed spoke of how, due to lack of air circulation, a small cloud would form just below the ceiling of the large third-floor room that constituted the top storey of their house. A neighbour living a couple of kilometres down the back road from me, occupying another of the designer's houses, told me once that he thought there should be a support group for people who live in the man's houses.

Still, the Whole is a striking-looking building, and its achievement as a location for valley residents to assemble is evident at the choir's Christmas concert. Before the music starts, and during intermission, the hall throbs with the noisy bustle of a capacity crowd greeting each other, while kids race around making their own fun. Refreshments are on sale, either as a benefit for the Whole or for some other worthy cause. Under Sharon's direction, year after year the choir offers increasingly sophisticated musical arrangements. Part of the program is also a sing-along of Christmas anthems.

While the religious aspect of the holiday isn't of much interest to me, on most occasions as the Yuletide standards reverberate through the hall, snow begins to descend outside, visible through the Whole's windows in the dimming afternoon. The much-vaunted spirit of Christmas—locally, the reconciliation of residents' feuds and divisions over political and social issues—feels momentarily realized amid the lyrics lofted by the voices of young and old together.

As the ideals of Christmas fade for another year, my daily life in winter revolves around, besides writing, clearing snow at Appledore, meeting the challenges of driving, and delighting in cross-country skiing. Overnight snowfalls are common, and snow-clearing—unless I have an appointment in town that morning—starts around 2 p.m. when I've had enough of words and shut off the computer.

Warmly dressed against the weather, I exit through the basement door and force my way through new drifts around the house's south side and up onto the deck via the snow-covered stairs at its western end. My snow-removal implements are kept on the deck, and to clear the latter, I employ a push-shovel to propel the snow out under the railings onto the white below.

When the deck and its stairs are finished, I pick up my snow scoop. My first winter at Appledore I realized my driveway was too long to attempt to keep snow off it wielding a conventional snow shovel. I witnessed people working in their driveways with a snow scoop, a tool I'd never seen before, and bought one myself.

The device consists of a sturdy plastic scoop about a foot deep at the back and with slightly lower sides, about 2 feet long. Snow scoops come in varying widths—I favour a 22-inch-wide one. The rear of the scoop is attached to the open end of a metal "U" that extends out 2 ½ feet behind the scoop and whose crossbar serves as the handle. Unlike with a shovel, snow to be removed is pushed out of the way rather than having to be lifted and tossed aside.

My first task with the snow scoop is to open a path from the deck stairs back to the basement door. Snow packed into the scoop is transferred to piles alongside the route via escape ramps I create in the snow at right angles to the path being cleared. The scoop's cargo is emptied by an abrupt jerk of the arms.

I clear completely the level area outside the basement door where my vehicle is parked. I keep the emptied space large enough that a visitor can park as well. Then the driveway is made functional not by removing snow entirely but by creating wheel paths: twin linear cleared areas a vehicle's tires can follow as they ascend or descend the drive. The wheel paths are the width of the snow scoop.

Since in any season, my vehicle has to slow to navigate the driveway's right-angle turn toward the house, in snow I am most likely to become stuck here if anywhere on the ascent. Prudence dictates that I remove snow completely at this location.

From the turn down to the back road, wheel paths are again all that is required. At the bottom, though, I once more clear the space entirely so I don't lose traction and hence momentum as I swing off the pavement and start to gun up the wheel paths.

Under ordinary circumstances, opening the drive—wheel paths and cleared areas alike—takes me a couple of hours. The task is excellent exercise, of course, strengthening muscles as well as improving my sense of balance as I manoeuvre a full snow scoop up a banked pile. The experience can be revitalizing on a cold, sunny day: I draw into my nostrils and throat chill air that seems so pure as to be medicinal. At certain stretches along the driveway, I pause at my labours to gaze across the valley at the glory of the snow-covered eastern ridges. Or I can stop to take in the loveliness of a snow-draped cedar or fir close by.

Snow-clearing becomes less appealing when the white stuff descends day after day after day. By the third or fourth snowy day in a row, I feel a kinship with Sisyphus. Also a drag is if the temperature is just above freezing and we get a foot of snow filled with moisture, which adds substantially to its weight. Some winters I tackle a driveway choked with snow so heavy that I give up clearing it after four or five hours, my clothes soaked with sweat. As long as I have no urgent need to leave the property, I decide to rest up and finish the job the following day.

However easy or difficult the task, when I've made the driveway navigable, Appledore is connected again to the greater world. Occasionally I've hired someone to clear the drive with a machine: Mickey Shkuratoff with his Bobcat, for example. During a teaching term, I would grow tired of returning from the Okanagan or Calgary for a weekend to face a dark driveway covered by a couple of feet of snow. So as an indulgence, I occasionally arranged in advance to have the snow removed before I arrived back.

Otherwise, I have three choices if I find myself behind the wheel at the bottom of my driveway deep in snow—on a late afternoon homecoming from a visit to the Coast, say, or from a shopping trip into Nelson. One option is to tighten my sphincter, gear into four-wheel drive, and hit the accelerator. My hope is that, because the driveway hasn't been packed down, the resultant traction will enable me to achieve the top, even if the climb involves the slipping and shuddering of tires, and maybe a near stall. The second option is to leave the vehicle at the bottom of the drive for the night and lug its contents—suitcases, grocery bags, whatever—to the basement door, plodding up and down through the snow in a series of round trips to bring everything up to the house.

The third option is to leave the vehicle at the bottom temporarily, trudge up to the house, change into working gear, snag the snow scoop off the deck, and, if night has fallen, by the light of the moon or a headlamp clear a set of wheel paths and the entire area where the driveway makes its sharp bend. Then I can motor up to the house to unload, aiming to finish the balance of my usual snow removal the next day.

My choice of which option is often not made rationally. Repeatedly, I've wished too late that I'd selected a more prudent option after, at the bottom of my driveway, I've heard a voice whisper in my ear: "Go ahead. Try it!" Before reason can intervene, my right foot is pressed to the floor and I'm urging the vehicle to "Go! Go! Go!"

Twenty per cent of my attempts to power up the snow-clogged driveway end with me stuck at the turn. I've sometimes left the immobilized vehicle where it's lodged part-way up the drive and unloaded it from there. In morning daylight, getting unstuck is much less of a challenge than in the pitch-black of night. Yet I've also, after a hurried change of clothes, been out in the chilly dark shovelling compacted snow away from wheels and spreading sand where the tires spun out. Freeing the vehicle might take several tries, each followed by more shovelling, more curses, and more sand.

I apply sand proactively to the driveway, too. Each autumn I purchase four or five sandbags at a gas station, although the material is available for free if I'm willing to sneak into one of the government gravel pits in the valley and fill some boxes. If a melt is followed by a freeze, especially if we get rain during a brief January thaw, the driveway transforms to a sheet of ice and sanding is a necessity.

During my first winters in the valley, driveways up and down the back road displayed wheel paths like mine through the snow. Nowadays the sight is rare: the drive is usually completely clear. If residents haven't hired somebody with a plough affixed to a pickup or tractor, or operated such a rig themselves, snow has been removed by an ATV with a blade, or by a snowblower.

In 2019 I finally purchased a self-propelled snowblower myself. Its size and weight mean it's a bit of a workout to handle. I should emphasize that "self-propelled" doesn't mean the heavy machine doesn't require help trundling uphill in deep snow or when its tires encounter ice. Nor is a snowblower a lot more adept at dealing with wet snow than I am with a snow scoop. Overall, though, owning the snowblower means snow-clearing is less work, particularly after a sizable dump of snow. And the snowblower means an end to only creating wheel paths, since clearing the full width of the driveway can be accomplished with a couple of extra passes.

Once I steer out of my driveway onto the back road, then onto the highway, my travel is affected by a much larger snow-removal project. This one has consequences for more than me.

The first time each winter that I feel my vehicle on the highway fishtail a little, the fear of losing control causes adrenalin to surge through me. Besides invisible black ice, other hazards of winter driving hereabouts include the rapid accumulation of significant amounts of snow on pavement from an unexpected storm, or having the windshield suddenly covered by a rooster tail of snow shot from a passing tractor-trailer.

By and large, the highway contractors do an adequate job of ensuring safe travel. Besides the weekday's shuttling of school buses, the enormous chip trucks continue all winter, trundling their load from Revelstoke down through the valley to the pulp mill at Castlegar. If the road is insufficiently ploughed or sanded, chip truck and other commercial drivers are quick to complain.

As are ordinary citizens after a harrowing trip due to road conditions. In the contractors' defence, I'm aware they can't remove snow from everywhere at once, given the finite number of their plough trucks. On the other hand, when road maintenance was shifted from the provincial Department of Highways to private contractors in 1989, the profit motive entered snow removal. Before the changeover, when people complained to friends and acquaintances about road conditions, the objects of their wrath were the supposed slackers employed by the "Department of Holidays." Nowadays we denounce the contractors, who can appear to be only too conscious of how the costs of sand, plough blades, diesel fuel and overtime impact the company's bottom line.

Drives are especially scary for me on a slippery snowy surface as my vehicle crawls past pickups or sedans that have slid off the pavement into the ditch, sometimes with hazard lights flashing, showing that the accident recently happened. Or I glimpse a pickup or van nose down over the bank amid the trees. Or I'm waved forward by a firehall first responder controlling a single open lane that passes a pickup upside down beside the shoulder, blankets draped over the cab's side window indicating a body hasn't yet been removed from the vehicle.

Mountain roads are always potentially dangerous in winter, with some stretches—like a shaded curve prone to icing up—inherently more of threat. On the 40-minute drive from my place north to New Denver, the route rises high into the mountains above Slocan Lake, and thus the road is subject to colder and more severe weather than either down in the valley where I live or down by the lakeshore at New Denver. Among the elevated highway's twists and curves, it skirts an out-thrust ridge far up a mountain, with a drop from the shoulder straight down hundreds of metres to water. The view from this elevation across the lake to the peaks of the Valhalla Range is beyond spectacular, but the margin for error in driving the stretch in snowy conditions is small.

The locals refer to the route across this mountain spur as Cape Horn. Constructing the road around this promontory in the sky was difficult. When I first moved to Appledore, the highway at Cape Horn still incorporated a kilometre of single-lane traffic: if you met a truck, bus, or even another car, one of you had to back up. In winter, with the snow-filled ditch on one side and the sheer drop-off to the lake far below on the other, meeting another vehicle and having to reverse was nerve-racking. The road at this spot was finally widened at great expense a few years after I came to the valley. The improved curves around the bluffs at Cape Horn still have to be driven at low speed, but at least traffic can proceed in two directions.

To this day, the mountain passes that lead into and out of the West Kootenay can provide terrifying winter driving experiences. When I taught in Calgary, I arranged my classes such that every three weeks I could drive home—eight hours each way—for a long weekend. Due to the shortness of a winter day, driving homeward-bound over Kootenay Pass, the summit of the Salmo–Creston Skyway, always occurred in the dark. One time, en route to Appledore on a December Friday, I ran into trouble.

On the day in question, I had been in and out of snowstorms the entire distance from Calgary. When I first experienced winter mountain driving, I had learned to observe the licence plates of oncoming vehicles if driving through even a mild snowfall. If the licence plates are caked with snow, I deduce that trouble lies ahead. After I left Creston with the last of the light and amid a steady descent of snow, the few cars that approached as I sped toward the start of the long, winding climb toward Kootenay Pass had snow plastered thickly against their plates and grilles.

As I ascended, darkness became total. I realized after about 15 minutes that the snowfall had become too heavy for the ploughs to keep up with. The road, illuminated by my headlights through the falling flakes, was pure, unmarred white.

I reduced speed to a walking pace. To pull over and stop didn't feel safe, since I had no idea if the shoulder invisible under snow was wide, narrow, or harboured a ditch. Nor did I think I could turn around safely due to the reduced visibility and uncertainty about the width of the road.

Whenever the route curved as it climbed, I would bring the vehicle almost to a halt until I could ascertain where the highway led. I could see ahead thanks to my lights, but when forested mountain, shoulder and pavement are equally white, the challenge is to confirm which direction the road leads. Intermittent snowbanks lined the route, left by the ploughs. Yet I couldn't trust that a given pile of snow really indicated the highway's edge.

For a long while, as I motored cautiously onward I encountered no approaching lights. I wondered if conditions farther along were bad enough that the avalanche gates either side of the pass were shut, closing the road. At last I saw through the snow-filled darkness in front flashes of yellow light. A few minutes later these resolved into a plough truck proceeding in my lane. The storm's severity, though, meant that until I neared the back of the truck, the road wasn't significantly less snow-covered.

Directly behind the truck, however, the pavement was free of snow for several metres, and I no longer had to strain through the dense tufts of white to determine the location of the road. I stayed in position close behind the truck. Our travel wasn't fast, but with my vehicle's interior lit up regularly by the pulsing yellow lights, the tension in my body started to ebb. At the summit, the truck turned off into the highways yard there. To my relief, the descent on the

West Kootenay side was ploughed and sanded. Several minutes later, I drove out of the storm entirely. The road led lower and lower, turn after turn, and I could even marvel at glimpses above the trees of a sky jammed with stars.

Yet my very worst winter driving experience happened only 15 minutes from Winlaw. Early one Saturday morning I was on Highway 6 headed to Nelson to teach my class in KSA's writing program. This was in the 1990s, before highway contractors began spraying a brine that causes snow and ice to melt at a lower temperature. The application of the brine often results in absolutely bare pavement. In contrast, on this day the ploughed highway retained a thin layer of white atop which I rolled along.

East of Slocan Park, the route enters a long straightaway before rising over Kosiancic's Hill. As I entered this straight section, I was thinking about the workshop I was about to lead. In the far distance ahead of me, I glimpsed two four-legged creatures in my lane, also travelling east. I had a hard time puzzling out what they were. But as I sped toward them on the white road, they eventually appeared to be two huge horses, Clydesdales, clip-clopping steadily forward, unaware of my vehicle nearing them.

As I drew closer, I eased my foot off the gas and hit the binders. Instead of the vehicle slowing, the brakes had no effect. I was skidding smoothly down the highway at speed in a direct line toward the rear legs of the animals, who loomed larger and larger. One now occupied each lane, bracketing the road's centre. My hope was that my brakes would eventually grip. But at a certain moment I realized I was going to collide with the creatures.

Desperate, I saw that some of the right shoulder had been ploughed. As I slid helplessly up to the animals, I swung the wheel hard to try to coast past them on the right.

Mere seconds from impact, my foot pressing the useless brake to the floor, I heard someone exclaim, *No-o-o-o.* I recognized the voice as mine. Later I thought how corny that at this perilous instant

I would involuntarily produce a word used in the speech balloon of characters in distress in any of a hundred comic books I had read.

A few years before, I had struck and killed a deer on the highway between Vernon and the Needles ferry across the Arrow Lakes. I had been motoring home for the weekend from my then-teaching job in the Okanagan. The autumn dusk had deepened as I drove down from Monashee Pass and out between fields. The road here at the western edge of the West Kootenay leads from farming country to the Edgewood turnoff and then an additional 8 kilometres to where the Needles ferry docks.

As I sped along in the growing darkness, a brown blur appeared out of the left-hand ditch just ahead, hurtling onto the highway. A micro-second later I heard the meaty thump of a collision with a large animal. Adrenalin coursed through me as, too late, I stood on the brakes and wrestled the vehicle to a halt on the shoulder.

I climbed out, shaking, my engine still running. In the day's final glimmers of light, I could see behind me along the highway the crumpled, still form of a deer on the right shoulder. I glanced at the hood of the vehicle—I drove a Nissan Pathfinder in those days—and all looked well, except the beam of my left headlight angled upwards instead of forward as it should. I walked round the front of the vehicle and stopped to stare at utter ruin. The grille was pushed inwards in a concave dent as though I had struck a pole. Coolant from the radiator was leaking onto the pavement. At least, I hoped anti-freeze was the only fluid that was slowly pooling under the car.

I gazed up and down the empty road. Nothing was visible but the dead animal, patches of forest, empty fields, and a distant farmhouse where no lights showed. I scrambled back into the driver's seat. Despite the obvious damage, my temperature gauge still read in the normal range. I knew a phone booth was available in the little park beside where the ferry puts in, and hoped my engine would last until I could call for help. No cellphone service existed in those days, even as today cell service is unavailable in much of the BC Interior.

Each kilometre I covered that evening, the stress in my body increased. Despite wanting desperately to cover the distance and phone the auto club for a tow, I resisted the temptation to speed up, figuring the cooler the engine ran the better. I glanced at the temperature gauge three times each second, prepared to shut down the motor the instant the needle lurched into the red zone. But the gauge continued to read normal. Almost dizzy with anxiety, I at last pulled into the parking area beside the phone booth. Four chilly hours after that, the tow truck from Vernon finally arrived.

Fearful memories of this earlier accident raced around my brain on that winter Saturday in the valley. I closed the last metres between my front bumper and the gigantic animals still trotting unconcernedly down the highway. I could see now they weren't horses, whatever they were. My last-minute yank on the wheel almost let me steer past. But with the same sickening sound as when I hit the deer, I clipped the right-hand one of the pair.

Instantly, just as the cliché states, the world shifted into slow motion. A solid wall of hairy back slid up the hood toward me and completely filled my windshield. The glass dissolved into a thousand shards. The hairy curtain disappeared to my left. The impact had slowed the vehicle, and 50 metres farther I drifted to a halt on the shoulder. I glanced in my driver's-side rear-view mirror to learn what the carnage was like behind me. The mirror was no longer there—torn off, I guessed, when the creature rolled from my hood. Keeping the engine running, I stepped out onto the snowy road.

Back down the highway, one of the beasts was sitting in the lane it had been trotting down moments before, while the other animal stood beside it, partially blocking the other lane. The standing creature's head was bent toward its companion, as if solicitously.

I glanced around, but the highway was empty in both directions. White fields extended away from the road on either side, with the valley walls rising behind them. A few houses were evident along this stretch, with long driveways leading from the road toward them.

I could see that my hood was dented where the animal had been propelled across it. My windshield had mostly evaporated, with heaps of tiny glass detritus scattered over the dashboard and across the front passenger seat. My face began to sting in the icy air, and when I passed my hand over my forehead, nose and cheeks, my hand came away with blood on it. Miniature needles of glass had penetrated my skin.

I moved to inspect the vehicle's front end, but except for a smashed left headlight, and crumpled fender and hood, everything seemed undisturbed. But given how slippery the road was, and the sight of the two motionless animals blocking the highway, I realized I needed to alert the authorities.

Rather than approach one of the houses in sight, I decided I would drive to the nearest public phone—as I had when I struck the deer—and report the incident. Only five minutes ahead of me, I knew, a phone booth stood next to a convenience store in Crescent Valley.

I gingerly pulled onto the highway. The absence of a windshield meant a constant stream of cold air flowed over the web of cuts on my face. I cranked up the heater. My plan was to flash my lights at any oncoming vehicle to warn them of the animals in the middle of the road, but I encountered nobody.

At the phone booth, my hands were shaking as I looked up the non-emergency number for the Nelson Mounties. I explained the reason for my call, that whatever I'd hit probably was still on the highway and somebody needed to warn motorists.

The person at the other end of the phone wanted my particulars. I gave him my name, but to my amazement blanked entirely when he requested my address. Luckily remembering that this information is on my driver's licence, I fumbled with vibrating hands to extract my wallet from my pants pocket, find my licence, and read out the address. I recognized even at the time that I must be in shock if I was unable to recall where I lived.

Back behind the wheel, at a slower speed than usual, I was able to steer another 20 minutes on to Nelson, where I washed the blood from my face and taught the workshop. I let the class know what had just happened, in case my behaviour seemed odd, but as far as I could tell, the session went fine.

I subsequently learned from friends that no one in the valley owns Clydesdales. The consensus among people I told my story to was that I must have struck an elk. A herd of elk inhabits the area, and I've subsequently seen a few by the side of the road near Crescent Valley, or once on the rail trail not far from the site of my accident.

The possibility of icy misadventure keeps me nervous to some degree while behind the wheel, whatever the apparent condition of our winter roads. Paradoxically, slipperiness is also a reason why—besides the desolate beauty of the frozen landscape—I love winter here: the chance to be out on cross-country ski trails.

Many folks in the West Kootenay journey somewhere warm for at least a portion of the winter months: Arizona and Costa Rica are popular destinations, and two couples I know who are active in the local literary community have spent the winter for decades in Mexican villages they return to year after year.

For me, easy access to cross-country skiing makes me eager for the snow to arrive and regretful when toward spring the snow starts to disappear. In the early 1980s I had been introduced to cross-country, but when I lived in Vancouver I only was able to enjoy the sport two or three times a year. I didn't care for the wet, heavy coastal snow, so I used to travel to Manning Park in the inland Coast Mountains to ski, about a two-and-a-half-hour drive each way.

My first winter at Appledore, I joined the Nelson Nordic Ski Club and have remained a member ever since. The club maintains a network of trails at a property a short drive southeast of Nelson, or about 50 minutes from Winlaw. My favourite trail is the Busk–Euphrates loop, named after a Boy Scout camp property the ski tracks pass through and a former mine at the trail's south end.

The loop, which used to take me an hour to complete and which I now finish in 45 minutes or less, is rated at a medium level of skill. A steep ascent near the start requires 150 herringbone steps to climb. Herringboning is accomplished by angling your skis outwards at about 45 degrees with each step as you proceed. The skis' inner edges dig into the snowy hill for traction. Meanwhile, your poles provide extra momentum while ensuring that a back-slip doesn't occur if a ski edge fails to catch.

On Busk–Euphrates, this strenuous ascent is followed by several steep downhill portions involving curves. Thereafter the trail follows for a distance a picturesque mountain creek, officially the Salmo River: the moving water purls between white banks lined with snowy evergreens, and around rocks and logs topped with snow in the midst of the stream. In the crystalline air, chickadees call and flit from snow-covered bough to bough. In the sky, ravens float over the forest, occasionally issuing a croaked comment on the scene below.

A more challenging ski club trail I also enjoy rises along a former logging road in the drainage of Clearwater Creek, a tributary of the Salmo River. This route winds steadily up and up and then, for a change, up some more for 7 kilometres, with only a few level stretches and one short downhill bit. The arduousness of the uphill slog is recognized by the club's placement of a bell at the top that you can ring to celebrate your achievement of the summit.

For years, my skills at cross-country were rudimentary. I loved being out in the cold mountain air, and prided myself on using waxable skis. But where I judged a downhill run as too steep for my skills, I would either sit back down on my skis and, in effect, sled down the slope, or else stay erect until I inevitably lost my balance and crashed. Often when I fell, I would tumble over and over if I was travelling fast enough. Amazingly, I never broke my glasses or snapped a bone—or a ski—although I sometimes ended up with legs still attached to skis in such a tangle that I had to free a boot or two in order to struggle upright once more.

Repeated experiences of such crashes at last led me to conclude that, after decades of skiing, I needed to take some lessons. I talked a former Appledale neighbour I often skied with into purchasing with me a lesson from Charles Arnold, the manager of a Nelson ski and cycle shop.

Arnold turned out to be an excellent teacher. The two of us met him one afternoon at the Nelson club site, and in one hour he gave us enough new techniques to work on for the next couple of years. Indeed, two years later we took a second one-hour class with him and, again, learned an inventory of new skills to hone in the years since.

Probably the most useful technique I learned from Arnold was how to snowplough down a steep drop—not only to snowplough, but to regulate my speed and direction as I do so. Snowploughing is the reverse of herringboning. Out of the set tracks, the skis are angled *inwards* at about 45 degrees, with the lower edges digging into the surface. The ski thus acts like a brake, and the lower you crouch, the slower you go. While you snowplough downwards, either ski extended ahead of the other means you turn in the direction of the extended ski. I'm now able to weave back and forth descending a hillside, or to skirt some obstacle I need to avoid on the slope. In the set tracks, if a descent isn't too steep I can reduce speed by keeping one ski in the track while snowploughing with the other. Gone are my days of sliding downhill out of control and hoping for the best.

Meanwhile, here in the valley, the committee in charge of the rails-to-trails route began to have it tracked for cross-country. I can finish writing at the computer at 1 or 2 p.m. and be out in the weather on my skis 15 minutes later. My goal each year is to ski the entire 50 kilometres, section by section. But my default run, my favourite, is from Lemon Creek north—the same route my brother and I walked the autumn we encountered the bear.

The Lemon Creek put-in is a 10-minute drive north from Apple-dore. The track leads away absolutely straight over the repurposed railway bridge over the creek, a stream that even in winter is much wider and more melodious than the Salmo River alongside the Busk–Euphrates trail. The rest of the route north toward Slocan, the winter trail cuts through snow-laden forest: straightaways followed by bends and then another ruler-straight stretch.

Much of the way, I can glimpse the Slocan River through the trees to my left. Ducks paddle on the current, and where the river narrows, a row of posts extends mid-channel, dating from when log booms were floated down the Slocan to mills at Koch Siding, between Winlaw and Slocan Park, and at Crescent Valley. The posts kept the booms from floating sideways and hanging up on a sand-bar or the river bank.

As I kick and glide along between the white-tipped evergreens interspersed with barren cottonwoods, birch and aspen, chick-adees announce their presence as on any winter trail. I hear the raucous squawking of ravens quarrelling in a tree; one rides the air ahead of me as if to show me where the trail goes. Farther on, two other of the noisy black birds draw my attention to a tall cotton-wood snag between the trail and the river. I'm suddenly aware an eagle is perched on a branch above a fork in which a large nest of sticks has been assembled.

Ignoring the ravens, the eagle is staring out at the water, on which float dozens of white swans. Tundra swans and trum-peter swans overwinter along this portion of the river, 80 to 100 of them in total. Unlike the romantic image of swans gracefully paddling a pond, many of these birds at any one time have their butts in the air as they search for food on the river bottom. Their young, presumably tidbits for the eagle when little, are grey. And among the swans of every age swim flotillas of mallard ducks and drakes, sometimes accompanied by small squadrons of their own offspring.

Audible through the still winter air, besides the mallards' familiar quacking, are occasional muted honks of the swans. A drumbeat accompanies a couple of swans' attempt to take to the air: for a distance they flap not far above the river's surface, with the sound of their wing-tips striking the water pulsing repeatedly as they struggle to achieve take-off speed. Then they break free and are silently aloft.

Also flying above me, and paddling on the river, are individual and strings of Canada geese, who have taken to overwintering here as well. I continue to kick and glide, kick and glide, until I reach a huge bench—the one where my brother and I ran into the bear. In the thickening light of late afternoon, I step out of my skis, climb up onto the bench and enjoy a few swallows of the water I've brought with me, along with perhaps a snack of energy bar or trail mix. I gaze west as I do so at the white bulk of Perry Ridge, or south down the river where ominous-looking clouds are maybe gathering. Soon the cold starts to bother me, and I clamber back down and click into my skis again.

Deer tracks abound in the snow along the trail. Paw prints that could be dog or coyote are everywhere on the route, although one wildlife biologist I know insists that wolves are also present in the valley. Once in February, I encountered grooves in the snow across the tracks: beaver had dragged a freshly toppled birch tree from the woods down to the river.

If I ski out to visit the swans on a weekday afternoon, I often have the trail to myself or perhaps meet one other individual on skis or a couple trudging along on foot with their dog. On a weekend, meeting one or two individuals per hour is possible. More often, even skiing on a Sunday further south down the valley from the Passmore trailhead to where the river curves from east–west to south–north, my hours in the cold amid the snowy trees beside the river are mine alone.

I know that endorphins from the exercise when I'm out on my slippery slats contribute to my feeling of exhilaration as I traverse the winter trails. Yet every place I am outdoors this season, I feel in awe of the grandeur of the white mountains looming above. The severe white ridges and peaks contrast with the oases of human existence below them, represented by a house, smoke angling away from its rooftop chimney, surrounded by snowy fields and the forest.

The cold winter world, with its edge of physical danger and its many gifts, becomes after a time simply how the planet is. The memory of fall has faded, and spring seems unlikely ever to occur again. Everything is snow, ice, and days far shorter than the nights. We winter-dwellers live our lives accordingly, appreciative of what we have by day of warmth and nourishment, human contact or solitude, and a weak sunlight providing us with vistas of unparalleled beauty. And throughout the long expanses of the night, above us the glacial air offers the bounty of a million stars.

Chapter Ten

THE ELEMENTS– HIGH WATER

AFTER LOSING MY GRAVITY-FED WATER MY FIRST SEPTEM-
ber at Appledore, I took every opportunity to learn more about the
system, despite having my well as a backup. I now know that about
a kilometre north of my place, a culvert carries Jerome Creek—the
system's water source—under the back road during the spring
freshet. The rest of the year the creek doesn't reach that far, due to
users absorbing most of the water. But following an exceptionally
snowy winter, in June the creek will exit the culvert and wander
downslope through scrub brush and somebody's former pasture,
slowly diminishing to a trickle. Some maps still show Jerome Creek
joining the Slocan River, as it originally did.

About 20 metres in elevation above the road, in every season
a rough wooden sluice diverts creek water into the inlet portal of
a somewhat-worse-for-wear rectangular concrete structure on the
east bank. This construction is the diversion box, about 6 feet long
by 4 feet wide and 3 feet high. The box is intended to function also as
a settling tank to allow debris in the water directed into it to sink to
the bottom. An outlet funnels water into a pipe that leads downhill

through the woods for 100 metres to a second, larger concrete box, situated 5 or so metres below the diversion box.

This second structure is the distribution box. Measuring 12 feet long by 4 feet wide and 4 feet high, and with a removable wooden cover sheathed by metal roofing panels, the distribution box has a concrete wall inside running the length of the box. The wall separates the distribution box's interior into two rectangular areas. The pipe from the diversion box brings water to the first of these areas. The second area is divided into nine equal-sized compartments, from which water is distributed to us water licence holders.

A notched metal weir tops the wall dividing the distribution box in two. When water is plentiful, the distribution box is filled almost to the cover, submerging the weir. An overflow pours out of the northern end of the box and puddles or streams away into the bushes and trees amid which the distribution box sits.

When the water level is lower, however, the weir functions as an allotment mechanism. Overflow from the first area bloops through rectangular notches in the weir, one notch for each compartment. The openings in the weir are sized proportional to the amount of water granted by the water licences awarded to the original user of each compartment.

These compartments, like the diversion box up at the creek, act as settling tanks, with an outlet a few inches above the bottom. Handmade screens with wooden frames are placed in front of the outlets. These screens are intended to block any waterborne debris from flowing into the water lines that snake downhill from the compartment outlets to our homes.

The system was constructed in 1961 by six Doukhobor families (Chernoff, Koozen, Relkoff, Chutskoff, Pereverzoff and Kalmakoff), along with two English-named families (Brooks and Corn) and one French-named family (Paquette). The original water licences, however, go back to 1912. Today most of the nine compartments serve multiple households. One list I have shows 17 families receiving water from our distribution box. The line from the southernmost compartment of the nine now brings water to three other households before reaching Appledore.

Glitches are plentiful on such a rickety system—one that resembles the works on most creeks throughout the valley. I learned at some point that the Jerome Creek system has a shadow volunteer guardian. He prefers that as few people as possible go up to the diversion and/or distribution box in an attempt to fix a problem with their water supply. Ignorance about the details of how the water system functions can potentially make it dysfunctional for more than just the homes on their own line.

The system guardian is Pete Relkoff, whose father was one of those who built the Jerome Creek system. I think of Pete as the mayor of Appledale. Unlike most of us, he has lived here his whole life. He bridges the gap between the mainly Doukhobor early inhabitants and the rest of us.

Hidden below Appledale's placid-seeming surface is the Doukhobor community's often-troubled history. In 1956 for example, the authorities separated Pete's wife, Shirley, then eight, from her family and interned her in a New Denver facility for three years along with other children of the religion's Sons of Freedom faction. Parents were permitted to visit their kids once every two weeks for one hour only. And the visitors could speak with their interned children only through a chain-link fence.

Pete's family farmed at Perry's Siding, Appledale's northern suburb, as it were. He attended the one-room Appledale school, now the Threads Guild building, where Perry's Back Road meets the highway. A former construction worker, Pete is a couple of years older than me, although he looks 10 years younger. As burly as Wolfgang, Pete, unlike Wolfgang, is a serious gardener. Also unlike Wolfgang, Pete wears an outfit that usually includes bright red suspenders advertising Husqvarna, maker of—besides chainsaws—lawnmowers and other useful implements. Those suspenders have been in evidence when I've been assisting him and others up at the diversion box—clearing it of stones, for instance, brought down by the spring run-off—and when I've been at a community meeting listening to him offer a Russian prayer.

He has tales about the origin of the water system. Since the builders were always short of money, they were overjoyed to get a deal on some used piping from the Trail lead-zinc smelter. Pete's laugh has a rueful tone: "Who knows what had flowed through those pipes before?" He also comments on why the water line from each compartment of the distribution box follows a separate route down toward the back road, rather than utilizing a common trench as far as the road before angling away to the different houses. "The guys who built the system, they were great for feuds," Pete notes. "'No way you're putting *your* pipe in *my* trench.'" Again his laugh.

Out of Pete's generous spirit, and unknown to a lot of his neighbours, he monitors water flow and how it impacts the system. In the spring freshet, for example, he'll check to make sure the diversion sluice hasn't been knocked askew by the force of the swollen, raging creek. He also will partially block the diversion box's intake with a piece of plywood. Reducing the incoming spring flow means less debris in the system and less overflow down at the distribution box.

Problems on my particular line, though, must be solved by me and the others who are served by this line. If our compartment up at the distribution box is full of water, the cause of low or no pressure at our homes could be—aside from a major leak—detritus blocking the screen covering the compartment's outlet. Or the issue could be at the compartment's outlet. Two narrow metal crossbars, set into the concrete at right angles at the entrance of the outlet, are intended to keep larger bits of junk out of the water line. But a piece of bark can sometimes float around the edges of the screen and become jammed in the opening. Other splinters of wood, fir needles and other natural debris then pile up against the bark and block or reduce the outlet.

Any remedial action requiring reaching into our compartment when it is full of water is a trial. Jerome Creek water year-round is teeth-rattling cold. In order to reach an arm and hand down to check the outlet, your face must be half-submerged in the icy fluid. Even retrieving the screen to clean it involves immersing your arms and hands in freezing liquid. The screen with its wooden frame will float free of the position it's supposed to be in unless weighted down with rocks. These rocks have to be removed to check the screen, and then, after the screen is cleaned, replaced. I learned the hard way to take a towel whenever an expedition to inspect our compartment is necessary.

If, when the distribution box cover is removed, I can see that all compartments are low in water, the problem of low or no pressure is a systemic issue. In that case, a trek uphill to the diversion box is in order once permission is obtained from the landowner on whose property the structure is located. At the upper box, perhaps an obvious cause of lack of flow is visible (other than late-summer low water in the creek).

When my original neighbour to the north, Lynn, sold her property to a Lynne with an "e"—Lynne Shalom—the solution of any issue on our water line fell to me. A few years later a partner of hers moved in, Ben Aubin, a laconic Quebecois timber cruiser, after which the two of us would tackle any water supply issues. His occupation made him a careful observer; his sharp eye was very useful at times in solving water line problems.

Why a line stops flowing or starts up again can be baffling. After many discussions with Ben in the midst of water crises, he finally convinced me that not everything can be explained. A kink in the line, or a small protuberance where two sections of pipe join or a repair has been made can cause material in the line to accumulate. Especially in the spring, when the snowmelt brings much debris down with it, the build-up at such a spot can significantly constrict flow or even entirely obstruct it. And these blockages can occur and dissolve seemingly at random.

In the face of a water loss, Ben and I might have done no more up at the distribution box than clear a screen not especially covered by wood chips or evergreen needles, and maybe remove a couple of twigs wedged in the outlet's opening. When we return home, discouraged, intending to figure out what else we might try, we might discover that normal water pressure had been restored.

Ben's speech in English can involve a drawl: "Waal," he might begin, as we stand at an outside faucet watching incredulously as water spurts forth where earlier that morning only a thin stream of drops had emerged. "Maybe the little extra water we let through because of what we did up at the box was enough to loosen a jam someplace. Maybe the line decided to fix itself." He shrugs. "We'll never know."

When Ben, Lynne, and her child, Chris, moved to Nelson in 2005, my new neighbours in the house to the north were Rod, Sharon, and baby, Evan. Rod, I've come to realize, can think like water does. Often Pete Relkoff will call on Rod to accompany him up to the water boxes on a maintenance or inspection visit. I sometimes go along in a helper role and leave the brain-work of rectifying our balky system to them.

One improvement on our portion of the system occurred before Rod and Sharon arrived. In August of 2001, hot weather settled in as though it would never leave, and by mid-month, as happened almost every year, water pressure on our line during the afternoon would drop to a level rendering the neighbour's and my irrigation sprinklers unable to operate. I suggested to Ben and Lynne that, instead of complaining to each other every year about the situation, or being suspicious that somebody up the line was using too much water, we should hire a knowledgeable civil engineer to advise us whether a remedy existed for this problem.

Lynne and Ben agreed, and in early November Ben and I toured around a representative of an engineering firm from Castlegar that had agreed to examine our set-up. Their report, given to us later in the month, suggested we install a holding tank at the top of our individual line that would be filled overnight when there was no draw from the households. After some calculations, the company suggested a size of tank such that, if each household on our line limited their irrigation sprinklers to two, the system would retain sufficient water pressure on those hot late-summer afternoons.

We decided to implement the storage tank idea. First, though, we had to contact the other users of the system and stress that our proposed tank would be *downstream* of the distribution box: in storing water we would not be taking any water our licences didn't entitle us to. We also had to secure permission from the landowner on whose property we proposed to locate the tank, just south of the distribution box. Finally, in April of 2003, a contractor installed an 1,100-gallon concrete tank, into which the outflow from our compartment now passes before rejoining the pipe that leads from the compartment to our houses.

The storage tank is buried in the ground, with only the concrete roof visible, containing a couple of hatches. Like the diversion box and the distribution box's compartments, the tank acts like a giant settling tank, with the outlet a few feet off the tank floor. This arrangement means the tank won't have to be cleaned for decades, but the topside hatches are large enough for a ladder to be inserted whenever the need to enter the tank to clean it occurs.

The local who installed the tank realized that in times of high water the tank potentially could fill to the brim and blow the hatches out, despite their considerable weight. Thus, an overflow pipe outlet is situated a short distance below the top of the tank, with that pipe leading away downslope into the trees. So far, the storage tank has worked wonderfully: a visit to it in spring includes the pleasant sound of water pouring out of the overflow. And those former late-August drops in water pressure at our homes have never recurred.

A side benefit is that when the tank was plumbed, the contractor installed a shut-off valve where our line exits the distribution box. Now if repairs need to be undertaken on our line, nobody has to arm-wrestle the flow of water I depict in Chapter Four. The tank set-up, in fact, involves two other shut-offs: one on the water line which, when closed, directs water into the holding tank. And one just before where the pipe from the tank joins the water line. Closing the latter and opening the former bypasses the tank.

When Rod and I were stumped one day attempting to account for a sudden drop in pressure, in desperation we shut off water to the tank briefly. This procedure for an unknown reason restored normal pressure. We could only speculate that perhaps the sudden surge of water down the line when we stopped directing water to the tank had blasted free an accumulation of debris somewhere.

Each time a water supply problem is tackled, however, there's no guarantee it will be solved. As a result, any time pressure drops, my anxiety rises. I'm blessed to have the well, of course, since as long as the well is operational, Appledore isn't without water even if my well-less neighbours have to do without.

And I don't want to over-emphasize difficulties with the system. Most of the time it works just fine. Whenever I turn on a tap in the garden to fill a sprinkling can, I think about how water has raced down the creek, been captured by the diversion box, directed through a pipe to the distribution box and storage tank, and then flowed down the line past three other houses to my standpipe. I'm astounded the system works as well as it does.

I'm aware that many people, both city and country, are unconcerned about where their water comes from. Since I have to count myself among them at the time I bought Appledore, I can hardly be surprised when I hear that people who depend on the Jerome Creek system have never visited the diversion or distribution boxes.

Maybe it's just human nature that when there's a problem, a percentage of people will sit tight, counting on somebody else to solve the problem. Or maybe the lack of curiosity is a by-product of how our society generally doesn't encourage us to pay attention to where things come from: to learn about the working lives of those who feed, clothe, house us, and more.

I remember being intrigued, while teaching at Colorado State University, when a colleague from the forestry faculty explained how snow fences are erected in the Rockies high above Denver. Snow mounds up against theses fences, he said, and thus melts slower than elsewhere, ensuring a longer-lasting run-off to supply that city's water system. Yet when I returned to Vancouver after that job, I couldn't have told you where that city's reservoirs are, the water sources that feed them, or if measures are taken in the back country around Vancouver, too, in order to enhance water flow during the summer.

Large or small, a water supply has dimensions that are unknown, hidden or mysterious to many users. Equally puzzling, at least to me, are some locals' behaviours regarding a water line.

In early July of 1996 water pressure dropped to near zero in all households on my line. Besides regular home and garden use of the water, two properties on the line now were also operating businesses. My then-neighbour to the north, Lynne, had opened a physiotherapy clinic in her basement. North of Lynne's, the first property on our line— formerly owned by Ed Jacobson—currently belonged to Arnie Castelli. Arnie, who had built an industrial barn, was operating a heavy-duty equipment and automotive repair shop. Both Lynne's and Arnie's businesses required water.

Rather than us determining what the problem was, at my suggestion we hired Ken Jensen, who three years before had replaced my well pump. Ken consulted with everyone he could regarding what they knew about the location of the water line, including Pete Relkoff and the original builder of Lynne's and my houses.

Based on Ken's experience, he concluded that a blockage on our line was liable to be at a junction point. No leak was discernible along the likely route of the line; I had retraced the course Ed Jacobson and I had followed when we combed Ellen Bazaroff's field nearly seven years before. At Arnie's place, Ken discovered that metal piping constituted the line there, rather than the plastic pipe evident up at the distribution box. Ken decided that the most probable place for a debris obstruction was where metal met plastic.

To excavate the water line starting at Arnie's, we hired Aaron Blakey, a young local guy who had a small backhoe. Aaron said he could only work after supper, due to his day job. I had given Mrs. Bazaroff's phone number to Ken, to alert her that a machine would be digging in her meadow south of her house. He phoned a couple of times, but she had no message machine, and he was feeling pressured by our households' urgent need of water.

The evening of July 11, Ken and Aaron crossed from Arnie's property onto Bazaroff's field with the backhoe and set to work. Some time later, the machine cut Pete Relkoff's line, which passed atop our line at a right angle as part of the invisible spaghetti tangle of piping originating at the distribution box. Pete came up from his house to see what was happening. While repairing Pete's line, Ken shut a valve some distance north in the field.

I had noticed this valve, contained in a decayed wooden box set in the ground, during my earlier traverse of the meadow in search of a visible leak. When I had told Ken about the valve, he had asked me to mark it with surveyor's tape, thinking the valve could well be the location of the join from plastic to metal, since it seemed to be on our line. Closing the valve would make any downstream repair to our line easier. In fact, this valve shut off water to Ellen Bazaroff's.

No one could have guessed that it had anything to do with Bazaroff's. The valve was in the field 100 yards to the south and downhill of her house, whereas the distribution box is much farther northwest and uphill of her place. Her water line *bypassed* her house, then swung back north to it.

In any case, now Mrs. Bazaroff had no water. The next evening, I was having supper with friends down the road when Lynne phoned over with the news: Ellen had discovered that people were digging in her meadow and not unreasonably was steamed that as a result her water had been cut off. I went up with the friends—who were also friends of Lynne's—to the water line where Ken was working, and Pete showed up to open the valve. Mrs. Bazaroff, an elderly widow, appeared herself and berated Ken and me. She asked us to stop repair work on the line.

Since both Lynne and I were to be away the following week for various reasons, we agreed. When we returned, we found that in the bewildering way water can behave, normal pressure had been restored. We speculated that perhaps the blockage on the line had been shaken free by the work done on the system to date.

Meantime, our line was exposed in Bazaroff's field and losing some water continuously through a few leaks the excavation had uncovered—none large enough to account for the major drop in pressure that had sparked the present situation. Arnie told us he wanted to replace this metal portion of the line rather than repair it, as it had come to the end of its serviceable life.

The situation regarding co-operation with Arnie was complicated because Lynne and I and some other neighbours were suing him. In 1991 he had built his big repair shop and commenced business, happily banging and clanging away seven days a week at any time from 7 a.m. to midnight. He had levelled off land and constructed the shop on the corner of his property next to Lynne's house and the Heinks' house immediately across the road. This location was hard to understand, since on the north side of his place, no one lived across the road and that large empty field stretched away toward Ellen Bazaroff's house.

The noise problem—besides the loud pounding of metal on metal, I found most irritating the whiny rasp of an impact wrench removing or mounting tires—was made worse by how Arnie had sited the doors to the workshop. The main entrance, which had a floor-mounted drive to haul large vehicles into the shop, faced toward Lynne's (and hence, my) place, rather than facing his own house. The large shop acted as an echo chamber whenever the door was open, which was most of the time.

I had asked Arnie twice to keep the door shut whenever possible and to observe regular hours, but he was resistant. He seemed to be of the "a man's got to do what a man's got to do" school. He told me he couldn't control when people showed up needing repairs to their skidder or logging truck or excavator. And that he only made noise when he had to.

After a lawyer's letter had been sent in 1993 with our two requests, and we experienced no change in shop functioning or hours, we launched the lawsuit. Arnie hired the Winlaw lawyer Kenyon McGee, already well known for—I discovered later—taking simple problems and expanding them into far more complex disputes. He in this case decided that our lawsuit represented an attempt to shut down all home-based businesses in the valley. Pursuing this strategy, Kenyon called into court as many witnesses as possible. He presented to the judge elaborate maps of the back road showing all the businesses that people ran out of their homes, including, with no touch of irony, Lynne's physio clinic. An added irony for me was discovering in conversation with Kenyon that he was a graduate of Colorado State University, having been a student around the time I taught there, before he moved to the valley.

The lawyer on our side was hard-pressed to refute the cascade of irrelevancy Kenyon devised on behalf of his client. I had two hours in the witness chair being cross-examined by Kenyon on individual poems published in my 1975 collection *Money and Rain*, about being employed for eight months on the hood line at

Canadian Kenworth's truck assembly plant in Burnaby. I couldn't fathom what Kenyon was seeking to show the judge by doing this. Presumably, after working in the deafening factory din at Kenworth I was used to, or even had a high *tolerance* for, industrial racket.

In court one afternoon Kenyon suddenly accused our lawyer of using Ontario court rules rather than BC's. No one present could understand that claim. And at one point Kenyon somehow discovered I was paying the lion's share of the suit, given that I was the only one of the neighbours with a steady income. He tried to claim I was guilty of champerty. This term describes a situation whereby a person not connected to a lawsuit funds it in return for a share of the benefits if the suit is successful. Since I was directly involved in the suit as one of the plaintiffs, that accusation didn't make sense. But these and all Kenyon's similar legal manoeuvres succeeded in dragging out the case year after year, court date after court date.

Our lawyer said that the dispute should have been settled in a single two-hour session, since the remedy we sought was so reasonable: the door shut except to move vehicles in, and regular hours. But the matter was still ongoing three years later when we were trying to solve the common issue of the water line repair.

More accurately: at the end of that June we had formally lost the case. The judge opined that he wouldn't want to live near Arnie's repair shop, but ruled that he didn't feel the neighbours had suffered enough to warrant a legal intervention.

His decision did state that, given the nature of the case, the losers wouldn't have to pay the defendant's costs. Kenyon appealed that aspect of the decision, and our lawyer was still mulling over whether we should contest Kenyon's appeal. As a result, the legal hassle with Arnie technically remained ongoing when the water pressure dropped in July.

I should add that by the time our total of eight days in court (on a noise nuisance dispute!) were finally over in June, Arnie had injured himself and was no longer repairing heavy equipment. This change in the shop's clientele had reduced significantly the cacophony emanating from his shop. Still ahead was that during the summer following the judge's decision, we awakened one morning to find the shop empty. Arnie had abandoned his property. It was seized by the bank and put up for sale, although the bank subdivided the house and 2 acres away from the balance of the 21 acres of Arnie's original holdings. That left the shop feeling to me like a loaded gun: what if somebody else bought it for similar purposes, and we were back to square one with the noise? Eventually, to my relief, the Vancouver artist Graham Gillmore, who works on large art pieces, purchased it. Graham converted part of the shop into living quarters and used the balance for his studio.

That happy outcome remained in the murky future, however, when our water line lay open to the elements in Bazaroff's field, its leaks ongoing. Ellen insisted nobody do anything on her property. Meantime, she had retained Kenyon, who began in his usual style by sending a letter accusing us of damaging the screen in our own compartment in the distribution box and thus causing ourselves the blockage we were trying to remedy. Equally incomprehensible was the letter's accusation that we had been excavating in Bazaroff's field to 5 feet down.

Our water line remained open for all of August, but in September winter loomed closer, with the unburied line susceptible to freezing. In late September, Arnie, his wife, Lynne and I met and agreed on the need to go ahead with Arnie's suggested replacement of the pipe. Lynne volunteered to clear the replacement with Mrs. Bazaroff, but instead received a letter from Kenyon demanding $660. Part of this amount was owed, according to Kenyon, for wrecking the wooden box around the valve that had been shut off causing Ellen to lose water. In fact, the box had deteriorated after who-knows-how-many years in the earth, as I knew from having had a good look at the valve myself when I first encountered it in her field.

The requested sum also supposedly covered "damages to land." Kenyon's contention was that because the easements that allowed us to repair our line said that the line would be buried 18 inches deep, any digging deeper than 18 inches constituted damage to property.

I pointed out in my reply that, besides the box having degraded due to natural causes, no person would agree to an easement that limited how deeply they could excavate in order to repair or replace a water line. Therefore no money would be forthcoming from us. Finally Mrs. Bazaroff relented, and the pipe was covered in early November.

Other threats to the peaceful flow of water to the system have occurred, though, besides leaks, blockages, lawyers and land-owners angry about accidents during repairs. The property around the distribution box was purchased by Aaron Blakey, who had operated the backhoe in 1996 that cut Pete Relkoff's line. Aaron intended to subdivide his newly acquired property, but he faced the problem of how to obtain water for the subdivided acreages. He tried having a well dug, apparently without success. He also ran a pipe under the road and then all the way down to the Slocan River, but water from this source would require a pump.

We were startled to discover in the early summer of 2015 that Aaron had applied to the provincial water authority to move the Jerome Creek distribution box higher up the ridge. Because of how he had subdivided, one potential home site was situated at an elevation above the box. On his application to relocate the distribution box, he said the purpose was to offer gravity-fed water to that acreage.

His application contained statements in support of his request that fell somewhat short of reality. He told the water authority that the connection to the subdivided property would not affect other people's waterworks, and that he had, as required by regulation, notified the rest of us licence-holders about this request to relocate the box. Actually, we had discovered the matter via a tip from a neighbour; we then asked the water authority for a copy of Aaron's application. People on the Jerome Creek system protested the application, and in October the provincial water stewardship officer on the file agreed that the request contained "incorrect and misleading" information.

Meanwhile, before we had heard back from the water official, in August the same neighbour alerted us to a new line tapping into the pipe that brings water from the diversion box. The line from this tap ran to where Aaron had been constructing a concrete holding tank several metres away. Once news of this illegal re-routing of water spread, a number of Jerome Creek water users had words with Aaron, confrontations that led in some cases to shouts and threats.

Aaron consistently claimed during these arguments that he had advised the other water licence holders as required and that he had permission to tap into the system. Except, no one had been notified. And we knew he didn't have the water regulators' okay, as we had copies of a 2007 request by him for an additional licence on Jerome Creek. He already possessed one such licence by virtue of buying the property surrounding the distribution box. This 2007 request had been refused on the grounds that all the creek's volume of flow is spoken for by the existing licences. We were aware that therefore any additional draw on the creek, such as Aaron's recent tap into the system, would never be approved.

We knew that the water authority would be slow to act concerning the illegal tap, understaffed as they are. Yet August can be when water is most precious, due to the creek being at its lowest at a time when nearly everybody is irrigating. On a hot morning that month, six of us went up to the box to disconnect Aaron's illicit set-up.

On first hearing about the theft, Rod and I had reconnoitred the site. Soil that ordinarily covered the pipe between the diversion and distribution boxes had been removed at a certain spot, and a hose connected to that pipe lay exposed, leading away toward Aaron's unfinished holding tank. We both marvelled that he hadn't filled in the hole as soon as his unauthorized tap was completed; no one probably would have discovered it for years, if ever.

I was plenty anxious the morning the six of us vigilantes hiked up the overgrown ruts of an access road toward the scene of the crime. One of our group had already been in a yelling match with Aaron over this matter, and others had stories of trouble he had caused on another local water system on which he held a licence, as well as an account of a fistfight he had gotten into recently with a neighbour. I had been relieved when, before we ventured out that morning, our bunch had discussed what we'd do if Aaron showed up armed to prevent our disconnection of his tap. Some of our group were more pugnacious than others, but all agreed that if a firearm was involved, we'd just leave.

Aaron had been advised by phone by one of us vigilantes exactly when our mission would occur. We wanted to be seen as acting openly, and also to let him know that his mischief would not be tolerated by the other Jerome Creek water users. Aaron's response, we were told, was to state that if we disconnected his tap he would return with his backhoe and destroy the distribution box.

I had no idea what the morning might bring as we trudged uphill. The six of us looked like a formidable unit, I thought. But I worried that someone who would brazenly steal water from his neighbours might be prepared to go to any lengths to defend his actions.

The disconnect was speedily accomplished, not least because we had with us Pete Relkoff's son-in-law, Scot Woods, whose occupation includes work on construction drainage systems. He had brought, besides the necessary tools, a plug to secure the pipe once the tap was extracted—this being the kind of detail I would never have thought of until in the midst of the job. While Scot worked, we took photos of the situation. As the minutes passed and Aaron didn't appear, I began to relax.

With the proper water flow to the distribution box restored, we ambled back downhill. We subsequently filed an online Natural

Resources Violation Report, and a month later, three of us vigilantes met at the site with the Natural Resource Officer assigned to the case. The officer arrived in his BC government pickup, attired in a bulletproof vest over his uniform. He explained that enforcement personnel such as himself weren't allowed to be armed, a situation he felt inconsistent with wearing body armour.

On the tailgate of the pickup, we spread out our documentation, including a sheaf of photos, and the officer took GPS readings of the crime scene, as well as his own photos. In October, Rod made a follow-up phone call to the officer, who said the decision had been made to fine Aaron for the unauthorized tap. However, the officer wouldn't issue the fine—in the order of $200—unless another officer was free to provide backup when the violation notice was handed to Aaron in person. Despite several subsequent inquiries to the water authority, we've never been able to learn whether in fact the enforcement branch has levied the fine.

Three years after this incident, however, Aaron, following prescribed procedures this time, notified we other users that he had applied for a legal tap on the pipe in question, on the same grounds as his 2015 request to move the distribution box, namely that he wanted to bring gravity-fed water to his subdivided property located above the box. Thirteen of us users of the system signed a letter to the water authority in response, explaining how this was a repeat of his 2015 actions, reminding the authority of their 2007 determination that no new licences would be granted on the creek. As far as we know, this request of Aaron's was also denied.

Despite these episodes of water line dysfunction, I'll stress that water continues to appear out of my faucets when they are opened, season after season, year after year, the majority of the time. That stream of clear, cold fluid is the ongoing reward for having to occasionally respond to challenges on the gravity-fed system. When these issues do arise, I remind myself that there are no paradises without snakes.

Rural water systems professionally rebuilt on certain creeks in the West Kootenay and administered by the regional district authorities have their own problems, albeit different than those on our user-controlled, do-it-yourself, Wild West system. With regional-district-administered systems, the increasing bureaucratization of governments at every level has led to top-down demands for expensive water purification schemes and to an ever-increasing number of top-down construction regulations. As a result, connection to a professionally administered water source can be costly for water users who agree to have their system be so run. Trouble on these waterworks arises not from aging infrastructure or rogue individuals. Difficulties originate from legal strictures introduced by bureaucrats either justifying their well-paid jobs or certain they are acting in the best interests of users.

Our system might be cobbled-together in appearance and operation, but given how government policies have mismanaged BC resources like timber and salmon, the authorities' ability to judiciously administer water is debatable. Often I've resented having to head up to the distribution box in response to some crisis. Despite me being peeved, the alternative means of ensuring a water supply isn't enticing, even if the others who depend on Jerome Creek would agree to it, which they wouldn't.

I think of the Anarchist saying: "Imposition of order equals escalation of chaos." The saying doesn't claim chaos doesn't already exist, as it seems to do on our water line from time to time. The maxim just points out that some intended solutions make problems worse.

Meantime, as with water from my well, I'm grateful each time I hoist a glass of gravity-fed water. I'm certainly aware this water hasn't appeared by magic. Yet given all I now know about how much can go wrong between the creek and Appledore, when such water splashes out of a faucet I can't help but feel *some* magic is involved.

Chapter Eleven

THE SEASONS—
SPRING

WINTER BEHAVES AS INDECISIVELY ABOUT STEPPING aside for spring as it did about arriving at the end of autumn. In late February or early March, a few days of melt can be followed by a cold front bringing a late-afternoon-and-well-into-the-evening snowstorm. Each day now, however, sunrise happens earlier and sunset later. And though overnight temperatures continue to dip below freezing, daytime highs gradually increase.

For three or four weeks a phenomenon occurs I've never understood. The white mountainsides transform to green as coniferous trees on the slopes shed their snow. Simultaneously, on the valley bottom the white stuff covers fields, woods, lawns and roofs as though in the full grip of winter.

Yet the rise in daytime temperatures is steady. My concerns about road conditions begin to ease. Unless I'm travelling late at night or am caught in one of the increasingly infrequent snowfalls, the chance of encountering black ice or other winter dangers is less and less likely. Eventually snow descending in daylight consists of flakes which waft downward only to dissolve the moment they touch bare pavement. I can drive through a haze of nearly suspended flakes without even slowing down.

Frozen waterfalls on the highway's cutbanks remain, though: icy stalactites attached to snowy rock. These formations and each ever-more-rare snowstorm and low overnight temperatures remind me that winter has not completely relinquished its hold. If I want to ski on the rail trail now, I have to do so before the set tracks decay in the morning's strengthening sun. And earth shows in a few places along the trail where overhanging boughs of a fir or cedar have caused less snow to accumulate. The tracks at the Nelson cross-country club site, due to their higher elevation, stay viable longer. But even the club's routes are degrading. My routine of writing in the morning and skiing in the afternoon reverses.

Finally the rail-trail tracks are too deteriorated to use any time of day. Soon, I make my last run of the season along the Busk-Euphrates loop or the Clearwater trail at the Nelson club's site. I'm always regretful when I put away my skis for another year, wishing I had spent more time on them.

At Appledore, patches of brown grass materialize amid the lawns' white covering, especially on the pathways I've kept open to the deck stairs and along the east side of the house toward the woodshed. Little by little, these snow-free areas expand. I clear the driveway after a snowfall for what I understand in retrospect was the final time this winter.

The warmer daytime sun continues to sparkle on the snowscape that my lawns and meadow mostly remain. Meanwhile, on the driveway, a different challenge than ice and snow manifests: mud. Water from melting snow either side of the driveway trickles onto newly bared earth where the wheel paths were. The first rains add more water. I begin to notice that my vehicle is leaving indentations in the wet dirt. Then deeper ruts. As I ascend the drive, the vehicle hesitates and shakes for a second or two as my tires spin, especially making that sharp right-hand turn.

For years, as the mire deepened I would charge up the drive, the vehicle slipping and shaking while my tires sprayed sodden earth behind them as they lost momentum. I never failed to obtain the top, but I experienced some dicey moments midway, barely inching forward in the clinging muck. My vehicle looked for weeks as if it had been mud-bogging, which in a way it had.

My driveway became an interlaced web of ruts, growing deeper each time I steered up to the house or descended. On a sunny day, a thread of water oozed down the bottom of these depressions. When the muddy channels approached unacceptable depths, I would spend an afternoon with a shovel and rake, coaxing the soppy earth to refill the longitudinal excavations my tires had dug. But my next passage down the drive carved deep ruts again.

After decades of spending hours each spring at this repetitive task, I adopted the technique for dealing with driveway mud practised by the majority of my neighbours. At an industrial supply store in Nelson I purchased a fluorescent red traffic cone. Ever since, from the moment I first am conscious of ruts forming behind my tires until the day two or three weeks later when I judge the driveway to be sufficiently dried out, I block it with a cone and park at the bottom.

Shutting down vehicular access means I have to haul groceries or other purchases up to the house in multiple trips. On balance, this expenditure of energy is less that that required to repeatedly reconstruct the driveway with rake and shovel.

These weeks of melting snow constitute another shoulder season. Skiing is finished, but too much snow lingers on the rail trail to bike. I commence the first garden chore of the growing season: pruning and spraying the fruit trees.

The aim of pruning is to get rid of the unwanted new branches, as well as to shape the tree. "You want the tree to produce fruit, not wood," I was told at a pruning seminar I took at Georama nursery in 2011. Previously my approach to pruning was based on advice from Bea, reinforced by observing pruned fruit trees in the area. At Georama, I learned that pruning has its fashions. I had always pruned according to the concept that a fruit tree's foliage must be open to light: the branches of a properly pruned tree spread out more or less horizontally at the top of the trunk, with the result resembling a capped mushroom. At Georama, I was told that the new belief is that a fruit tree should be shaped to resemble a rocket. One vertical branch is identified as the leader, and all other branches are cut back so the tree looks pyramidical. The idea is that, pruned in this manner, all branches have access to sunlight but the tree doesn't expend energy trying to push one branch aloft as the main stem.

I was advised that, unfortunately, my pruned-the-old-fashioned-way trees can't be reconfigured into this up-to-date shape. Which means the latest pruning style has been applied by me only to fruit trees purchased since that seminar.

Some years I launch into pruning when a foot or more of snow remains at the base of the trunk. If the weather is cool enough that the snow crust will hold my weight, I can stand on the snow to deal with the shorter trees. More often, most of the snow is gone before I start to prune. Pruning thus requires use of my 6-foot-high orchard ladder. These devices have three points of contact with the ground: two at the bottom of a set of rungs, like a conventional ladder, and the third at the bottom of a pole hinged to the top of the ladder. In theory, the orchard ladder thus functions as a tripod, ensuring stability on uneven or sloping land. In reality, the ladder can be tippy, especially when I reach over too far to clip an unwanted shoot with secateurs rather than climb down, reposition the ladder, and climb up through a tangle of branches again to more safely remove unwanted growth.

I also employ pruning shears atop an extendable pole for situations beyond my reach from the ladder. This tool is harder to manoeuvre than the hand-held secateurs, as the weight of the elongated pole has to be compensated for as the shears are positioned to cut a shoot high above me.

Pruning for me is a matter of compromise. A not-yet-pruned Appledore fruit tree can resemble the back of a bristling porcupine, with a proliferation of new shoots rising vertically everywhere along its branches. Such new growth has to go. But in shaping the tree to its final configuration, how much new *horizontal* growth to remove at the ends of limbs is a judgment call.

Pruning can take several afternoons to complete. Then, before a tree breaks dormancy, I need to spray it with a mixture of lime sulphur and dormant oil to destroy any harmful overwintering insects. The spray's ingredients are organic, but the lime sulphur reeks and the spray often blows back onto my face and clothes. By the end of an afternoon of spraying, I smell like a match, and my glasses, face and beard are coated with tiny droplets of the stinky yellow concoction.

My sprayer is a hose-end one, which means I have to join together several of my 50-foot garden hoses in order to span the distance from an outside faucet on the east side of the house to trees as far as 80 metres away, down near the road. The hoses are brought one by one out of the shed where, neatly coiled, they have spent the winter. Prescribed amounts of lime sulphur and dormant oil are added to the sprayer, which is refilled repeatedly as tree after tree is doused. Any snow remaining near the base of a tree displays bright yellow patches by the time I'm done.

Three aspects to spraying are particularly unpleasant, besides enduring the smelly mixture on my glasses, skin, hair and clothes. One annoying component of the task is that the linked lengths of hose have to be hauled across the lawns to bring the sprayer to a tree. While I'm tugging at hoses, they seize every chance they get to display their displeasure at having been awakened from their cozy winter's nap in the shed only to be yanked across snow-covered or chilly ground. The hoses kink and snag, as well as leak water from where they're joined to other hoses.

Each year my language gets worse when I pull the trigger on the sprayer and nothing happens. I trudge wearily back up the line toward the tap to see where the kink in a hose has occurred this time. Or when a hose balks at being pulled to a new location, I have to go discover what obstacle is preventing it from shifting position. I find myself loudly threatening certain hoses with dismemberment or consignment to the garbage should they continue to be unco-operative. My warnings result in little improvement in a hose's behaviour.

The second reprehensible component of spraying is that often dirt has accumulated inside the stored hoses, presumably debris left over from the summer. Whatever the cause, the filter on the sprayer becomes clogged, meaning the spraying process has to stop while I disconnect the sprayer from the hose-end and clean the filter.

The third facet of spraying I dislike is that the trees have to be sprayed twice, with time for the droplets to dry between the two applications. I'm not sure why two applications are needed, but my sprayer's instructions insist that once the mixture dial is set to 30, spraying has to be repeated a second time. This requires yarding that long line of joined-together hoses, heavy with not only their combined weights but also that of the water filling them, from the cherry trees at the edge of the woods west of the house all the way down to the pear and plum trees beside the road. And then do it all over again.

Because of the aggravating and odoriferous nature of spraying, I attempt to accomplish it in a single day, forgoing any literary efforts. Usually the sky has dimmed to twilight by the time I re-coil the last hose to return it to the shed, strip off my fragrant coveralls, and head for the shower, exhausted.

My next spring chore is lifting the mulch from garden beds. I tackle flower beds first. Where the snow has melted, a purple crocus or two may have broken through last fall's mulch of birch leaves compacted by overlying snow. But as I start to remove the mulch and wheelbarrow it to the compost pile, I discover considerable activity has been occurring below the covering of leaves. Shoots have emerged from the soil and risen 2 or 3 inches: hyacinths, daffodils, tulips, as well as more crocuses.

These bulbs' stems are often yellow when first exposed to light. I apply bulb food and mix it into the soil. A few days later the shoots have turned green, and I'm often astonished by how much the little shafts have grown in such a brief time.

Soon many more crocuses, including a few white ones, are in bloom. The lawns become light-brown expanses of dead grass, with only a few heaps of snow lingering where the snow scoop piled snow extra high. Dangling from twigs in the hazel trees now are 2- or 3-inch-long light-brown catkins. After I become accustomed to observing these, one day I notice the catkins have vanished, replaced by tiny slips of green: the tips of leaves emerging.

I start to prepare the vegetable beds. As with the flower beds, I remove the mulch. Where I planted the rows of garlic cloves in autumn, below the mulch 3-inch-tall stems are evident.

I make my first visits to local garden stores and nurseries, purchasing bags of fertilizer. After this is spread on the veggie gardens, I turn them over with a fork to work the fertilizer in. The soil is damp and heavy, and the effort involves muscles I haven't used over the winter.

Vegetable seeds are available at a couple of garden supply stores in Nelson starting in January. But not long after I took up residence at Appledore, a friend put me on the mailing list for a seed catalogue from a Manitoba supplier. I fell into the habit of ordering my veggie seeds by mail. Currently I obtain my seeds from two companies: T&T and Veseys, located in Manitoba and PEI, respectively. In February I spend a couple of evenings poring over the brilliant colours of the catalogues' offerings while outside my window the landscape is deep in snow. I consult my notes from the previous summer's garden to recall how well or poorly certain seeds from one of the suppliers did.

Besides vegetable seeds, I also buy gladiolus bulbs from the catalogues. And over the years I've tried some of their other products: caragana hedging, peonies and asparagus roots.

The greenhouse, too, has its beds prepared: a simpler job because I don't mulch these. Yet because the beds have been out of the weather all winter, the soil is very dry. So once my seeds have arrived, I give the greenhouse beds a good soak. Then the first of the cold-weather veggies are planted there: lettuces, radish, peas, spinach, onions. This sowing is the launch of the vegetable growing season, even if many nights I continue to light the wood furnace in the house to remove the chill from the air.

The lawns continue to green up. Yellow flowers blossom on three forsythia bushes—always a welcome sight during early April days, which can be cool, wet and dreary. One afternoon I observe that a purple hyacinth has bloomed, soon followed by more. The first yellow daffodil opens. Miniature leaves speckle the branches of the mountain ash, although cottonwood, aspen and birch are still clusters of sticks.

I make my second run to area nurseries, this time in search of trees. My destination is Georama nursery outside Nelson, Four Seasons Greenhouse south of the Winlaw Bridge along the back road, or Dig, a newer nursery at Playmor Junction.

At each establishment I acquire a few 3- or 4-foot-high pines, firs, hemlocks or birches, and maybe an apple or plum to replace a newer tree in the orchard not producing fruit. Since Appledore's lower boundaries are now successfully lined with mature evergreens, in recent years I have purchased fewer new trees than previously. But for each acquisition, a site has to be selected, hole dug, and a mix of fertilizer, bone meal and water placed in the hole and stirred to the consistency of mud. The tree, carefully extracted from its container, is lifted into place, with soil packed around it and watered. The sapling has to be staked, too, so wind won't shift the root ball below ground. Such motion would delay the little tree's roots securing its spot.

A trip to Nelson now is a kind of time-travelling: as in autumn, the lower valley and Nelson can be two weeks in advance of Winlaw with regard to growing things. I'm always amazed when I see en route to town a grove of deciduous trees whose branches now bear a tentative haze of green. When I drove past the week before, their limbs were as barren as the ones still empty at Appledore.

Each afternoon on the grounds, though, I witness evidence of returning life: a red tulip blooms that was shrouded by its green leaves yesterday. A blue primula is in flower in the bed between the house and the abandoned water feature. Two days later, other primulas display explosions of different colours. The first thin stems of columbine break the soil in the bed that runs along the east end of the house. Hollyhock shoots are visible in a bed below the south side of the deck.

I gather the vegetable seed packets whose instructions say, "Plant as soon as the soil can be worked." First the various veggie beds have to be planned: where will arugula go this year? Cilantro? The idea is not to sow heavy feeders in the same location as the year before. Once I decide what will be grown where, I plant in the kitchen garden beds and in the lower garden a second round of the same cold-weather crops whose green beginnings can now be seen in the greenhouse.

Lettuce seeds are tiny. Before the seeds are positioned, I remove small impediments like minuscule pebbles and crumbs of earth or of fertilizer along a shallow trench barely inscribed in the soil. As I kneel or squat over the row, I use a small hand-held plastic seed dispenser to release seed after seed—ideally one at a time, but more often in clumps my thick fingers have to try to separate.

In a few weeks, veggies such as cucumbers and squash that require warmer soil will be in the ground. I bring into the house the first of the year's cut flowers—daffodils, hyacinths, tulips. One afternoon, the air is warm enough that, until the sun slips behind the ridge about 5 p.m., I'm gardening in a T-shirt.

Another afternoon, despite my long to-do list of garden chores, I attach my bike rack to the rear of my vehicle, load my bike, and pedal the rail trail between the Lemon Creek put-in and Slocan that I last traversed several weeks before on skis. Trailside bushes display tufts of green. No swans grace the river, since they migrated north as the weather warmed in March. Plenty of ducks and geese remain, and I see high in the air an eagle coasting on the breeze. If I ride the trail south of Winlaw, the yellow of skunk cabbages dots swampy areas I pass.

I pay a visit to my two main sources of annuals, and of those foods like tomatoes, peppers, basil and kale I grow from starts rather than seeds. For the first 20 years at Appledore, I acquired my veggie starts and my marigolds, dahlias, lobelia, petunias, nicotianas, fuchsias, nasturtiums, and other flowers from Elderbee Greens. This seasonal nursery was situated about 4 kilometres north of Appledore along Avis Road, an unpaved lane that veers off from the back road west of the Perry's Siding Bridge.

The nursery's name was picked because the husband of the couple who owned it, Gail Elder, raises bees for honey. For decades he taught music at Winlaw's elementary school, retiring in 2003. Gail conducted the valley band for 42 years, plays the tuba-like euphonium in it, and raises organic potatoes on a bench above their house and greenhouses. "I like potatoes better than my students," he told me once, a twinkle in his eye. "Potatoes will stay in a row if you tell them to."

Gail's wife, Brenda, remains the plant expert. She started Elderbee Greens around 1985, and the nursery was certified organic in 1999. She has a fine sense of what grows best where in the valley. One year I asked her, for example, when tomato starts should be planted. She pointed to a small clear-cut visible high on the east valley wall, a patch of white surrounded by the mountain's green. "Don't plant your tomatoes until the snow is gone from there," she said, a rule I observe to this day.

After decades, Brenda passed the business on to a younger couple, who relocated it farther north on Avis Road and renamed the nursery Bee Greens. As with Elderbee Greens, most of the successor nursery's sales are wholesale, rather than to customers like me. Yet Bee Greens' owners, Hamsa Gooderham and Pete Slevin, enjoy—as Brenda did—the interactions with the locals who stop by to shop. Much of the enjoyable conversation at Bee Greens is about plants, but valley gossip and the larger issues of the day—forestry practices, wildfire threats, the state of the economy—appear among the words as well.

My other source these days for veggie starts and annuals, along with the occasional perennials like delphiniums or foxgloves, lies in the opposite direction on the back road, a few kilometres south of the Winlaw Bridge: Four Seasons Greenhouse. This year-round operation, larger than Bee Greens, also operates a retail sideline to their wholesale business. As with Bee Greens, selling direct to the community is more about interaction with neighbours and friends than for the dollars netted.

At Bee Greens, I can get involved in fascinating conversations with either Hamsa or Pete. But at Four Seasons, more of a difference is evident between the owners, Pearl and Fred Dutoff. Pearl, who has a day job as a hospital nurse, is more business-like than Bee Green's owners, less inclined to pass the time of day. Fred, a mainstay for many years of the Winlaw volunteer fire department, enjoys sharing his wide knowledge about plants, valley history and especially Doukhobor history. As well as discussing the features and preferred growing conditions of whatever plant I inquire about, he loves a good yarn and will take the time to tell it. Often he'll ask me what writing I'm working on. I dedicated one short story, "The Shed," to him in my collection of Slocan Valley tales, *The Shadows We Mistake for Love*. In describing to him one spring afternoon what can spark a piece of writing for me, I was reminded of a mysteriously half-torn-down building alongside the valley highway that intrigued me, and which became the basis for that story.

When I mentioned once the premise of this book, he was quiet for a moment. "For anyone who has never lived in the valley, moving here is a voyage of discovery," he mused. He related an incident that occurred during one of the Winlaw Fall Fairs he and Pearl organized for several years. He was at the Fair, he said, in his fire department uniform. A valley newcomer he didn't know approached him and announced, "My well has stopped working."

Fred said his initial response consisted of, "So? What am I supposed to do about it?" But he realized that the newcomer was used to having access to some civic authority to whom he could turn when difficulties arose. Fred in his uniform was the only identifiable representative of organized civil society; hence the person expected Fred to solve his problem. As Fred talked, I could sympathize with both protagonists of this tale, having been completely bewildered myself by the loss of my water supply my first September here, and having now had decades of experience dealing with such developments.

At either nursery, cruising the tables jammed with annuals and healthy vegetable starts is one of my favourite spring experiences. As my eye travels over the riot of colour and the robust green of veggies, I'm imagining how my gardens will look this year and what abundance of kale or tomatoes I will enjoy in the months ahead.

Beginning with my first spring at Appledore, I followed local consensus and launched my blitz of planting annuals and warm-weather vegetables on the May 24 weekend. I take a day or two off from writing, and work in the garden from after breakfast to the supper hour, or even later. By the end of the first week of June, everything is in the ground. Most recently, I've begun earlier in May. In 2021, for example, the planting rush was *finished* by May 28, an all-time record. Is global warming letting me start planting before I used to? Or am I more efficient in the garden? Since I have lots more beds under cultivation than my first years here, my guess is the earlier finish is due to a combination of these factors.

Vegetables are my first focus during the May planting. Onion sets, seed potatoes, and basil and pepper starts are positioned where the year's plan decrees. Once I'm done with the edibles, dealing with all the annuals that I've brought home from the nurseries looks like a daunting task. I ease into it by first readying my hanging baskets and deck pots. Fuchsias, lobelia, and cascading petunias go in pots suspended from the eaves over the deck and also from a joist under the deck by the basement door. The much larger deck pots hold cherry tomato starts as well as geraniums, lobelia, nicotiana for evening fragrance, and other blooms-to-be. I also prepare a few other flower-filled pots, including the one I place down by the road at the bottom of the drive to welcome visitors.

I wait until the spring bulbs have died back in the beds before planting annuals—and always a few perennials I've acquired. Tulips linger the longest in bloom. Often a few are continuing to entice the bees when I start to prepare the bed for the annuals. As I plant, I bear in mind where various flowers are best placed, and the heights specific flowers will attain. For instance, impatiens and begonias do best where the beds are mostly shaded. The tallest marigolds are planted where I've earlier buried gladiolus bulbs, since I've never found I can depend on glads actually showing up later in the summer.

Around me nature is busy, too. Overnight, lilac bushes near the top of the driveway are redolent with the sweet scent of purply-blue blooms. The big rhododendron off the southwest corner of the deck has produced an array of reddish-purple blossoms. The first purple iris is out, with more to follow. At the edge of the woods, and a few places on the lawn, lupins have burst into bloom: most of their flowers blue, but a few a pale pink.

With the garden planting underway, a couple of firsts for the year happen. At some point in May, my neighbour Rod strolls over to see if I agree that we should turn on the irrigation water. We together lift the cover off a depression in the earth north of his driveway where the irrigation shut-off valve is located—the valve I changed with great trepidation long ago. Once water starts to travel through the line, at his place and mine we shut the irrigation stand-pipe taps, left open when we drained the system in the fall. When the last standpipe is closed, one of us is sure to announce, before we each head off to the rest of the afternoon's chores, "That's it: another year begun."

Now I can stop watering the greenhouse plantings by hand and rig up a soaker hose with a battery-operated timer. When the lower veggie garden is planted, I place a sprinkler there, connected to another standpipe and timer. Thanks to the timers, irrigation water will flow to the lower garden sprinkler each morning from 6 a.m. to 7, and then to the greenhouse's soaker hose from 7 to 7:30, the kitchen gardens' sprinkler from 7:45 to 8:45, and finally the Grave of Literary Ambition's soaker hose from 9 to 10.

The other beds receive water every couple of days via hand, soaker hose or a movable irrigation sprinkler. By late May the grass is overdue for its first cut. Once the power mower's engine is coaxed into life after its winter snooze, the first complete mowing of the lawns, as with opening the irrigation line, is a milestone of the season. To mow all Appledore's lawns takes me about eight hours, spread over three or four days. With so much uphill and downhill on the property, and so many obstacles in the midst of the lawns—trees, the bird bath, the kitchen gardens—manhandling the heavy mower can be exhausting. People ask me why I don't buy a riding mower, since many of these are in evidence in the valley. My excuse is that I need the exercise. And given the slope of some portions of my lawns, I'm not sure how safe operating a riding mower would be.

In these spring months, no sooner have I cut the last of the grass than the first area I trimmed is looking unkempt again. By fall, I'll have cut the lawns nine or ten times, with half of these mowings occurring in May and June.

The weather continues to warm. In the day, I leave screened windows and doors open. Outside, I work in shorts for the first time. Tree after tree around me has produced their full complement of leaves. After months of only seeing empty branches, I'm overwhelmed by the abundance of leaves evident in every direction. An aspen, cottonwood or maple can transform in a matter of days from showing only traces of green at its twig-ends to displaying a dense cloud of green that envelops trunk and branches, shimmering in the spring air. Roadside bushes, too, burst into leaf. As the season advances, every shade of green is on display at Appledore, and wherever I travel in the valley: jade, emerald, lime, mint, verdigris and more. Stretches of the highway form an alley of green I steer through. A profusion of intermingled greens rises either side of the pavement from asphalt shoulder to treetop.

This time of year is what a friend calls "peak green." Soon enough some leaves will fade, curl and brown as insects do their worst. But for a few weeks, the view in every direction is green, green, green. Not so long ago, I remind myself, the world was white, Now, astoundingly, everything is green. From my deck I admire my Japanese maples' million emerald shards. I'm impossibly rich in leaves.

More than sap is rising during these weeks. As the ever-hotter sun melts the snow on distant summits, the area's creeks fill and become tumultuous. The Slocan River runs wider, deeper, faster. The June rise has begun.

At either end of the Perry's Siding Bridge, roadside water meadows develop puddles, which become pools, then are transformed to lakes. One spring ritual I have enjoyed for years is to hoist my canoe onto my vehicle on a sunlit afternoon, unload it where the back road and Avis Road meet, and launch the vessel into reedy water covering what is a meadow much of the year.

My friends from south of Silverton, Phil and Emma, usually accompany me. Phil occupies the bow to paddle, while I take the stern to paddle and steer. Emma sits between us on the canoe's flat bottom, enjoying the ride. Avoiding the main channel of the river, we glide north over flooded land alongside Avis Road.

Our pace is leisurely. Coming upon water lilies or spotting an eagle in a nearby tree provide excuse enough to stop paddling and just drift while we savour these finds.

This seasonal waterway beside Avis Road ends at the oxbow Bea and I encountered when I first moved here: that former bend of the Slocan that now is a placid loop out of the main stem's powerful current. The oxbow's landscape in flood resembles my vision of the Everglades. Swampy-looking vegetation encircles the island formed when the river's main passage bypassed its former meander.

Floating on the oxbow's tranquil waters, Phil, Emma and I meet fleets of ducks, who with squawks and splashes lift off into the air if we approach too close. What appears to be a log floating midstream turns out to be a beaver swimming toward the south shore, where between the trees and the water a large pile of branches must be a beaver lodge.

A stroke or two of my paddle directs our lazy progress around the west side of the island. None of us says anything for a time as we drift, sun-drenched. I can glimpse the roofs of the Elders' house and greenhouses amid the forest on the western shore. A barbed-wire fence marks the oxbow's northerly banks, enclosing the pastures of the farmer whose property extends upriver. We glide in that direction, and two cows from the herd of Black Angus in the field beyond notice us and start to amble our way. Over the calls of robins, the chittering of a squirrel, and the chirping of some bird I can't identify, I hear low moans of the cattle. A raven croaks out a guttural protest as he laboriously flaps overhead. A Steller's jay beelines from a lone meadow cottonwood across the oxbow and disappears into the island's woods.

Portions of the northern field are submerged, so we sail above a barbed-wire fence and amid half-drowned grasses toward a grove that borders the river's principal channel. Between cottonwoods and aspens to my left, I can see in the distance sheep grazing in a meadow and an old barn. Beyond them, the huge bulk of Perry Ridge lifts green under a faultless blue sky.

The canoe's bottom grates on land. Waterlogged grasses and bushes surround us, and the way forward between trees looks wet. But this route is impassable with all three of us in the vessel. Phil hauls himself out of the canoe, lightening the bow while I back-paddle. When the craft is afloat again, Phil clambers aboard, bare feet dripping, and I manage to swing us around towards deeper water. A few strokes of my paddle, and we're coasting back over the underwater fence into the oxbow once more. Phil soon has a joint going as we drift. Emma produces a sketch pad from her knapsack, and her drawing pencil starts to capture a nuthatch or swallow resting on the few inches of a fence post rising clear of the water. When Phil hands her the joint, Emma—who never indulges—passes it to me.

Somehow in the sunshine we've wandered close to where the northern leg of the oxbow meets the river surging downstream. I direct us back nearer to the island. Emma one year saw a bear among the island's cottonwoods and cedars, although by the time she drew Phil's and my attention to the animal, it had vanished into the understorey.

Close to the island, the leaves of its trees are reflected on the scarcely moving water. Phil is leaning over the port side, looking for fish. The water is absolutely clear, the bottom devoid of vegetation. Emma is munching an apple she brought. I'm keeping an eye out for another sight of the river's eagles. Spring has returned to the valley. At Appledore, the grass needs cutting again.

"There's one," Phil says quietly. "No, more! There's three." I lean over the opposite gunwale to see if I can spot them.

Chapter Twelve

THE ELEMENTS–
FIRE

THE SAME MONTH I TOOK POSSESSION OF APPLEDORE, MY friends David and Judy mentioned that although we were enjoying August heat, winter would inevitably come and I needed to obtain firewood for my basement furnace. Natural gas remains unavailable in the valley even today, making one's choices for home heating wood, electricity or, as at Appledore, a combination.

After Peter Christensen's attempt after the Headwaters conference to show me how to operate a chainsaw, I decided I didn't want to buy one and master how to use and maintain it. Not having a pickup in those days, I also didn't know how I would bring firewood home after cutting it in the woods. I asked Lynn, my then-neighbour, where she obtained her firewood. She gave me the phone number of Larry Nestor in Castlegar, whom she said provided cut, split and delivered pieces.

Lynn mentioned she burned four cords over the winter, and since our houses were almost identical in size, I figured I'd order that amount as well. She explained I'd need to specify the length I wanted my firewood chunks cut, and also the tree species desired—she recommended a mix of birch and larch. These were not details I would have thought of. After measuring some firewood left in a small pile beside the shed north of the house—16 inches long—I picked up the phone.

When I dialled Larry's number, the response provided an inkling of his sense of humour. "Hello," a voice boomed out, cheerful and energetic, after the third ring. A silence followed. I promptly started babbling about who I was, and that my neighbour had passed along his phone number, and how I wanted to buy...

The voice in my ear cut me off. "This is a *machine*. Please leave a message. Thank you. Thank you very much." On the recording a dog barked in the background twice before the beep sounded for the caller to speak.

Larry's answering machine message remained the same, decade after decade: I became his customer for 30 years. I would phone at the beginning of May each year, and, ignoring the silence on the recording that had fooled me the first time, wait for the eventual beep before ordering my wood. A month or so later, a large battered stake truck would slowly rattle up my driveway, its box jammed with a couple of cords. I wanted the load dropped on the lawn by the northeast corner of the house, a location handy to the garden shed, alongside which I established my main woodpile. But to unload on the lawn meant Larry had to turn around on the area where I parked outside the basement door, a manoeuvre that took considerable skill even after I moved my vehicle, given the size of his truck.

Once he had backed to the right place to unload, he opened the rear gate on the truck box, then shifted a lever, and the vehicle's hydraulics slowly raised the back. The pieces of firewood roared and tumbled out, quickly mounding up. Always two or three pieces of firewood stuck to the nearly vertical floor of the raised box, and he would toss another chunk of wood at any recalcitrant piece to loosen it.

Larry, a heavy-set middle-aged guy in work clothes, didn't engage in small talk. A few times over the decades he showed up accompanied by a dog, and twice had a woman in the cab with him. Most years he was by himself. Deliveries were always in late afternoon. He once mentioned that his operation was on the site of a former sawmill that he and his father had owned. I assumed he spent the day cutting logs into rounds and then used a mechanical splitter to produce a load before driving it to his customer.

Always he phoned a day or two before he made the delivery, and at that time he let me know that year's price per cord. After the cost of gas crossed over a dollar a litre, a delivery charge was added. For years I handed him a cheque just before he left my place. If I had an appointment away from home on the day he planned to drop off the load—often he called the evening before he intended to bring my wood—I left the cheque for him in an envelope thumbtacked to the basement door.

After one delivery, however, when I handed him the cheque he asked, "Do you have money?" Since over the years his price per cord steadily rose, I thought his question was a way of inquiring whether I could afford his newest rate. Or perhaps, I thought to myself, he's asking if my cheque is good. Maybe he had been stiffed by one of his clients.

"I've got money," I reassured him. "The cheque will clear okay." He stared at me. "Do you have money?" he asked again.

I stood bewildered for a moment, cheque in hand. Then I got it. "You mean, ah, you'd like to be paid in cash?"

He nodded.

Henceforth I had to withdraw from my bank in Nelson the payment for my cords. Since the area's illicit marijuana growers are famous for cash-only transactions, I felt nervous standing in front of a teller requesting a sizable cash withdrawal from my account. I'd explain each time that my wood guy had asked me to pay in cash. Even to me, my explanation sounded false. The teller always

229

remained professionally poker-faced as she counted out the stack of bills.

Most years I only saw Larry twice, when he delivered my two loads of wood. In 2012 he informed me he had bought an even bigger truck, capable of hauling *three* cords at a time. To ensure I obtained my needed four cords each year, I started buying three cords one year and six the next.

By now I understood the importance of having extra wood stockpiled. Acquiring nine cords instead of eight over two years would let me slowly build a surplus. An exceptionally long cold spell one winter had meant that by spring I had used up nearly every stick I had. Because I like lighting a fire on cool, rainy spring evenings to counter the damp chill, that April I was reduced to burning what wood I could. Year after year I had stacked the latest delivery on top of the residue of earlier firewood loads. Now these elderly chunks of wood at the bottom of the stack were the only fuel I had available. The pieces were so desiccated they were almost weightless, and they produced the same BTUs when alight as a piece of Kleenex. I understood then that I needed a cushion of burnable wood as insurance against an unusually frigid or long winter.

I was also aware that some neighbours took pride in having three or four years' worth of extra wood on hand. Having that much firewood felt to them, I suspected, like money in the bank: the volume of one's woodpile indicated to others how competent you are at practical matters, how good a provider you are for your household.

My neighbour Rod told me that not only guys pay attention to how much wood somebody has stacked. In the fall when the valley's single women are looking for a bachelor to link up with for the winter, Rod said, one factor in their choice is the size of the potential partner's woodpile: "Naturally, she wants to stay as warm as possible during the cold weather."

I only saw Larry in his home environment once. Following his change to a cash-only operation, one of his night-before-delivery phone calls meant I lacked sufficient funds unless I made a special trip the next day into Nelson to my bank. When I suggested a different delivery day, he replied that he'd deliver tomorrow according to his plan and that I should drop off the money when I was next in Castlegar.

I discovered the following week that he lived on his wood yard, next to an industrial barn where the former sawmill had been located. His house looked somewhat run-down from the outside, but when he invited me in, I was impressed. Gleaming samples of polished wood were featured as windowsills and trim throughout the well-appointed interior. When I commented favourably about his place, Larry spoke knowledgeably about the different kinds of wood used in finishing carpentry.

He was cooking something savoury on the stove when I arrived, and I joined him and a pal seated at the kitchen table for a beer. I learned he and the friend were gourmet cooks, and I listened as the two men ranked menu items from the best area restaurants. Larry's conversation was a long way from his gruffly terse statements when he delivered my wood. We kidded around about my failure, as Larry viewed it, to sufficiently trim back the trees lining my driveway, branches of which Larry often requested I cut so as not to damage his truck. I did prune these some, but almost always after the truck had come and gone, freshly broken bits of tree limb littered the drive.

Another beer was offered, and I was encouraged to stay and sample the food Larry had been preparing. I had other errands pressing, however. As I was leaving, Larry commented: "You know, you clean up real good." I realized that on the afternoons of his deliveries he had only seen me in my grubby outdoor work clothes. Similarly, I had only known him to be dressed in *his* work gear. He had formed an impression of me that was as limited as my sense of who he was. Probably he viewed me as some hippie who had lucked into inheriting money and so had been able to purchase a valley property. Or as one who had amassed sufficient wealth by growing weed.

During my annual phone call, Larry mentioned sometimes that he'd be tied up for a month working for Teck Cominco's smelter at Trail as part of their annual maintenance. Either at the smelter or some other side job, he injured a leg. Each spring when he arrived with my wood, the leg seemed worse. Watching him lower himself from the cab and limp to the back of the truck to open the box's rear gate became distressing for me to watch. He was evidently in pain, though stoic about it when I inquired. One winter I ran into him by chance in the Castlegar Safeway. He admitted the leg wasn't improving but insisted that nothing could be done about it.

At last, in 2020 when I called him to place my annual order, he phoned back to say he was shutting down the business because of his injury. Rod's wife, Sharon, did some neighbourhood research for me and found a young guy in Castlegar just starting a firewood business. The following year, my new supplier even purchased some of Larry's equipment, so I have some sense of continuity.

The furnace that came with the house was simple, yet highly effective: essentially a big metal barrel on its side with a door at one end to load wood and, below that, a flap which served as a damper. A metal label on the furnace read: *Valley Comfort, Winlaw, BC*—the company having begun here before relocating west to the larger market of the Okanagan Valley. A chain also connected the damper to a thermostat mounted above the door. The idea was that as the ambient temperature declined, the chain would retract, opening the damper and thus causing the fire to ramp up. But whether or not the appliance was new when the house was built, the thermostat was no longer operational by the time I acquired the place.

When the cold weather arrived and I kindled my first fires, I learned that the furnace threw an incredible amount of heat, so once the fire was lit, the damper stayed shut. The barrel was enclosed in a larger metal box, open at the top. At first I wondered why heat from the furnace wasn't ducted upstairs—a flange around the top of the box indicated where a duct system would be installed. But when a fire was merrily alight, so much warmth poured up the basement stairs and through vents in the upstairs floor that I understood why ducts, like the thermostat, were unnecessary. Even on the coldest nights the house was toasty: I generally wore a T-shirt and no socks indoors in winter, the same as I did during the hot days of summertime. All electric baseboards except those in the living room, bathroom and basement study, which are connected to their own wall thermostats, were shut off by me as unnecessary. (In 1990 I had an office built for me in the northeast corner of the basement; the short portion of the L-shaped living room was repurposed as a dining room.) Some winter nights I closed the upstairs door to the basement to try to cool the house for a better sleep.

The furnace was so basic in design and worked so well I thought it would chug along forever. But after two decades I noticed that high heat in the furnace had deformed the metal of the barrel in a few places, causing ripples in its sides. I showed these to my brother, a metallurgical engineer, during one of his visits to Appledore. He informed me that metal is weakest where folded, and that the potential for a leak is greatest there. His concern was that carbon monoxide might escape through a hole in the barrel, a potentially deadly situation.

When I decided to purchase a replacement furnace, I discovered that the design of these had advanced considerably since mine was fabricated. The manufacturers of modern versions claim their products not only are more efficient, they also emit less smoke. In 2009 I purchased a new model with a glass door, a firebox lined with special bricks, and an arrangement of tubing inside that, according to the manufacturer, Regency, brings secondary air into the firebox to allow the smoke to be "reburned."

Installation of the new furnace meant, however, that to bring my heating system up to code a new metal chimney had to be installed.

Also, current regulations now required a dedicated source of air for the heating unit, since new houses are expected to be airtight. My place is snug, and I'm never aware of drafts, but for 20 years the furnace consumed the ambient air in the dwelling without any noticeable negative side effects on me. Yet no one would install a new furnace that wasn't up to code. A hole had to be drilled in the north side of the house and a stovepipe set-up constructed to convey outdoor air to the base of the new unit.

While the new furnace certainly keeps the house comfortably warm, gone are the days of heat pouring up from the basement in tropical quantities. When I first light a fire, with the damper open or partially, I can still step out on the deck and watch smoke lifting from my chimney toward the sky. When the furnace is dampered down, though, only transparent waves of hot air escaping from the chimney reveal to an observer with a sharp eye that a fire is burning within.

The technology built into the new furnace also means it is more fragile than the old one. The latter functioned for 29 years without any maintenance, assuming it was new in 1980 when the house was built—which I doubt, since the builder wasn't financially well-off. But after a mere 10 years, the interior of my new furnace had to be completely rebuilt with new ceramic baffles, firebricks, air tubes and insulation around the firebox door. This maintenance cost me 20 per cent of the original price of the unit, although, to be fair, some financial inflation doubtless occurred over that decade.

The new furnace, like the old, provides an adequate supply of heat, so I shouldn't complain. Yet despite the claim of greater efficiency for the new unit, I burn the same four cords of wood most winters.

To make feeding this wood to the furnace as easy as possible, every spring when I clear away the heap of new firewood dumped in the designated spot on the lawn, I stack about a cord-and-a-half in the basement. This amount lasts until after Christmas. Then I have to break out the wheelbarrow again, and, load by load, trundle wood through the snowy afternoon from an outside stack to be re-piled in the basement. After a couple of weeks, the stack in the basement is as big as when the cold weather first arrived. If I'm lucky, this rebuilt indoor woodpile will last the rest of the winter. Otherwise, in March I'm back outdoors filling the wheelbarrow once more.

Fire of course burns more places than in a furnace's firebox. For many years the chief of the Winlaw volunteer fire department was Richard Meissenheimer, whom I knew through a couple of different connections. His wife, Bonnie Baker, is a faithful attender of literary events in Nelson, as well as someone who writes herself. Bonnie also kept sheep—and one donkey to protect them from coyotes—and sold sheep manure as fertilizer. For a few years I would muck out their barn each spring in partial payment for a load of the good stuff, which I shovelled into my tow-behind trailer. As well, Richard's mother, Joyce, was a political activist all her life—a "banned" person in South Africa, due to her participation in the anti-apartheid movement before she and Richard immigrated to Canada. She had liked some of my poems, and when she visited Richard and Bonnie from Montreal, I was occasionally called in to entertain her.

Richard told me Winlaw experienced very few house fires, because of adherence to building codes. Most fires the department attended were caused, he said, by the local custom of people burning off their lawns each spring. The motivating belief for these blazes is that they cause the grass to be greener when later it grows up through the ashes. Trouble arises, Richard explained, because when people stand around the flames, leaning on a shovel while making sure the grass stays alight, they frequently drink. Drinking leads to poor judgment. Indeed, for the first couple of decades I lived here, scorched grass was common, but also charcoaled wooden fence posts and blackened siding on many an outbuilding wall.

Slowly the concept of setting fire to your grass has fallen out of favour. Richard meanwhile died in 2006 of brain cancer. I had always enjoyed chatting with him because of his droll sense of humour. An auto mechanic by trade, he mentioned to me once that he wished he'd studied instead to be a doctor. "A doctor only has to be familiar with *two* models," he pointed out.

For everyone in the valley, forest fires are a larger concern than a house fire. Some summers smoke from wildfires thickens the air day after day. The surrounding mountains disappear, and in the worst weeks the smell of smoke permeates my house. To wake in the pitch-dark night with a heavy odour of smoke in my bedroom is disconcerting. Living as I do in a wooden house heated by a wood fire, the cloying scent of smoke indoors is associated in my mind with catastrophe.

Such smoke often originates from fires in our area, or in the Okanagan. But since the prevailing winds in summer are from the south, smoke from forests alight on the eastern slopes of the Cascade Range in Oregon or Washington also frequently drift this far, adding to the astringent, eye-watering air.

Any nearby fire brings with it, besides smoke, the noise of aircraft fighting the fire. Helicopters hover to bucket water from the Slocan River, pulling their load upwards at the end of a long cable as the machine clatters away toward the blaze while another chopper loudly edges in to dip its bucket in the same part of the river. Water bombers drone or buzz overhead all day as well. Once the water bomber was a lone, huge, multi-engine airplane. Now fleets of three or four much smaller craft are employed to, one by one, drop their cargo of fire retardant on a burning mountainside.

During one visit from my brother in fire season, we hiked the Galena Trail, a rail trail extending 7 kilometres from the edge of New Denver east to the former site of Three Forks, a once-thriving mining and railroad town. In the woods as we strode along, the smoke suspended in the air obscured our surroundings only 10 metres from us in every direction. Another summer, for a few days if I stood in my lower meadow down by the road, I could watch flames and a pillar of smoke rising high on a mountain to the northeast. A different fire that year, at Enterprise Creek between Slocan and New Denver, closed the highway for a day when flames swept down to the edge of pavement.

My biggest worry is a blaze on Perry Ridge itself. A historic photo exists of the forest on the ridge completely burned off. The picture was taken before homes like mine were established along the base of the ridge, but obviously the possibility of an apocalyptic forest fire on the mountain is not zero. Every few years a fire does break out somewhere along the ridge's crest. Provincial wildfire crews are quick to respond, and while one rages, I check daily a BC government website that reports on the firefighters' progress toward containment of the blaze.

To date I've never had to be on evacuation alert, although in the summer of 2020 friends who live several kilometres away below the southern end of Perry Ridge had to be poised to evacuate for six weeks when a fire that had started high up as usual began to spread down toward numerous homes. And in July 2021 an evacuation alert extended to this side of the river in response to a fire burning along the eastern summit ridges directly across the valley from Appledore. Luckily, the alert for my side of the valley only extended as far south as Ellen Bazaroff's property.

An evacuation alert sparks an existential crisis: out of all your possessions—which some say define you—what do you pack to take? Where will you go? Should you leave now, or wait until the alert is perhaps upgraded to an evacuation order? For people with animals, an alert triggers more problems. Horses, sheep, cattle, goats, chickens all have to be moved to safe ground, since if the alert is changed to an evacuation order, no time is allowed to deal with livestock. Wherever the animals are removed to, meanwhile, they have to be tended there daily for the duration of the alert.

During the 2020 fire at the end of Perry Ridge, I would bike south periodically to see how far the flames and columns of smoke had reached. From a vantage point on the rail trail, I watched from close by the incredibly noisy choppers hovering one after another to refill their buckets in the river before slowly angling off toward the mountain again. When in the far distance the bucket was emptied, I could only observe a tiny flash of silver against the green blur of as-yet-untouched trees. Compared to the magnitude of the blaze, the contents of the helicopters' buckets resembled a thimbleful of water poured on a campfire.

But the choppers stuck to their task hour after hour, and presumably had some effect on the conflagration. I've noticed, however, that BC Interior forest fires seldom are pronounced 100 per cent contained until after significant rainfall or the advent of fall's cooler weather.

A downpour is most welcome in fire season only if it is not part of a thunderstorm. Most West Kootenay wildfires are caused by lightning, When I acquired Appledore, I experienced my first summer storm involving thunder, lightning, torrential rain and high wind that bent birches and aspen far over. If such a storm is intense enough, the Seven Sisters sway to an extent that I begin to wonder if one is going to topple. I stare out at raindrops bouncing off my deck in their fury, while clouds low overhead light up again and again amid thunder that resounds almost continuously.

Initially I reassured myself regarding lightning by telling myself it would strike high on the ridge above me rather than down on the valley floor. A few years after my move here, however, a tree in the vicinity of the Winlaw general store was hit by lightning. Since then, I'm more cautious when I'm outside and hear thunder grumbling in the distance. One summer afternoon I was working in the lower garden, keeping one ear on a slowly increasing rumbling in the sky. My plan was to finish, before the storm arrived, the overdue weeding of my raspberry canes.

I waited too long. Suddenly a wind of tremendous force sent a hail of twigs, moss, leaves and a few good-sized branches sailing through the air in my direction. I could hear other boughs or maybe entire trees crack and crash in the forest west of the house. A thunderclap abruptly detonated, many times louder than I'd ever heard before. I abandoned wheelbarrow and tools and sprinted madly up the slope of the lawn toward the house, passing through debris-filled air and hoping no tree limb of size was being lofted my way at hurricane speed. As I panted uphill, a wall of rain descended, leaving me soaked to the skin by the time I reached the door into the basement. I stepped inside to safety the same instant a simultaneous flash and boom of thunder deafened me momentarily.

Any valley storm with strong winds, in any season, can result in the constrained fire that is electricity ceasing to flow. At least once every couple of months a power outage occurs at Appledore, lasting from an hour to more than a day. The official reason given is usually that a tree fell on the line someplace. Or, from time to time, a vehicle accident on the highway has taken out a pole.

Power rates continually increase, always with a notice explaining that the money will be used for improvements that will prevent future interruptions to the electrical supply. Despite this assurance, the frequency and duration of outages has never decreased for as long as I've lived here. Which means Appledore, like every dwelling in the region, is prepared for life without power. With the gravity-fed system to provide water, and the wood furnace to provide heat, some basics for survival are taken care of. A supply of candles, an old-fashioned kerosene lantern, and several flashlights provide illumination if necessary. A Coleman two-burner camping stove can be used on the deck for cooking, or the flat top on my new furnace is, in effect, a stove top when a fire is lit inside.

Lack of electricity means the computer is dead—not always a bad thing, if I've been spending too much time at it. Of course, losing the computer is a pain if I'm in the middle of crafting something, or am overdue replying to an email or a letter. If power isn't restored after several hours, my concern is that the contents of my small basement freezer will thaw, and other food in my fridge will begin to go bad.

One December when my brother was visiting, the power disappeared Christmas morning, leaving me to contemplate trying to cook a turkey out on the snowy deck using the Coleman stove. After five hours, however, the electricity was restored, early enough that I could rush the bird to the oven and sit down to a Yuletide feast only an hour later than I'd originally planned. A couple of years ago, as a fall outage lasted into its second day, Rod offered to activate my freezer using a portable gasoline-powered generator he and Sharon had bought. Because Sharon bottles, cans and freezes a good deal of what their garden yields for them to live on through the winter, loss of the contents of their three freezers would result in a financial disaster. Rod had already put the generator to use restoring cold to his freezers and refrigerator before offering the machine to me. We hauled the heavy device across their lawn to my house, and energized my freezer. Later that afternoon the power came back on.

The restoration of power itself can be fraught. For a couple of years, each time after an outage when the electricity was turned on again, a power surge resulted. People's fridges, stoves, audio equipment, and computers were fried, and the utility company accepted no responsibility. I was fortunate in that all I lost were two surge protectors. Eventually the company figured out again how to reinstitute power without sending a burst of electricity up the wires. Nevertheless, each time the power goes off at Appledore, one chore, besides switching my water supply to the gravity-fed system if I'm using the well, is to pull the plugs bringing current to my computer, printer and fax. Just in case.

Lack of power renders my house's telephones useless. They have portable receivers and therefore function like tiny radio sets dependent on electricity. For emergencies, I keep one phone whose receiver jacks directly into a phone wall outlet. The phone system operates on its own electrical current, so by using this old-fashioned unit when the power is off, I can get a dial tone and send and receive calls.

The problem with my phone during my first few years at Appledore, though, wasn't that it failed to remain operational through downpours, strong winds and dumps of wet snow. The difficulty with it was that everyone in the valley was on a party line. At least the phone only rang when the call was for me. But when I went to make a call, often somebody was chattering away on the line.

A particularly bad situation occurred if I was in the middle of a stressful call—talking some matter over with Bea, or discussing with P'nina a personal issue I wanted feedback on—and another person picked up the phone to make a call. At times the other person dialled without listening to the receiver first, so all conversation on my phone was drowned out by the loud whirr and click of the dialling mechanism. "Oh, sorry," they might say, when after dialling they lifted the receiver to their ear.

I also had some teenagers on the party line, who indulged in the practice of clicking repeatedly the off button on their phone to encourage me (or, I presume, anyone else using the phone when they wanted to make a call) to terminate my conversation. In addition, Wilf Heink's wife across the road asked everybody on their party line, which included me, not to use the phone Sunday mornings because each week her husband phoned relatives in Germany then. Another issue arose if I wanted to arrange a call with someone for a certain time. Because I could never *count* on the line being free, I had to warn whoever I was arranging to converse with that the connection might be impossible.

I thought that having to endure a party line in 1989 and 1990 was absurd. Friends in Vancouver and other cities were incredulous that party lines still existed. A couple of times a BC Tel repair crewman I was speaking with advised me to complain to the company.

"They send all the crappiest, outdated equipment to Winlaw," he said. "And we're supposed to keep it running." BC Tel merged with the Edmonton-based Telus and changed its name to the latter in 1999. The current reluctance of Telus to provide cellphone service to the Slocan Valley might be regarded as the contemporary equivalent of the company offering its customers hereabouts only party lines long after these were discontinued almost everywhere else.

Learning who exactly shared my line besides the Heinks took me a while. Valley people I got to know would sometimes brag about how few people were on their phone line. My four-household line was one of the busier ones; I met people who had only one other household whose use of the phone they had to navigate.

One of the many drawbacks to party lines was that we users couldn't access the internet, which in those days was accomplished via a dial-up connection. If somebody had gone on the internet via dial-up, they would have blocked phone service for everyone else on their party line. So I lived without online research or email, although lack of email wasn't as unusual in 1989 or 1990 as subsequently.

Party lines weren't ended by the phone company, but by an initiative of the BC government that decreed the lines had to be phased out by a certain date. I can no longer recall when in the early 1990s BC Tel converted my party line hook-up to an ordinary phone line. I do remember that after the service guy had finished changing the connection on the side of the house, his BC Tel van wasn't all the way down my driveway before I was on the phone to the local Nelson internet service provider, arranging for a link to the modern world.

Chapter Thirteen

THE SEASONS—
SUMMER

U NLIKE WHEN ANY OF THE OTHER SEASONS CHANGE, nothing dramatic marks the transition from spring to summer at Appledore. Summer has unquestionably transformed to fall when hazel, birch and aspen leaves have changed colour and begun to float down, and the temperature at night plummets ever closer to frost. A permanent blanket of snow confirms winter's arrival. Snow's disappearance, crocuses blooming, and the sighting of the year's first robins indicate winter has decidedly shifted into spring.

But trees that leafed-out in spring mostly stay that way until September. Some birds that arrive in spring, like robins, hang around until after the leaves turn. Early June days can be as hot as August's. Overall, the valley appears the same across the divide between late spring and early summer.

This absence of change brings to mind my early unexamined assumption that valley people lived as they always had and always would, and that the appearance of the valley—its houses, barns, fields—was how it had always looked. David Zieroth had tried to alert me, on our drive to the Headwaters conference, that change is part of the rural no less than the urban. Now I better understand what he meant.

I mention in the previous chapter the change I have witnessed over the years of the near-total abandonment of the early spring practice of people lighting their lawns on fire as soon as they were free of snow. The arrival of the internet slowly transformed the concept of rural home-based business, previously limited to such enterprises as in-home hair dressing salons, heavy equipment contractors and truck loggers. For example, my closest neighbour to the south runs a business from his home helping companies increase their presence and effectiveness online. And Facebook has greatly increased the speed at which gossip—accurate or not—spreads through the valley.

Then, too, I gradually became aware that my own presence in the valley altered it. Attitudes and expectations I brought represented change, as did some physical modifications to my acreage I initiated, such as my annual planting of trees until the lower part of Appledore now more resembles forest than the meadow it was when I purchased the property.

I estimate that in the past 30 years, people subdividing their properties has meant about a third-again as many houses have been built on the back road between the Winlaw Bridge and my place. My neighbour to the south when I moved here, Jim Warner, told me that at the time he constructed his house, nobody lived between his place and the Bazaroffs'. Then the house where Ed Jacobson lived went up, followed in 1978 by the one immediately to the north of me, and then in 1980, the house I bought was built. From Jim's perspective, the empty land to the north of him was relentlessly filled, house after house, neighbours closing in on him as the decades passed.

Change can also be people moving *out of* the valley. When the lumber mill at Slocan began to cut shifts, then finally shut entirely in 2011, people affected who couldn't find other employment in the area had to leave. And sometimes people with young teenagers tire of their constant demand to be driven into Nelson—the bright lights—and relocate to town. Or valley parents seek more educational choices for their kids than are available at the centralized high school in Crescent Valley, and move to Nelson or even the Coast.

Some changes I noticed since arriving in the valley are less significant than who lives here or population density, but illustrate in their own way that the rural is anything but static. I think of fluctuations in vehicle models commonly seen. When I moved here in 1989, many vehicles in the valley were Ladas, Russian-built Fiats. A four-wheel-drive model was even available. Ladas were especially popular among the Doukhobors. But the Russified Fiats lived up to their parent Italian company's worldwide reputation for poor engineering (the company name is reputed to stand for a customer's plea to "Fix It Again, Tony"). Today Ladas have vanished from our roads; no Lada dealer exists in the West Kootenay.

Also at the time I moved here, counter-culture inhabitants were at last abandoning their vw Beetles and microbuses. A longtime valley vehicle repair enterprise specialized in vws, calling itself Organic Mechanics. Yet VeeWee owners one by one replaced their vehicles with the Toyota Corolla station wagon. These, once numerous on valley roads, in turn have been supplanted by RAV4s, Subaru Foresters, and other small SUVs. The attributes of a SUV, a vehicle much denounced by Green urbanites, turns out to be perfect for a rural mountain environment of steep terrain and severe winters. Among the proliferation of SUVs, an imported right-hand-drive minivan, the Mitsubishi Delica, can be frequently spotted.

Another minor but tangible change involved Italian coffee concoctions. In 1989 in the valley (and Nelson), coffee was coffee. But as an espresso tsunami roared inland from the Coast as a consequence of the Starbucks earthquake, for a time three dedicated coffee places existed along the 25 kilometres of highway between downtown Winlaw and the junction with the Nelson–Castlegar road. Two of the coffee enterprises had names that reflect how local people love wordplay (Winlaw has an Our Road, a Sesame Street and a Lois Lane). You could pick up a latte or cappuccino in downtown Winlaw at a coffee stand called Sleep Is For Sissies, or in Crescent Valley at Pony Espresso. Now that every area restaurant and café has an espresso machine, these stand-alone coffee bars have vanished.

So changes to the valley are continual, whether the changes are as in-your-face as a new house suddenly under construction in what previously was a pasture or woods, or as muted as new fencing along the road or that almost imperceptible transition from spring to summer. Traditionally, the summer solstice—June 20 or 21—marks the official launch of the season. For me, however, maybe summer begins that first day the temperature has warmed enough for me to work outside in shorts all afternoon. To feel hot sunlight on legs that for months and months have been shrouded in jeans or ski pants signifies a tangible change, whichever calendar month I initially enjoy that experience.

Or, if I define spring as the time of intense green, maybe summer starts with the arrival of the annual insect attacks on the leaves of my apple, cherry, plum and birch trees. The chief villain is a leaf miner (*Lyonetia prunifoleilla*), which causes many of these trees' leaves to curl and turn brown, altering them to a blotched version of their former healthily green selves.

The leaf miners are tiny, half-inch long, bright green (ironically) worms suspended on spider-web-like threads. In the midst of the infestation, these threads can form a clump reaching from tree branch to tree branch and to the ground, establishing a barrier across pathways and under trees. The webbing sticks to my clothes, face and arms if I push through one of these gossamer obstacles on my way someplace around the property. I wear a bill cap to work outdoors, and one or two lengths of thread, each with a dangling worm, can be suspended from the bill after I've forced a passage through a sticky screen. The threads with worms swinging in front of my eyes are an irritating distraction until removed.

Most years, the leaf miners are only in full-on infestation mode for a week or two. But even when just a few threads remain hanging from trees, with no further sign of the worms, the shape and colour of affected trees' leaves have significantly degraded. Thereafter, the trees commence again putting out fresh, wholesome leaves, and very gradually the tree regains a semblance of its springtime prime. But until the leaves are shed in autumn, the tree's leafy branches never again look quite as robust as they first did in spring.

Or maybe summer officially begins for me when I eat the first of this year's grown-on-the-premises vegetables. These will be from my greenhouse: romaine and buttercrunch lettuce, arugula, radish, cilantro, spinach. Thereafter the gardens yield their harvest according to nature's schedule: peas, onions, beans, raspberries, strawberries, blueberries. But it will be mid-July before I eat a salad of ingredients *entirely* from my gardens, including cherry tomatoes, baby carrots, a green pepper.

Certainly the difference in taste between store-bought and home-grown food is a hallmark of summer. Savouring the sharp tang of one of my own radishes on my tongue is entirely different from sampling the generic vegetative blandness of a purchased radish, even one marketed as organic.

Food aside, perhaps summer starts when the first rose blooms. Or the first day of summer could be earlier, when in the midst of a hot afternoon's garden chores, I take a break around 4 or 5 to sit in the shade on the lawn in an Adirondack chair. Sipping apple juice, I watch white clouds larger than mountains float eastward above the tops of the Seven Sisters.

I know summer is unquestionably underway when friends from elsewhere show up for a stay at Appledore. Scheduling visitors is usually no problem, although occasionally I've had one lot leave on the same day another bunch are slated to arrive. Having back-to-back guests like this means frenetic activity for me, as beds are stripped and remade, laundry started, the house vacuumed and swept, kitchen and dining-room tables reset, and flower vases refreshed. I've never had the vehicle of departing guests meet the vehicle of incoming guests halfway down my driveway. But once or twice the window between the two group has been a matter of a few hours.

Some visitors are content to mainly hang out on my deck, or on the living-room sofa, cooled by breezes wafting in from opened windows and doors. But curiosity about the West Kootenay or a desire for exercise leads others to want to experience the region. I don't mind showing visitors more of the area, since they provide an excuse for me, too, to renew my appreciation of the area's rivers, lakes and mountains.

At the height of tourist season, I might seem to be running a B & B (or, more accurately, a B & B, L and D). Except acquaintances who operate a real B & B complain about the unending heaps of laundry involved, as well as difficult guests. Whereas in my case, the people arriving are ones I'm glad to see.

I should say, I'm glad to see *most* of them. I've learned the hard way to be careful who I invite to visit in the summer. The difficult folks are the ones unaware that the country is different than the city. Not only different due to the absence of cellphone service. Once this sort of visitor gets over the shock, despite having been forewarned, they realize they can use my internet connectivity to keep up a semblance of their normal existence in cyberspace. But if a visitor has a disinclination to step out into nature, a visit to Appledore can be boring or otherwise dissatisfying.

One remedy I have for such folks is to take them on a great circle day tour. From Appledore I drive them north on the highway, where after the village of Slocan they can enjoy the panorama as the highway climbs far above Slocan Lake, with the mighty ranges of the Valhallas extending apparently endlessly to the west. A lookout high above Silverton lets them gaze in wonder at this spectacle. We descend again to lake level, and 4 kilometres north of Silverton, in New Denver, the Japanese internment museum is reliably a fascinating stop for my carful. Reconstructions of internment housing and other displays portray the awfulness of the World War II displacement and impoverishment of so many innocent people, and the life they subsequently built in the Slocan.

From New Denver I steer east 14 kilometres to the ghost town of Sandon, a former mining metropolis that by 1897 had electric street-lights and hydrants and at peak boasted a population of 4,000, the largest burg around. Now the site is reduced to only a few restored and semi-restored buildings and a museum. The orneriness of some current West Kootenay characters is also evident at Sandon. In the midst of the heritage townsite, a large collection of decrepit Vancouver transit buses are parked on a large, privately owned lot. The buses have nothing to do with Sandon's history, to the despair of local historical societies and committees who can envision the ghost town as a tourist draw, rather than the present dog's breakfast presenting artifacts from wildly different eras and locales.

On we go another 43 kilometres east, where I conduct my visitors through the town of Kaslo, on Kootenay Lake. We halt at the restored CPR paddle sternwheeler, the S.S. *Moyie*, which formerly ran freight and passengers up and down the lake from 1898 to 1957. The *Moyie* is a national historic site, which means, unlike Sandon, every detail on the vessel is appropriate, well presented and explained. If kids are part of the excursion from Appledore, one aspect of the now-landlocked ship they delight in is that up in the wheelhouse they can activate the ship's whistle: a satisfyingly loud blast that reverberates over the town.

Then we head south 70 kilometres along the lakeshore to the metropolis of Nelson. The usual city attractions of shopping, bars and many restaurants are available. After supper there, it's back to Appledore, driving home through the warm dusk.

Is the Journey

While this circle tour occupies an entire day, I'm still left with trying to amuse for the balance of their stay visitors not interested in the out-of-doors. For this reason, I've learned to limit the stay of people I don't know too well to a couple of days. On occasion, that second day has seemed everlasting.

I had one visitor from the East who, while resisting all temptation even to go for a stroll, spent his second day downloading crossword puzzles from the internet and labouring over them in my living room. I was fine with his choice but couldn't help feeling he had travelled a long way to complete a crossword puzzle.

Another type of visitor not interested in exploring the local milieu wants instead to help improve Appledore, or at least help with the chores. When my parents visited in my early years here, they were like this. Breakfast was no sooner done than my mother would be outside weeding some flower bed before I could stop her, and my father would insist we install a railing for the basement stairs, or that the two of us should be stacking the latest heap of firewood Larry Nestor had delivered.

My friend Ron Riter is a born-to-work type like my parents. I know Ron from our days together on the UBC student newspaper; he eventually worked as an editor on various Canadian dailies, mainly the _Vancouver Sun_. Since I've owned the place, Ron has steadily contributed to it: two tall maples on the property were originally seedlings he brought from his yard in Vancouver, for instance. When he's about to visit, I have to prepare in advance a list of chores he and I can undertake. The alternative is that I'll be still doing the breakfast dishes while Ron is out lighting the burn pile I've been saving until the summer restrictions on burning are lifted.

A few years ago, he and I replaced the split-cedar posts of the tumbledown barbed-wire fence along the road. Before Ron drove up from the Coast, I purchased new split-cedar posts from Bernie Clover, a logger neighbour along the back road. As a joke, Bernie advertised these on a sign beside his driveway as "organic fence posts." Ron and I over three days somewhat improved the look of the fence. Yet even as Ron was leaving, he pointed to where the couple I had bought the house from had raised Irish setters in dog runs off the southwest corner of the lawn near the Seven Sisters. The dog runs' now fallen and teetering 4 × 4 posts and sagging chain-link fencing are being absorbed into the forest. "Next trip, all that has to go," Ron said.

A visitor like David Zieroth is the opposite of Ron. For years David spent a week here every summer. During his stay he'd spend his mornings working on poems at a temporary desk I rigged up for him on the dining-room table. When in the afternoons I'd offer to let him help with the gardens, his response was that he grew up on a farm and never wanted to have to do garden chores again. On the other hand, he was always happy to go for a walk. As we strolled along, I learned a good deal from his encyclopedic knowledge of birds—their differing calls, habitats and habits. And he delighted in the country lanes we followed, saying they brought back memories of his rural Manitoba childhood.

The majority of visitors are glad to be out in the summer air, with canoeing, biking or hiking on the agenda. Canoeing in summer can involve a put-in at the Perry's Siding Bridge, followed by a hard paddle upstream against the river's current to the oxbow for a relaxing float around the meander. Late in August, when the river is as warm as it's going to be, we can exit the oxbow, dig our paddles in again, and fight our way upstream to a certain sandbar for a swim. Or a canoe journey can be a relaxing three-hour drift downriver from the Perry's Siding Bridge to the Winlaw Bridge, scarcely paddling while observing the wildlife above, on and in the river.

My companions for summer outings can be local friends, as well as visitors. My pilot friend Phil and I once canoed the 40-kilometre length of Slocan Lake, leaving from Slocan village and camping along the west shore, much of which is Valhalla Provincial Park. Our pace was unhurried, seldom involving more than three hours a day of paddling. Phil likes his comfort, so brought along gourmet foods freeze-dried for high-end campers. He did the cooking, and we ate like kings.

My only complaint was how little sleep I got on the four-day trip. In the evening, we'd suspend our food in various packs and bags from a line thrown over a branch high enough to be out of the reach of bears. Then we'd cram into my little two-person tent. In that small interior, no escape was possible for me from the horrendous bursts of snoring emanating from Phil's nose once he zonked out.

Also, Phil regarded the trip as a chance for hours of uninterrupted trolling, which left me to do the bulk of the paddling. Phil sat in the bow, amiably stoned, and tried this or that lure as his fishing line trailed behind our craft close below the surface. Under a hot sun blazing down, my paddling across the mildly rippling water was hypnotic and peaceful, so I didn't mind being the sole source of propulsion as we progressed up the lake.

We only caught two things on the trip. At one point a gull swimming on the water's surface seemed to be following us. The bird tailed the canoe for a half hour before we realized to our horror that Phil's fishing line was in its mouth. Somehow the bird had become hooked on his line.

I suggested he cut the line, but Phil insisted the responsible thing to do was to reel in the bird and attempt to dislodge the hook from its bill. I had visions of a desperate battle between a terrified gull and a determined Phil: a flurry of beating wings and sudden over-the-transom lunges by Phil as he tried to secure the creature in order to pry loose the hook. The struggle would be taking place at the bow of a rather tippy vessel.

I paddled us toward shore while Phil steadily cranked his reel, drawing the bird ever closer. Slocan Lake drops off quickly from the shoreline to an average depth of more than 200 metres. I was shoving water behind us as fast as I could, aiming the canoe toward low boulders at the lake edge.

The gull was only 4 metres behind the canoe when suddenly it stretched out its wings, flapped them, and flew away. Apparently the bird was simply holding the line in its bill and wasn't hooked at all. I felt tremendously relieved, but Phil calmly finished reeling in, inspected the lure at the end of the line, and fumbled in his tackle box for an extra weight to attach.

Two hours later, we caught a Conservation officer. As I paddled, I became aware that a runabout powered by a huge outboard was angling toward us. As the craft neared, I could see someone in uniform at the controls. Catching Phil's attention, I gestured toward approaching officialdom. The patrol boat throttled back and pulled alongside our canoe, its wake catching up and causing both vessels to start bobbing.

The officer demanded to know if we had the requisite life-jackets and bailing can, which I showed him. Then he asked Phil if he had a fishing licence. Phil assured him he did.

"Can I see it, please?

"It's in my backpack," Phil said.

"Get it out. I'd like to see it."

Phil slowly lowered his fishing rod to the bottom of the canoe, and half turned to draw his pack toward him. Swivelling in the bow seat so his back was to the representative of the law, Phil undid various straps securing the pack's top flap, then the drawstring underneath. He began to rummage in the top of the pack.

The minutes ticked past, as the engine on the craft beside us rumbled and gurgled in neutral. "Can't you find it?" the officer asked after what seemed to me an eon of Phil fumbling in his pack.

Phil, absorbed in his task, didn't reply.

"I think I'll issue you a citation," the officer declared after a further few minutes. "If you find your licence, show it to the RCMP in New Denver. They can void the ticket."

"Here it is," Phil announced, in what I thought was the nick of time. I didn't relish having to paddle the 3 kilometres across the lake to New Denver, walk from the beach to its small cop shop, then have to paddle back to the west side again to resume our journey. In addition, the RCMP detachment in New Denver is tiny. If no police were in the office when we arrived, presumably we'd have to wait around until a constable returned.

Phil passed the piece of paper across to the other craft, where it was briefly inspected, and handed back. Without a word, the Conservation officer gunned his engine, swung his bow away from us, and tore off northeast.

"Lucky you found the licence," I said to Phil when we stopped rising and falling in the wake the departing runabout created and I had our bow facing the head of the lake again.

"I knew where it was in the pack," Phil said. "Trouble was, I had my bag of weed lying right on top. I didn't want that doofus to see it. The trick was to bury the weed in the pack while extracting the licence."

A less eventful canoe trip I frequently take visitors on also leaves from the beach at Slocan but follows the west side of the lake for a couple of hours, only as far as a beach at Evans Creek. If the day is hot, by then a swim at the Evans Creek beach is in order. A trail winds inland 100 metres from the beach to a large metal footbridge that crosses the creek in front of a scenic tall waterfall.

During the paddle to and from Evans Creek, a place to pause is at a cliff on which aboriginal pictographs are visible. The sheer face of the rock is angled inward from top to bottom, which has preserved the markings. Two of the few interpretable symbols among the many painted with red ochre are a sun with a face, and a curved object with three parallel projecting vertical marks (presumably three people in a canoe). At a meeting of the Slocan Valley Historical Society in Slocan, I heard a talk on the pictographs by an expert. The speaker said the various images might indicate a boundary, a record of travellers' tales, or commemorate individuals' vision quests. How old they are is also debatable, we were told.

Three different tribes claim the valley, which seems to have been used seasonally by all of them. One of the groups is based currently in the Okanagan, another in the East Kootenay. The third, known as the Lakes Indians, or the Sinixt, have been declared extinct in Canada following their removal in the 1800s to the Colville reservation in the southern part of their territory, now in Washington state. According to their late spokesman, Virgil Seymour, deaths from post-contact diseases made local communities unsustainable; hence the decision to concentrate survivors in the south. Who exactly painted the Slocan Lake pictographs—more of which are found on the lake's east shore—is as much a mystery as their meaning and age.

Some summer activities, I'll experience by myself. I originally encountered the pictographs on my first solo canoe outing on the lake. I observed that another canoe had stopped just below the cliff, with the people in it staring intently up at the rock. Once they paddled on, I headed over to learn what they had been gazing at.

Not that every summer paddle on Slocan Lake is a pleasant and/or educational experience. On August afternoons, a wind often starts to blow from the north down the lake, which can change from a dead flat calm to whitecaps in a frighteningly short time.

Twice in my first years at Appledore I was enjoying a solo paddle northward when the sky clouded over and the water became increasingly choppy. As the breeze picked up, any forward motion ceased despite me desperately applying all my strength to each stroke of the paddle. The waves around me steepened into whitecaps, and I became scared. I swung the canoe about, intending to head back to the beach at Slocan. But even that plan quickly seemed a mistake, with the water ahead of me now a roiling sea of breakers. I steered instead toward the closest rocky shore, where I managed to scramble onto solid ground holding the bow line, and pulled the canoe out of the water to wait out the storm.

A guaranteed pleasant excursion is a hike on the 8-kilometre trail along the west shore of Slocan Lake to Evans Creek. From

Evans Creek another 4-kilometre route inland climbs 500 metres in elevation through the forest to Emerald Lake, and then a farther 4 kilometres and a 215-metre elevation gain to Cahill Lake.

A different rewarding summertime journey is a hike into the Valhallas to Mt. Gimli or the Drinnon Pass. These I wouldn't do by myself, though. A trip to the Mt. Gimli trailhead involves driving former logging roads for about 26 kilometres, with road conditions so poor the last time I went, the trip took nearly two hours. Washouts had narrowed the road to barely a single lane in a few places, and in others, rocks that had fallen from cutbanks onto the right-of-way had to be bumped over or steered around.

From the Gimli trailhead, the 4-kilometre path leads unremittingly, steeply uphill. Despite vows to pace myself, and despite believing myself to be in excellent shape from months of gardening chores, I've never done the hike without reaching a moment where I simply cannot take another step. Usually my collapse face forward is just before or just after the trail breaks out of a scrubby alpine fir forest and continues its climb above treeline.

This last part of the route leads up a shoulder of Gimli Peak, 600 metres higher here than the trailhead parking lot. The peak itself is a gigantic plug of black granite looming another 400 metres above the trail. On the shoulder, several metre-high stone windbreaks offer places in which to catch one's breath, eat some lunch, drink deep from a water bottle. Basically, to regain strength while protected from the chill alpine wind.

Around a spur of rock from the windbreak, the parks service has erected—or, more likely, lowered from a helicopter—an outhouse. From here, a user has an unbelievable 180-degree view to the south of summit after summit, ridge upon ridge, stretching to infinity. Gigantic cumulus clouds sail above the ocean of peaks.

Leaving the windbreak, visitors can proceed for another 45 minutes of clambering up and across open country. This route ends 115 metres higher, at a ridge narrow enough that, to peer over the far side, I'm most comfortable lying on my stomach. Below the ridge to the north, the world drops 300 metres straight down to the lakes of Mulvey Basin.

Since snow comes early to these summits, and stays late, mid-summer is one's only chance to view first-hand what the high country offers. For me, though, such excursions as the Gimli hike, or a similar one into the Valhallas to Drinnon Pass and on to the Gwillim Lakes basin (a rise of 556 metres from the trailhead), are infrequent. The epitome of my summer is more me bending over a garden bed to thin a row of carrots, or staking up delphiniums or corn stalks that have grown higher than the plants' ability to keep them vertical. Or, resting on my deck between chores, contemplating the summer while a hawk high in the blue over Appledore circles and circles. And with my lazy thoughts interrupted by a hummingbird's buzzing whirr as it rockets centimetres over my head toward one of the deck's feeders.

In late July and August, the very hot weather settles in. Inside the house, besides opening everything that is screened, I have a couple of portable fans that I employ to move the thick air. The basement, however, is always cool. My study thus is a welcome refuge from the main floor, which can be baking all day despite the fans' best efforts. And because Appledore *is* in the mountains, the temperature drops at night, making sleeping never a problem.

During those weeks of scorching days, watering every garden bed not irrigated via a timer, in addition to every deck pot and hanging basket, becomes a daily necessity. I start to long for rain. A day following an overnight shower or afternoon thunderstorm, when I don't have to water, feels like a holiday.

By this time, Rod will have drawn my attention to the first of the dogbane that have yellowed. Toward the middle of August, I begin to tire of garden work, other than harvesting what has ripened. For months I've laboured in flower and vegetable beds, but at a certain juncture I don't have much inclination to weed, sow another crop of lettuce, or thin the latest planting of radishes. Luckily, the heat slows the proliferation of uninvited growth, and veggie plants like squash, cukes and potatoes are now established enough that weeds are no threat to their thriving.

Friends are busy canning and freezing, and making salsas and jam. All I have energy to accomplish along these lines is to concoct pesto with my basil and store-bought cheese, then freeze it for winter consumption.

Days, though still hot, gradually become shorter. Darkness falls by 8:30 p.m., then earlier. The cooler temperature in the evenings is welcome. But the sense that the season is winding down makes me impatient for summer to be over.

This season is the only one I grow somewhat tired of. Fall, with its beautiful coloured leaves and invigorating crisp days, could linger longer each year, in my opinion. And I'd love winter to be twice as long, so I could be on my cross-country skis more often. Spring, with its magical transformation of the landscape into cascades of green, plus all the garden dreaming I indulge in as planting gets underway, could also tack on some extra weeks without a complaint from me.

When I was teaching, I looked forward to the resumption of classes immediately after Labour Day. Detailed preparation of my fall courses began in early August, and once that chore was completed, I was eager for summer to finish so I could try out fresh teaching techniques and introduce students to books and literary ideas new to me, too. I couldn't wait to discover which of my planned new approaches or material functioned successfully in the classroom and what needed rethinking. When I retired, Labour Day's significance evaporated. Summer lingers on into September, even as initial signs of fall appear and slowly proliferate.

Maybe late summer's predominantly dry weather, with its interminable need to irrigate, helps trigger my wish for fall to arrive with its rains. Yet I can simultaneously appreciate the cloudless blue continuing to arch overhead from green valley wall to valley wall. For a few more weeks, T-shirt-and-shorts days remain the norm. In the absence of any serious frost, the gardens carry on producing tomatoes, peppers, corn. Below the dense covering of the squash plant's leaves, I discover additional gourds taking shape since the previous week's inventory.

Given my dislike of cold water, late summer is also the only time I really like to swim. The glacier-fed lakes and river of our region are as tempting during these weeks as they're capable of becoming. In the ongoing heat, I'm finally eager to plunge head-first under the surface of Slocan Lake or the Slocan River, and enter that cool and unfamiliar world. Or from Shoreacres beach, just south of Playmor Junction, I float supported by a foam noodle half a kilometre toward where the Slocan River joins the Kootenay River. Before that confluence, I clamber out of the water, struggle up the bank, follow the trail back to my starting point, and do it again.

Or, if dry land rather than water appeals, I drive to the Passmore rail-trail parking lot but from there bike the back road from Passmore north to Winlaw. That route has hills so steep I give up shifting gears near the top, and walk the bike the last part of the rise in the hot day. Reaching Winlaw, I'll have lunch outside at the café, and take the easy route back down the rail trail to the Passmore trailhead where I left my vehicle.

Then one morning I'm aware that although the scene around me hasn't changed from the previous day, a subtle alteration has occurred. The sunshine bathing everything is thinner. "Fall light," I declare to myself.

Weeks of warm weather remain ahead before in the middle of the afternoon I have to re-enter the house to put on a long-sleeved shirt. Or later in the calendar, before I wake to lawns white with frost. But the great wheel of the year has turned. In the changed light, a season that seemed endless suddenly appears to have passed too quickly after all.

Chapter Fourteen

THE ELEMENTS–
EARTH

IN THE 1970S MY PARENTS PURCHASED A 100-ACRE FARM near Rice Lake, north of Cobourg, Ontario. A vogue had begun among Torontonians like themselves to own, if they could afford it, rural land as a getaway rather than the traditional cottage. Since my father didn't like to have the farm's rolling pasture land unused, he let a neighbouring farmer run cattle on the fields in return for keeping up the fences. Whenever I visited from BC, I was struck by how the cows there were familiar with every nuance of the land they occupied. The herd of 20 or 30 cows and calves slowly travelled around the property during the day depending on their desires: shade, being out of the wind, being in the wind, being up at the barn to be fed if the farmer arrived with something extra for them besides the grass underfoot.

After decades at Appledore, I resemble those cows in that I'm intimately familiar with every inch of the portion of my land that contains the lawns, gardens, fruit trees and meadow. I'm conscious of each bump in the ground, every variant of light and shade at any hour of any season. I can tell you why this spot on what should be lawn is nearly devoid of vegetation (year after year I temporarily stored a pickup-load of horse manure here atop a sheet of plastic; the grass died underneath it and has not yet recovered). I have a favourite roost on the grass near the basement door under the Japanese maple, where I can sit (or recline) in blessed shade to gulp down water when I'm parched from heavy work on a blistering July day.

From a distance, Appledore's lawns when freshly mowed resemble expanses of manicured grass such as on an English estate. But knowing them up close, I'm aware they are composed instead of a very high percentage of dandelion, buttercup, wild strawberry, a ground cover whose name I don't know that produces tiny blue flowers in the spring, clover, moss, and hawkweed. My mowing also keeps down shoots of aspen, mountain ash and bracken that appear in the grass. Lupin and mullein sprout in the lawns as well, although sometimes for variety I'll leave little islands of these flowering plants.

Beyond having absorbed the land's manifold details, and the effects on these of season, weather and time of day, I feel most bonded to my fragment of the valley during May planting sessions, when I'm closest to the earth. Kneeling at a vegetable bed to dispense minuscule carrot seeds, I often think of the American poet Theodore Roethke (1908–1963), whose father owned 25 acres of greenhouses. Roethke's poems can zero in on the tiniest acts of a seedling breaking into air. In "Cuttings," for example, he describes how:

> One nub of growth
> Nudges a sand-crumb loose,
> Pokes through a musty sheath
> Its pale tendrilous horn.

The feeling I have of close attachment to the earth here is at once calming, humbling and inspiring. I have no idea if cows experience affection for the meadow they co-exist with, but I certainly feel surges of love for Appledore's earth, its topography. In spring and summer, with the air warm and the world about me pulsing with life, I sometimes experience an urge to lie down on the grass and... what? Embrace it? Sink into it? Fall asleep and dream what the birch and lupin dream? I resist this impulse, since my actions would be alarming or at least hard to explain if my neighbours wandered by to ask if they can borrow my extendable clippers and observed me stretched out on the ground.

I know I'm not the only one who feels this way. My neighbour Rod's dad for years operated a sawmill in the Cariboo and can fix or operate any machine. His first inclination in any problematic situation is to reach for a powered tool to overcome the difficulty. Yet once during a visit to his son's, he was over to my property and stopped suddenly as we were walking. "This is all that really matters," he said. He gestured toward his feet. "To stand on your own land. To feel that connection to a place." I could only agree.

And whether I'm projecting or not, I believe that, at times, the land gives me back what I need. I can fall into a depressive obsession with some misunderstanding between myself and another person, or with a wrong-headed political development in the wider world. Then after a few minutes outside, I'm given a jolt of beauty that redirects my thoughts to astonished thankfulness: the first pink peony of the year that has blossomed overnight, or butterfly that wanders past me while I tie up a drooping rose stem.

Of course I believe nature is indifferent to my existence. I might be lifted out of a bleak mood by observing the rarely-seen-around-here orange-and-black varied thrush. But the planet just *is*. No nicotiana scent I inhale, chickadee I hear, or the first raspberry of the year on my tongue had me in mind when it came to be.

Still, I underwent an experience at Appledore that, like that laughing cloud over Slocan Lake before I moved here, reinforces my sense that the Earth is not entirely disinterested in my well-being. In January of 2014 I fell on my right side at the bottom of a hill at the Nelson cross-country ski club site. A day later, I was loading the wheelbarrow with firewood to bring indoors and misjudged the depth of snow when I took a step. When my right foot hit bottom, a spasm of excruciating pain shot through my lower back on that side.

The intensity of the agony dulled somewhat after a few moments, and I tried to resume loading the wheelbarrow. Once more a flame seared my back muscles. I left the wheelbarrow half-full, and gingerly made my way through the falling snow toward the basement door.

I thought the torment would subside after a break. However, when I stood again after half an hour on the computer, the scorching anguish in my lower back had not diminished. Upstairs, I managed to make supper, grabbing the counter or table edge for relief when a wrong move unleashed a fresh stab of severe pain.

Next day, a Saturday, my back was no better. I debated whether I should drive to Nelson to the hospital's emergency department. Since lower back pain is common and usually disappears in a day or two, I decided I would phone my GP for an appointment on Monday if the problem persisted.

It did. Bringing in more firewood or going for a ski was unthinkable. I found I could temporarily suspend my attention to the pain if I became lost in my writing. Yet each time I stood to fetch more coffee, keep the fire going, or make a meal, I suffered a devastating reminder of why my ordinary life was suspended.

Nights were worse. I figured bed rest was likely what my doctor would prescribe, but climbing into bed without inflicting more suffering was impossible. In bed, I couldn't get comfortable, and a pill brought little relief. In the dark of my bedroom, I began to imagine the pain was caused by a tumour, that these were my last days alive.

Monday, early as I could, I phoned my GP in Nelson. Friday was the earliest appointment they could let me have, so I took that. I also phoned a physiotherapy clinic in town and made an appointment for Friday after the doctor's appointment. I thought a physio might be able to complement whatever treatment the doctor prescribed—assuming cancer wasn't the cause of my ongoing distress.

Living through the week was an ordeal. Any wrong move brought instant retribution. Sometimes a fiery poker jabbed me in the lower back by for no reason I could figure out. Whenever such a random assault took place, I berated the body: "What was *that* for? What did I do to *you*?"

On Tuesday, Rod dropped by on some mission. He suggested I visit one of Nelson's two walk-in medical clinics rather than wait for my Friday appointment. But I assured him I could last until Friday. Later that day he and Sharon came over and offered to bring in firewood for me. I was touched by their thoughtfulness. I insisted I probably had enough pieces on hand for the week, but they brushed aside my concerns and wheeled in wood until quite a surplus was stockpiled. Rod, knowing my habits, even stored the wheelbarrow under cover where I usually kept it.

Then I was alone with the pain again. Several times during the balance of the week, especially during the nights, panic suffused me. For the first time in my life, I had a glimmering of why someone with incurable pain might seek a medically assisted death. With the present restrictions on my functioning, I wouldn't be able to continue living at Appledore. All that I enjoyed doing here—gardening, skiing, biking, canoeing—had become impossible to undertake. Yet where could I live, if not here? How could I even look for a different place, racked by so much pain? Each morning, though, in the light of the new day, I told myself that I had made these medical appointments for Friday, and that seeking help before then would be wrong.

Matters came to a head very early Friday. The torment overnight notched up: the pain was so severe I got out of bed about 5 a.m. and sat in a chair in the kitchen in my bathrobe to wait for the end of the night. Once I had managed to lower myself onto the chair, the slightest motion triggered stabs and waves of anguish. I wasn't sure I'd be able to climb into my vehicle, or drive it into town to keep my appointment. Would I have to call an ambulance, an act I'd find incredibly humiliating?

At 7:30 I steeled myself, and successfully stood up. I amazed myself by cautiously but steadily managing to shave, take a shower, and pull on my going-to-town clothes. My climb into the driver's seat was painful, but once behind the wheel I felt relieved at how the seat cushioned and supported me. I had less discomfort by far than sitting up in bed or in a kitchen chair.

My doctor didn't think my condition was as dire as the past week had led me to believe. I like my GP, who has the fine Kootenay name of Dr. Dharma McBride—although he originates from the same part of Ontario's Ottawa Valley where I was born. He's a serious mountain biker, trekker and back-country skier, so understands the body in motion. Because he alternates between serving as an emergency room physician and conducting a family practice, my problem likely seemed minor compared to those of a car crash survivor or logging accident victim he encounters at the hospital ER.

I did get a prescription from him for a muscle relaxant, as he attributed my torment to my body trying alternately to immobilize a stressed part to relieve pain, and then the rigid immobilization itself causing pain. Reluctantly—he is far from a pill-pusher—he at my insistence also gave me a prescription for a stronger pain medicine than I had been taking. Then I was outside in the street again, easing into my vehicle to head to my physiotherapy appointment.

I was assigned to physiotherapist Anna Weber, a beautiful young woman who proceeded to work no less than a miracle. She listened attentively to my symptoms and diagnosed a sacroiliac issue. As she stretched my bent legs toward my chest, where I lay on my back, the pain began to ease for the first time in what seemed like months.

I couldn't believe her skill as she pushed and pulled. When I left the building an hour later, I felt I had crawled in and was walking normally out. Eighty per cent of the agony had vanished. In my hand I held a sheet describing exercises that would continue what she had started, plus an appointment for a week later, when we would review my progress.

I drove to the pharmacy, and then home, elated. But as darkness fell, my mood of desperation returned. The pain wasn't entirely gone, and I feared it would flare up into unbearable anguish again. Before bed, I took the pills Dr. McBride had prescribed. But would they really work? How much of my current relief from feeling my lower back was aflame was due to having been attended to by medical experts? I knew that people sometimes feel briefly better after medical attention, then relapse.

In a highly anxious state, I stood in the bedroom, rehearsing in my mind a new technique I had conceived to minimize pain while getting horizontal. Earlier in the week I had formulated a routine to counter the blistering explosions as I tried to go in one smooth motion from standing to lying in bed on my right side. Dr. McBride had advised, however, that I should avoid lying on that side, where the pain was. My new idea was to follow the same procedure as before, but from the far side of the bed so as to end up on my *left* side.

But what if this unfamiliar approach triggered fresh shots of pain? I had suffered so much torment during the past week, I was weary to the core of being hurt. Paralyzed by indecision and worry, I tried to summon the courage to attempt lying down. My body seemed frozen from fear as I stood by the bottom of the bed.

In my agitated state, the Earth came to my rescue. I watched with awe as through the bedroom doorway entered, single file, a row of the evergreens that stand closest to my house to the west. The silhouettes of the firs and spruces west of the building were familiar to me from sitting on my deck or looking through the living-room window. Outside, the trees tower over my house. Here as they approached, they were only 7 or 8 feet tall, some of their tops just brushing the ceiling.

The foremost in the file of trees moved around the corner of the bed toward me and stopped. The others lined up behind the leader along the side of the bed closest to the door.

"You will be alright," the nearest evergreen said. The voice was part comforting, part a command. I felt a frond touch the top of my head reassuringly. "You will sleep tonight." The trees stood waiting.

Obediently, I moved to the other side of the bed, switched off the light, and lowered myself onto the mattress as I had planned. No pain registered at all. I pulled up the covers and moments later I was asleep. I enjoyed the first long, restful sleep since my injury.

A hallucination? My mind inventing a restorative waking dream? The trees only appeared once more: the next night while I was falling asleep I saw, or imagined, a smaller delegation of the evergreens clustered within the bedroom doorway, as if checking up on me.

An occasional shock or twinge of pain happened during subsequent weeks, but after the evergreens' timely intervention I never again was as devastated by the anguish my body could inflict. I followed Ms. Weber's exercise regime to the letter, augmented by further treatments at the clinic and by additional exercises suggested by her as I slowly improved.

The evergreens, however, aren't the only emissaries from the landscape that have entered my house uninvited. My first fall here, I became aware that a squirrel was scrabbling repeatedly up the siding at the east end of the house, pushing into the attic via an unsecured mesh over a ventilation opening in the soffit near the peak of the gable. I didn't like the thought of animals roosting in my attic, and Nelson's Hipperson Hardware sold me sturdier mesh—varmint wire—which I stapled into place over the soffit vents at both ends of the house.

This procedure was tricky: it involved work from the very top of my extension ladder, which in turn was placed on a portable table in order for the ladder to reach high enough. I have a fear of heights, so this effort was an ordeal for me. As well, I had to wait and watch until I was sure the squirrel had left the attic before sealing its entry portal.

The helpful sales guy at the hardware store had suggested the squirrel probably had babies in the attic. Indeed, once the entry to the attic was blocked, the squirrel started to desperately gnaw the wooden siding under the gable at the east, then the west, then again the east end of the house, as though seeking a way in. I once more had to climb the precariously situated ladder to cover that gnawed area with varmint wire. For hours after I finished, the squirrel dashed madly around under the soffits, trying to locate a way inside.

And one March evening, during the early years of this century when I taught in Calgary, I arrived home to Winlaw for a weekend after the long day's drive from Alberta, the last couple of hours done in darkness. At Appledore, I stepped out of my vehicle into the valley silence, and unlocked the basement door intending to start the fire in the furnace before unloading.

When I flicked on the basement light, I saw on the floor by the clothes washer a smashed flower-pot containing a geranium that ordinarily rested on a window-sill. I'm aware that sometimes a house plant grows in such a way as to unbalance its container, although I hadn't thought this geranium was in any danger of tipping over.

En route to fetch a broom to sweep up the mess, I glanced into my study through its open door. Framed photos and other knickknacks that had been on the window ledges were strewn across the desk and floor. Another geranium plant on a window-sill was knocked onto its side, with spilled earth reaching a couple of neighbouring framed cards that now lay face down.

Somebody or something had obviously broken into the house, even though the basement door had been locked when I arrived. I checked in a desk drawer for my passport and some US cash. They were still there.

I crept up the stairs to the main floor, in case whoever or whatever was still in the house. Once I left the last step I half-expected to see, around the hall corner, the door into the house off the deck kicked open or otherwise ajar. It looked closed.

I walked over to confirm the door was still locked. As I did, I observed that some candles that had been on a kitchen window-sill were lying below it on the kitchen table. Glancing toward the living room, I noted that a potted begonia and geranium were intact on the nearest window ledge. But another geranium was missing that had been there when I'd watered everything two weeks previously.

When I entered the living room, more carnage was evident than the plant pot on its side on the rug. Plants from the west window's ledge were toppled onto the couch under that window. A colourfully embroidered bedspread I was using as a couch cover was scrunched up in places and partially pulled onto the rug at one end.

Disturbing as all this damage was, its cause was visible on the rug in front of the sofa. A squirrel lay stretched out on its back—dead, or asleep.

I cautiously stepped closer. The animal didn't respond to my approach, and I could see no sign of breathing. I deduced that somehow it had gotten into the house and freaked, racing from window to window, frantic to discover a way out. The squirrel didn't look particularly thin, so I guessed it hadn't starved to death during the weeks I'd been absent at work. In its panic, the critter must have suffered a heart attack.

I quickly checked the bedrooms, but nothing appeared amiss. All seemed normal, too, in the dining area adjoining the living room. I reasoned death must have arrived for the squirrel before it had dashed along *every* window-sill. The sofa coverlet, when I peered more closely at it, was ripped and badly stained: mute testimony to the creature's frenzied attempt to return to the wild.

Puzzling over how the beast could have entered the house, I headed to the basement to light the fire before proceeding to the shed for a shovel to remove the dead squirrel. As I hooked the damper open on the old furnace, a solution to the mystery occurred to me. The squirrel might have been exploring the chimney top and tumbled in—once the snow is gone, the sound of a squirrel racing across the roof is common. Assuming the squirrel survived the fall down the chimney, the animal would have ended up in the firebox, and the flap that formed the damper could easily have been pushed ajar from inside.

Thereafter whenever the furnace wasn't in use, I jammed a piece of wood against the damper to render it immobile. Also, in the fall when I went to light a fire for the first time since the spring, I opened the firebox door gingerly, nervous about what I might discover. I thought, too, about a procedure to follow if I ever heard scraping and rattling inside the secured furnace. Should I ignore the animal's attempts to free itself and let it die of starvation? Or try to secure a garbage bag or cardboard box against the damper to capture the rodent?

My potential dilemma never arose. The new furnace, purchased in 2009, is a fortress compared to the old one, with no potential exit into the house for a squirrel. And the appliance's glass door means no surprises are possible with regard to what might be within.

As in any country dwelling, mice have appeared in my house. Because it is so snugly built and the basement is concrete, they've only gained access twice, when the basement door had been left open for hours while work was being done inside. On one occasion, a snap-trap I'd set in the basement to rid the house of the unwanted guests captured but did not kill a mouse, who was pathetically trying to drag the trap behind itself across the basement floor when I went to check on my trapline. I had to fetch a shovel and brain it, a task I very much didn't want to have to do, but the alternative was worse.

I've also had to deal with less likely interlopers than squirrels or mice. One summer day I had used a basket to hold a number of tools when I was changing the catch on the door into the anti-deer fence around the big garden. Task completed, I placed the basket of tools on the ground for a few minutes while I checked on the irrigation timer in the greenhouse.

I retrieved my tools and headed up to the house, bringing the basket inside through the basement door. As I stepped across the threshold, a garter snake wriggled out of the basket, fell to the floor, and speedily writhed under the clothes washer.

I was stunned. Three or four times a summer I encounter one of these snakes, which are green with a yellow stripe down their sides. The West Kootenay has no poisonous snakes, but I'm always startled at unexpectedly sighting one of these reptiles as it slithers across the ground. One snake magnet is the former cold frame near the lower garden, used to store straw for autumn mulch. Snakes like to hang out atop the straw bales during the colder months, and sometimes in the summer as well. If I lift the cold frame lid, I raise it carefully.

Now, though, I had a snake in the *house*. My anxiety surged. I armstronged the clothes washer a foot to one side exposing the snake, which, after a second or two of immobility, slithered under the repositioned washer.

No mice or other food for the reptile were in the basement, so I considered doing nothing. As long as the snake couldn't climb the basement stairs, I reasoned, it would die for lack of nourishment within a few days, or else find some crack or knothole unknown to me through which it could escape outside.

Ranged against adopting this plan was the thought that I could never be sure exactly where in the basement the creature was. Such uncertainty would increase the chance for me to be unpleasantly startled when I reached for a tool on a shelf or, in my study, lifted a book or paper from a pile on my desk. And what if a snake *can* climb stairs? I imagined a heart-attack-quality shock if I opened a cupboard door for a fresh set of towels, or turned back the sheets to climb into bed, and revealed a snake equally alarmed at being discovered.

Ignoring the reptile didn't seem a viable option. Obtaining a cardboard box, I yarded the washer to one side. Quick as I could, I dropped the box over the momentarily motionless reptile. Since the basement door has no raised threshold, I nudged the box inch by inch across the floor toward the doorway. Once the box was outside, I shut the basement door and freed the snake. Ever since, I check thoroughly any basket I take outside before bringing it back indoors.

Hitchhiking reptiles haven't been limited to snakes. A year after the snake incident, I had used a plastic bucket from the basement to refill the bird bath. The bucket was left on the grass while I became distracted removing a sizable tree branch that had blown down overnight onto the driveway. When I returned, I looked to be sure no snake had taken up residence in the bucket and, indoors again, left it in the basement sink to dry. Next afternoon, I lifted the bucket out, intending to store it in its usual place. In the sink was a lizard.

The creature's presence on the white porcelain of the sink seemed unreal. I'd never seen a lizard on the grounds in all my years at Appledore, and now a 25-centimetre-long one had materialized in my basement sink. The challenge, once I calmed down, was how to relocate the lizard outdoors while ensuring it didn't escape mid-removal and dart somewhere else in the basement where I'd never find it. I guessed it must have attached itself to the bottom of the bucket left in the grass, and clung on when I lifted the pail to bring it indoors.

I decided to adapt the removal procedure I had used with the snake. Once I had the lizard covered by a small cardboard box, I reasoned, I could work a piece of cardboard under the container to secure the reptile while I hoisted the box out of the sink. When I attempted to put the plan into effect, however, the lizard stuck close to the sink's walls, repeatedly ducking out from under the descending box.

I was engaged in matching wits with a reptile when Rod happened to drop by. Once I'd explained the situation, he calmly reached into the sink, grasped the lizard's body, carried it through the basement door, and lowered it gently to the ground.

I expressed my gratitude. In truth, the thought had occurred to me to put on a pair of gloves to manually push the reptile into the box. But I never would have solved the problem the obvious way Rod did.

A different animal I encounter from time to time, albeit one that's never—so far!—been in my house, is livestock anybody would expect to meet in the country. A couple of kilometres south of me on the back road, a wiry middle-aged farmer, Neil Baranov, raises a herd of cows. Neil, who also sells straw, hay and manure, customarily wears a wide-brimmed hat that resembles a scaled-down cowboy hat. Call it a five-gallon hat.

Two or three times a year, Neil conducts a cattle drive down the back road, taking the herd toward pasturage he's arranged either north or south of his own acres. I first became aware of him moving the herd when, my second spring here, I was lifting mulch from the Grave of Literary Ambition and heard an unrecognizable tumult of sound. The increasing cacophony came from south of me, and I couldn't think what could produce such a strange racket, resembling a vinyl record played at too slow a rate. I stared up the road toward where the noise seemed to originate. A pickup with its hazard lights flashing was proceeding north along the asphalt at a walking pace. Behind the truck a cluster of cows ambled into view, lowing as they approached.

The herd was abreast of the driveway of my neighbour across the road when one of the animals broke from the group and darted down the neighbour's drive. A guy attending the herd dashed past the cow to head it off. A different beast, meanwhile, made a lunge toward my driveway and had begun pacing up it when another person raced past the creature and blocked its path. The cow turned, and retreated to join its peers. The bulk of the cattle followed the pickup, moaning and mooing continuously. Behind them stretched a trail of cow flop on the pavement.

In the years since, I've also come upon the cattle drive when in my vehicle, either stuck behind it as it moseys forward or having to push my way very slowly through massed cows when I've met them headed toward me. Neil generally regards the back road as an extension of his farmyard: I'll encounter at the bottom of his driveway a semi-trailer rig blocking one lane of the road while unloading hay. Sometimes a large tractor is stacking giant circular hay bales on the road's shoulder in front of his place. Or if that space is filled, the tractor will pile them not far south of Neil's farmstead at the wide junction of the back road and a loop road, McKean Road.

I like the idea of a person nearby making a living from the earth as a farmer, even if Neil is rumoured to have formerly supplemented his income with illegal as well as legal agriculture. I take that rumour with a huge grain of salt, since someone is likely to whisper to me, regarding *any* West Kootenay small-scale commercial enterprise, that drug money is involved.

Yet the West Kootenay is fabled as a major BC marijuana-growing region. Local participants in the weed industry claim it is a major contributor to the economy. No question wholesale and retail crops are raised hereabouts in converted barns, chicken coops and basements, as well as deep in the woods. And very little of the local harvest so far is government-sanctioned, although lately here and there in the region a few industrial barns have been erected, complete with air purifiers, to produce an above-board crop. The wholesale buyers of the illegal stuff are alleged to have a particular fondness for motorcycles.

My own sense is that the industry is less of an economic driver than its practitioners claim. If black-market growers were raking in sizable profits—enough to be a significant factor in the regional economy—I believe our area would boast the same disposable-income establishments that relieve the well-paid employees in the oil patch of their dollars in burgs like Fort McMurray: auto dealers specializing in high-end muscle cars or dualies (pickups with dual rear tires), for example. Both sorts of vehicle are scarce around here.

Though many folks grow their own herb, and some sell their surplus, I'm convinced most illegal weed is the product of mom-and-pop operations and not of large-scale operators generating loads of dough. Indeed, spokespeople for a new local weed produc-ers' organization complain that the government's insistence on quality control, not to mention other bureaucratic flaming hoops and barrels growers seeking legal status are asked to leap through, has prevented West Kootenay producers from ramping up the scale of their activities in order to cash in on legalization.

Whether or not locals engaged in agriculture are law-abiding, crime is the main activity of a particular area resident through-out the growing season. Deer—white-tailed and mule deer—will munch the springtime blossoms on a fruit tree, wiping out the entire future crop. A whitetail or mulie will attack a row of ready-to-be-picked carrots, yanking them out of the ground by their tops one after another and biting each one to be certain to ruin it. Similarly, deer will tug down and bite every tomato on a plant, or on a *row* of tomato plants, wrecking them all for the sheer pleasure of denying anybody else enjoyment of the harvest. Squash as well: as if the next gourd chewed on will be more appetizing than the last one sampled. Or the one after that.

Such garden vandalism constitutes wholesale destruction of foodstuffs for no good reason. Flowers are prey, too. Starting in the spring with tulips, as the weeks go by Bambi and her Evil Hordes will strip the leaves from roses, impatiens, hollyhocks, sunflowers and many other plants.

In response to my complaints about the deer early in my time in the valley, a friend informed me that the only defence against the malicious quadrupeds is: "Big fence, big dog, or big gun." Some people pay for a deer fence to be built entirely around their property. The effect can seem imprisoning rather than liberating, however. "When I'm working in the garden, deer are on the other side of the fence looking in at me," one fencing enthusiast who lives down the road admitted to me. "I can't help but think that instead of fencing the deer out, I've fenced myself in."

A dog wasn't a good idea for me during the many years I taught elsewhere and travelled frequently back and forth between work and Appledore. Acquiring a gun meant mastering a technology which, like learning to operate a chainsaw, I was reluctant to do.

In 1998 I did erect an 8-foot-high chicken-wire fence around my lower vegetable garden. But I didn't want to construct such deer-proof fencing around every bed and balked at the expense of enclosing the whole portion of my property that holds house, lawns and gardens. The successful deer-protection technique I eventually adopted on the advice of a valley master gardener is a protein spray. Bambi, being a hardcore vegetarian, is turned off by even a hint of protein. Every two or three weeks in spring and summer I spray the gardens and fruit trees with a mix of a half cup of milk and one egg added to a gallon and a half of water in a two-gallon sprayer. The spray takes me about three-quarters of an hour to apply to every bed, pot, rose-bush and fruit tree. The concoction is nearly 100 per cent effective.

Nevertheless, the kitchen garden beds and the Grave of Literary Ambition receive an extra layer of deer defence in the form of motion-activated sprinklers. These devices are attached to hoses, and by day or night shoot a stream of water at anything that moves within range of their built-in sensor. Unfortunately, during the summer I frequently head out for the kitchen garden to secure an onion or lettuce for the evening's salad, and, preoccupied by my goal or something else I'm thinking about, forget to first shut off the water to the sprinkler. Being abruptly soaked by a jet of ice-cold water is a disagreeable reminder to pay attention to what I'm doing.

To date I've been lucky that the other garden-wrecking ruminant in the lower valley, elk, have not yet appeared along the Winlaw back road during the growing season. The huge beasts, popularly known as "deer on steroids," raid and damage gardens around the Playmor Junction area and as far up the valley as Passmore. Folk wisdom insists that an elk's strength is such that it will plough through even the sturdiest fence, like a bear.

A couple I know who were plagued by elk raiding their vegetables had a dog that would chase away any deer, skunk or even bear that threatened the garden. But when elk showed up, the worthless canine retreated to their front step and passively watched the fiends do their worst.

A valley tale features a resident incensed because he looked out to see several of the giant animals busy chomping on his pea and bean vines. He came charging out of his house with his rifle and fired a warning shot. Then he realized that a dead elk lying in the garden would be as difficult as a dead horse to remove, let alone to bury. A tractor would be required to drag the corpse out of the veggie beds, and a backhoe would have to be hired to dig a hole large enough to bury it.

In desperation, the gardener approached one of the gigantic thieves scarfing up his vegetables and repeatedly poked the rifle barrel into its flank. The gesture was meant as a threat to convince the elk that it was in mortal peril unless it immediately stopped stealing what it never toiled to plant. But the elk being prodded merely stepped sideways a pace or two in the direction the barrel was nudging it, without pausing from hoovering up the greens.

Probably *my* most unsettling encounter with one of Earth's creatures happened on a June morning in 2018. The day was warm and promised to be hot. I had the wooden door to the basement open, while through the screened window in the closed storm door a refreshing breeze blew into the basement and on into the study where I was writing. Upstairs, I had my screened windows open and the screened bottom half of the storm door leading to the deck was also letting in fresh spring air.

I was absorbed in my keyboard and screen when I heard irregular thumping sounds that seemed to come from outside, somewhere above the basement door. From time to time Steller's jays or flickers will fly under the house soffits to look for bugs, and the bumping and clunking noises that result were like what I was hearing.

Yet such sounds were only *like* what I was hearing. The slight difference drew me outdoors to confirm my presumption.

When I emerged from the basement and turned to look up at the eaves, no birds were visible. I did observe, however, a big rip in the screen at the bottom of the door from the deck into the house. Had a dog pushed through the screen and, once inside, been the cause of the noises I had heard? Yet what would lure a dog to crash through a screen into a house? After breakfast as usual I had done the dishes and tidied everything edible away, nor had I left out any meat to defrost on the counter. Since I'd owned Appledore, a stray dog had never approached the house, let alone been motivated to tear through a screen in order to enter. And could the dog still be inside?

I stood staring up at the house, trying to account for the ripped screen. Suddenly a face appeared at the kitchen window above the basement door. The face of a bear.

Adrenalin pulsed through me in an instant. I had a bear in my kitchen? The face scanned from left to right and back again, as if taking in the view of the mountains. The animal must be standing on my kitchen table, I realized. At no time did the face angle down to spot me standing gobsmacked below it. As abruptly as it had appeared, the face vanished.

My brain throbbed with fright and confusion. How was I going to get a bear out of the house? Bears in the wild will attack when a food source—a deer kill, say—is threatened. Given that a kitchen is one big food source, how could I possibly convince a bear to stop pigging out and leave? Attempting to scare the bear into departing would mean I risked serious injury or death if the bear interpreted my actions as an attempt to separate it from food.

A neighbour across the road from me, Stuart, is an experienced hunter. He told me once he likes to take a bear each fall, since the diet of apples, pears and plums that bears in our area are eating in the autumn make their meat especially flavoursome. If Stuart was home, I could call on him to dispatch the bear. But having a dead bear bleeding all over my kitchen wasn't an outcome I was keen on. And was Stuart even home? The longer the bear was in the kitchen, the more damage it would cause. Did I have to abandon my house until Stuart returned from wherever he was and agreed to shoot the bear?

I was rooted to the spot, mouth ajar, mind whirling. Then out through the torn screen onto the deck loped a very small bear. I surprised myself by yelling at it: "Get out of here!" The bear, whether it heard me or not, increased speed and scrabbled down the deck toward the stairs, bounded across the lawn and vanished into the forest.

Hands and arms shaking, I stepped back into the basement, up the stairs, and braced myself for a scene of total mayhem. I peered around the hall corner into the kitchen.

Everything looked normal. The only disturbance visible was a tipped-over vase of flowers on the kitchen table, and a table decoration—a wax candle in the form of Appledore's eponymous apple—lay on the floor. The refrigerator door was not pulled open. Food cupboard doors weren't ajar, nor were their contents shovelled out by a hairy arm onto counter and floor.

Stepping closer, I could see a few bits of dirt from the visitor's paws on the tablecloth. The wax candle, when I picked it up from the floor, had a tooth mark and some slime on it but was otherwise unaltered. Nothing else in the kitchen had been disturbed. Odd that atop the refrigerator a bowl held oranges and *real* apples that the little bear had ignored.

As my brain geared down closer to its normal functioning, I wondered if the small size of the bear maybe indicated it was an orphaned yearling, untaught by its mother to stay away from people's houses. Evidently the bear's lack of training meant that in the middle of a food cache like my kitchen it didn't know how to exploit its situation.

Lucky for me, but not so lucky for the little guy. I later heard a small bear had been hanging around people's places a little distance south of me. It tried to enter another house, whose owner shot and killed it.

Such a death was regrettable, but I had considered asking Stuart to bring about the same end for my visitor. And of course death is part of the biosphere's natural cycle. Even so, I don't deal well with death. I'm still startled and perturbed when I'm busy with a chore outside and come upon a dead bird on the grass or the deck. After fetching a shovel, I've grown used to carrying the feathered bodies on the blade into the woods not far from my compost pile. There I commit these creatures of light and air to the dark soil.

Once I had to clean up half a rabbit. Tracks of these animals are evident in the snow around the house, and occasionally in the fall I'll encounter one near the shed. But also present and seldom seen are feral cats, fierce hunters that likely killed and half-consumed the bunny.

My current neighbour to the south keeps chickens and stores their feed in an old barn. To discourage mice, rats and other critters from helping themselves to chicken chow, my neighbour feeds barn cats that are more or less wild. Sometimes early in the morning, I catch a glimpse out the kitchen window of a cat trotting down my driveway.

I was pleased when these cats killed off pack-rats that had made their smelly nests in my shed and woodpile for a few years. Before the felines took an interest, the pack-rats' audacity extended to making nests in the engine compartment of my pickup. They obtained nest material by ripping out large swathes of insulation from under the engine hood and from the firewall separating the engine compartment from the pickup's cabin.

Pack-rats are famed for making a mess, and that's what they accomplished under the hood. I phoned the Chevy dealer for advice. He suggested strewing dryer strips around—the small paper sheets used to reduce static in a clothes dryer. The dryer strips' strong chemical smell, er, fragrance jams the pack-rat's olfactory warning system. I was also told by the dealer to leave the hood ajar, which makes the engine compartment feel like a less secure environment for the rodents.

This technique worked, although having to remove the dryer strips before each use of the pickup, and then reposition them whenever I returned home, was a drag. So I was happy when I saw several times a cat waiting patiently near my woodpile. The pack-rats disappeared from the property within a few months of the cats' attention to them. But during that time I was less pleased to find once the mangled remains of an animal by the shed that could have been a mostly eaten pack-rat. I didn't look too closely at it while burying it.

For me, dead things radiate a powerful negative energy that frightens me. Paradoxically for somebody like me with such trepidation around death, I've arranged reminders of my own family dead around the grounds. At the wellhead, a memorial plaque I had prepared names the well after my mother's sister, Beryl Lowry, whose bequest largely paid for the original well's installation. At the foot of the house's south lawn, beside where the drilling rig spun out, I planted a magnolia tree under which is a plaque for my uncle Alex. Its inscription reads, "He did what he figured was best." At the edge of the lawn by the northwest corner of the house is a flower bed labelled with my mother's name. A couple of feet away I put a bench in memory of my father. The bench plaque's inscription is a quote adapted from a poem by one of my father's favourite poets, A.E. Housman (1859–1936): "[He] walk[ed] the resounding way / To the still dwelling." Suspended from a pine bough beside the bench is a construction consisting of two back-to-back picture frames, each holding a poem. My father loved to recite both of them aloud: the untitled second poem in Housman's 1896 collection *A Shropshire Lad*, "Loveliest of trees," and a five-stanza excerpt about Kew Gardens from "The Barrel-Organ" (1904) by Alfred Noyes (1880–1958).

I took family politics into account in siting these memorials. From my father's bench or my mother's flower bed, you can see the wellhead with the plaque in honour of my mother's sister. She and her acoustic-engineer husband were at times part of my parents' circle in Toronto, although I wouldn't characterize the relationship between my mother and her sister as warm.

However, I had to position the plaque in memory of my father's brother where it couldn't be viewed from the bench, since my father had very little contact with his brother for decades. While my uncle was proud of my father's accomplishments, this respect wasn't returned. Alex contributed a lot to society: as a union construction labourer, he helped build, among other structures, Vancouver's Granville Street Bridge and the Alcan aluminum smelter in Kitimat. Like a lot of the guys who helped construct the smelter, he was offered employment there once it was complete, and he served on the smelter pot lines for 21 years.

I never knew for sure why my father wasn't closer to his brother. Did Alex's life as a manual worker represent to my father what he might have become had scholarships not enabled him to continue his education? My parents were raised amid Toronto working-class economic uncertainty. My father's—and Alex's—father was a machine operator in a Tip Top Tailors factory when he worked; my mother's father a cabinet-maker when he could find employment. To my parents living through the Depression in their twenties, education was the only means to achieve a stable existence, even though they were both left-wing, staunchly pro-union, and wherever they lived were involved in the community. My parents, especially my father, were active on library boards, PTA councils, Boy Scout group committees, and community projects such as a new swimming pool for the Prince Rupert civic centre when we lived there, and later the realization of the Queen Elizabeth Playhouse in Vancouver. Both parents participated in seniors-oriented volunteer initiatives in retirement. Still, to keep peace in the remembered family, I felt that not being able to see my uncle's plaque from my father's bench was best.

One visitor commented after a tour of Appledore, "Jeez, it's like a graveyard around here." I hadn't thought of the family memorials that way. To me, having the reminders of these relatives near me is a way of keeping their memory freshly present as I pursue my seasonal tasks.

I should add that death is not the only dark component of our earthly existence that manifests itself where I live. In this book I've touched on a few difficult local characters. Overall, Winlaw is an incredibly safe community. Many residents don't lock their houses or vehicles. Yet there are worlds within worlds in Winlaw, the same as anywhere else. In the 30-plus years I've lived here, two murders have happened, one solved and one where no person has ever been charged. Both killings were extra shocking because each involved a small cluster of seriously dysfunctional individuals. Since Winlaw exists on a planet of wounded souls, we could hardly expect to be exempt from such people.

My neighbour Rod, who interacts with far more of the community than I do, will sometimes warn me: "Stay away from that guy." But the individual isn't anybody I'd ordinarily have anything to do with. A group of sketchy fellows Rod deemed prudent to avoid gathered daily one summer at a picnic table under the spreading branches of a cedar across the highway from the café in Winlaw. Mostly in their twenties or thirties, the six or eight individuals would drink coffee and smoke, seemingly with nothing else to do all day. Rod and his son Evan called the cedar under which this bunch gathered "The Seedy Tree."

A couple who are friends of mine forbade their daughters from visiting the home of a particular school classmate. The schoolmate's parents were growers who mainly sat around the house all day. My friends said they didn't want their kids to think that working at nothing was acceptable adult behaviour.

Then there was a local family whose teenaged kids about the time I arrived were blamed for anything out of the ordinary in Winlaw: beer bottles along the roadside, tire skid marks where somebody did a doughnut on the asphalt in the middle of the night, a break-in at the post office. I thought of them as the Snopes, after a blighted and destructive family in the US South featured in several stories and three novels by William Faulkner (1897–1962). The Winlaw Snopes moved away after a couple of years, and I've never heard them referred to since.

Societal dysfunction has been a focus of a lot of my writing over the decades, albeit emphasizing the effects on people of the authoritarian structuring of daily work rather than considering family or community problems separately from employment's influence on our lives. Still, I'm aware that an occasionally brutal underworld exists in Winlaw. Because its inhabitants don't usually interact with Appledore, I try to ignore their existence.

My life here has been to date one of overarching delight. The tiny minority around me who are exemplars of society's—of the earth's—dark shadow are seldom in my thoughts.

Chapter Fifteen

THE ELEMENTS– AIR

THE MOUNTAIN AIR I INHALE, MOVE THROUGH, FEELS ABSO-lutely pure as it enters my nostrils and lungs—most of the time. The atmosphere can be smoky from forest fires, of course, or in season a downdraft can bring a whiff of smoke from my own or a neighbour's wood furnace. Yet usually I breathe an elixir, air that seems to vibrate with health itself.

Being out in the fresh air every afternoon, for work or recreation, means I'm in the weather. I have work clothes that are a match for almost any conditions, except for a serious blizzard or very heavy downpour. Whatever the weather, paying attention to how it can change makes me a connoisseur of clouds. Most often the weather flows up-valley, so I'll pause at a task to peer at cloud formations to the south to learn if one that looks menacing is advancing this way. Or, if a west wind is blowing, I'll check out what sort of sky-moun-tains are sailing over the top of Perry Ridge. Alternatively, a glance at the treetops might inform me that a rarer north wind is bringing clouds from that direction I need to keep an eye on.

In chill temperatures, chimney smoke can hint at changes in air pressure. If the smoke streams absolutely vertical into the sky, I'm confident that whatever weather the current pressure system has brought will hang around for a while. Conversely, if smoke no sooner leaves the roof than it curls toward the ground, an alteration in pressure is underway: different weather is due.

Besides bringing the weather, the air outdoors carries scents. In autumn, I experience that sweetly spicy odour of yellow birch leaves I've raked into a pile. Icy winter air has its own smell: a combination of crisp freshness and threat. As snow melts, the odour of wet earth rises. Later my nostrils take in the tang of chicken manure or other fertilizer I've worked into flower and vegetable beds before planting starts.

As gardens start to grow, I inhale the scent of daffodils I've just cut to bring into the house. Of a lilac bush in bloom. Just-mowed grass. The heavy perfume of my peonies in flower. The smell of my Joseph's Coat roses: a blend of honey, chocolate and cilantro.

Before even the daffodils blossom, though, if I enter the springtime woods, my nostrils fill with the scent of new growth: a green musk. When the brown forest floor transforms into ivy-like ground cover, when tiny leaves appear at the ends of aspen twigs, I smell the earth's sweat from its exertions to reawaken life.

The Appledore air throughout the year is filled with birds and their calls. While I'm removing snow or replenishing the basement stack of firewood, around me resonate multiple enunciations of *chick-a-dee-dee-dee*. Both black-capped and mountain chickadees are noisy in the trees. An aerial creature's plaintive *Phoe-be, Phoe-be* invokes the Titan goddess who is the daughter of, appropriately enough for a bird, the Earth and the Sky. A different winter resident's extended whistling note repeats two or three times. I wish I knew more of the aerial song-makers' names, but I enjoy anyhow the soundscape they constantly create.

When the bird census swells in spring, warblers and nuthatches flit past amid the cottonwood seeds drifting on the breeze. The summer soundtrack includes—besides the occasional loud passage of a motorcycle or dirt bike down the back road—a half-chirp, half-rattle repeated five times, then after a pause, uttered another five times. A single shrill whistle-like call rings out again and again, then is silent. All the while a sequence of *chirp-cheep-twitter, chirp-cheep-twitter* strikes my ear: a robin's song.

And throughout the calendar, ravens ponderously flap overhead, wings creaking. Or the black birds fuss loudly with each other in the treetops. Whatever errand they engage in, ravens provide their hoarse commentary.

Birds' presence at Appledore doesn't only occur by chance. In mid-November, when I'm sure the bears are settled into their dens, I hang a couple of feeders from trees near the house. I fill and refill these with black oil sunflower seeds until I judge from the warming April weather that the bears have received their spring wake-up call.

Flocks of chickadees and pine siskins mainly consume these seeds. Both kinds of small birds are sloppy eaters, so those individuals not squabbling for a turn at the feeders' ports are hopping around underneath, pecking at fallen seeds. Occasionally a Steller's jay will appear, gigantic in size compared to the usual devotees of the feeders. The jay's bright blue feathers contrast as well with the muted attire of the majority of birds consuming the seeds. Flickers, also looking enormous compared to a chickadee or siskin, will from time to time sample the spill under the feeder. They also like to peck at bugs under my eaves, before flying off to hammer at a tree trunk down by the road, as any self-respecting woodpecker should.

The feeders also cause Appledore's squirrels to become airborne, albeit briefly. Before the feeders are out, as early as when the dogbane begins to yellow, the rodents shift into mad activity to cache food for winter. The creatures are nonchalant about tracing at impressive speed a path through the trees in their single-minded pursuit of storable edibles. One route might involve a dash out along a certain hazel branch until it bends under the squirrel's weight. Whereupon the animal jumps to a branch in an adjoining fir which, in turn, leads to a pine trunk it scrabbles down, followed by a zip across grass to a fence post, climbed in an instant. Then a sprint along the knife-edge of the topmost fence rail as far as the soil-sweeping branches of a spruce into which the squirrel vaults, presumably to stash something in a winter food depot between the evergreen's roots.

When I first put the feeders out, the squirrels try several times to acquire seeds from them. A squirrel will rush out along the branch from which one of my feeders is suspended, then leap head-first onto that device's steeply pitched metal top. Unable to grasp hold, the squirrel slips off, tumbles through air, and lands on the ground below. My other feeder's design incorporates a flatter top, but access to the feeding portals below is protected by a down-sloping transparent plastic shield. Again, the squirrel's feet get no purchase. A thieving rodent occasionally manages to retreat with considerable effort to the horizontal top again, but more often loses traction and sails off the plastic to collide with the lawn. After a few such failures, the squirrels limit themselves to scavenging seeds beneath the feeders.

A different occasionally airborne annoyance often seen below my feeders showed up in the region in the second decade of the twenty-first century: feral turkeys. Herds of these pests migrated north from Washington state, perhaps due to climate change or a human-caused decline in predators. Perpetual whiners, the birds complain with equally loud emphasis about any incident perceived as a threat, whether a slavering dog chasing them or a sleight feint in their direction from another turkey. When the turkeys are not producing their self-pitying barks, they click to themselves, as if for self-reassurance that they are entitled to feel put-upon. Mostly, though, they spend their day noisily snivelling about their sorry lot.

In the colder months, the Appledore-based turkey flock—which can number 30 or more—roost for the night high in the spruces, firs and pines west of the house. That a bird so huge can fly at all is astonishing, and where they settle for the night is 7 or 8 metres above ground.

The turkeys are always dissatisfied with their initial choice of bedroom up in the sky, selected as the afternoon dims. Picking a branch to sleep away the night involves much grumbling, nit-picking and denouncing of peers. The birds try out various spots in search of the perfect perch, flapping from one tree to another or, in the same tree, fluttering from one branch to a different one. Sometimes they want to be alone in their perpetual misery, and sometimes so many crowd onto a single branch that, if I'm outside, I'll hear a *crack*, and then the sound of a tree limb falling through foliage to the ground. The broken-off branch's descent is accompanied by an explosion of turkey insistence on personal innocence, claims of systemic oppression by other flock members, and denunciations of every former occupier of the branch but themselves.

When in spring, robins fill the air again with their songs, tom turkeys strut their stuff for a couple of weeks and then the pests are seen less and less on the valley floor. "They're up in the woods having more turkeys," is the local explanation. By the end of summer, the birds reappear: a couple of hens will be shepherding a dozen miniature nuisances. The males, identified by a projecting feather mid-chest—known as a "beard"—have formed separate, smaller groups who wander the same territory as the mobile kindergartens, although not at the same time.

Since the ability of the local environment to support an ever-increasing number of this invasive species seems doubtful, I keep waiting hopefully for a population crash. I long for a spike in the presence of coyotes, cougars or any other predator that might enjoy a meal of turkey. The legal human hunting limit is only two per year, and the meat is reportedly tough and stringy.

One bird whose population crash I regret is owls. When I first moved to Appledore, at night I could hear owls hooting from the forest south of me on the ridge. Then in 1994 my neighbour at the time to the south clear-cut those acres, and I've rarely listened to an owl since. They haven't completely disappeared from the area, though. I saw one on a telephone wire near the Winlaw Bridge once, and a small northern pygmy owl hung around near the bird bath at Appledore for a wonderful half hour one summer afternoon.

Birds aren't the only airborne creatures here. Bats circle the house continually at night in summer to scarf up bugs. Indoors, I've learned to expect a Bug of the Month: one particular insect whose presence in the house peaks in visibility during a given month. Not all such bugs are airborne. For instance, each February for some years, several ants appeared daily on the east wall of my bedroom. In 2009 I called a pest-control outfit, who knocked them back, and simultaneously eliminated carpenter ants in the south wall of the living room who had begun to deposit a little pile of shavings each winter beside the sliding glass door to the deck.

Another crawling insect designated Bug of the Month most years are spiders. Webs spun by spiders of all sizes span the airy spaces throughout the house, but their preferred habitat is the basement with its seldom-visited corners, levels of shelving, and bare-bulb lighting amid exposed floor joists.

The Bug of the Month honorific is granted to two decidedly airborne insects during the year. In either September or October, stink bugs claim the title. Known as "cedar bugs" as well, these slow-moving brown creepies smell like an old banana if annoyed or crushed—hence their common name. The stink bug population explodes in early fall, when they emerge from cracks and crannies to whiz through the house and land on any flat surface, vertical or horizontal. The challenge is to relocate them outdoors without having them release their pungent stink.

Mosquitoes earn the Bug of the Month designation anytime from late June to late August. For reasons that I've never been able to determine, homes along the back road experience each summer a plague of the irksome critters, whereas across the river, the east side of the valley is mosquito-free. The eastern shores of the river don't have any less swampy stretches than our side, and puddles or other examples of standing water aren't more plentiful west of the river than east. At the height of the mosquito plague, I'll race from my house to my vehicle pursued by a lynch mob of mozzies. Safely inside, I can then motor to downtown Winlaw after crossing the river and eat a meal outdoors on the Winlaw café patio unbothered by even one of the wretched mini-vampires. Similarly, I can ride my bike up and down the rail trail—which is east of the river— unmolested. But back at Appledore, I'm stabbed innumerable times while removing my bike from the vehicle's bike rack.

I have only mixed success at keeping the flying irritants out of the house, which accounts for their Bug of the Month designation. Once the mozzies appear, work outside would be unbearable without potions like Off! or Muskol. Occasionally a summer happens where the aggravating cloud of suicidal bloodsuckers is of such low volume that I only have to douse myself in repellant once or twice all season. Far more standard is having to retreat to the basement every couple of hours on a hot afternoon because I've sweated off the insect spray and need to reapply it.

Any foray without protection—venturing quickly out to the kitchen garden at suppertime to pick a green pepper or onion for the salad—is a race with sanity as the miniature harpies relentlessly attack. Their ferocity reaches a peak once the sun sinks below the ridge and the long summer twilight begins. The mozzies seem to understand that if they don't find blood immediately, they won't survive the pending night. The risk of being slapped into oblivion is of no consideration as the light slowly fades: die now or die later seems to be their motto.

Dealing with the infuriating mob becomes second nature as summer wears on, so I'm always taken aback toward the end of August when abruptly the mosquitoes vanish. Nothing has changed with regard to daily temperatures or precipitation. While picking raspberries or the last of the beans, though, I suddenly realize that no hideous *Eeeeeeee* is buzzing around my ears and face. Since they don't migrate, the mosquitoes' precipitous absence remains a mystery.

Other flying insects that can cause more pain than mosquitoes are yellow jackets (locally called mud wasps), hornets, and paper wasps. These stinging insects' nests abound under eaves and deck furniture, and in deciduous tree branches, the greenhouse, and the ground. Their nests range from a few inches in length to 2 or 3 feet tall. I suspect wasps and hornets live in my house's outer walls as well, since I've seen the bad-tempered critters exiting and entering cracks in the siding. Because they seldom appear indoors, however, they fail to ever qualify as a Bug of the Month.

About every two years I'm stung. This usually occurs because one of the species has constructed a nest near the basement door or the door into the house off the deck, or in the greenhouse. My coming and going past their nest is interpreted by one of the guardians, whom I presume is having a bad day, as a threat. I've also been stung because my lawnmower runs over an unnoticed yellow jacket nest in the grass.

In the years between stings, I forget how intensely painful these punctures are. I'm always shocked by the *degree* of pain. Luckily, the hurt rapidly fades, although I worry about anaphylactic shock. It's never happened to me, but my understanding is that people can develop this reaction at any age. I keep antihistamines in my medicine chest, just in case.

Because of the pain, I operate on a zero-tolerance model for stings. I can overlook nests of any size being built anywhere, but once I'm stung, war is declared. As the instructions on the can of anti-wasp foam advise, I wait until after dark when the perpetrator and her or his enablers are quiescent. Then I return to the scene of the crime, foam can in hand, to wreak mortal revenge—collective punishment, really.

Having to take such drastic measures is an infrequent experience, though. If I'm out in the night air, more often I'm there to revel in the sight of the myriad stars and constellations slowly turning overhead. Or to watch the stunning progress of a full Kootenay moon rise out of the trees atop the valley's eastern rim and ascend toward the zenith.

On balance, the aerial world provides me with immeasurably more beauty than disagreeableness. Whether I walk around my grounds or drive anywhere in the West Kootenay, the vistas never appear stale to me, no matter how many thousands of times I pass that way. Ever-changing combinations of clear or misty air, of light or gloom, of all the other atmospheric effects keep the prospects fresh whatever the season. These views of mountain, forest, water— up close or in the distance—unfailingly grant me much-needed perspective on my days, console and inspire me, and fill me with happiness.

Travelling through the air toward me from this geography, I hear a music. I've tried repeatedly to describe in words the melodies I discern originating from stone, field, woods, river. The tunes are not perceptible to the ear, but they sing in my mind. Since science tells us all the senses occur in the brain, the music that the landscape generates is as real to me as anything heard through an audio system's speakers, or as the sound created by a musician or singer performing in front of me.

In 2017 I published a book of poems about music, *Helpless Angels*. Repeatedly in these poems, topographical features—ranges, forests, lakes—are linked with melody. The collection includes a sequence, "Elemental Musics: Selkirk Mountains," which won the 2016 "Sonic Geography" literary contest organized by Musicworks, a Canadian organization dedicated to encouraging innovative music. The poems depict sequentially the harmonies emanating from wind in the alpine, from a breeze passing through a grove of trees on the valley floor, and from a creek burbling down a mountain toward the Slocan River.

A reinforcement of the concept that the West Kootenay air is imbued with music arises from my wind chimes. The house came with a home-made set of four suspended metal cylinders, producing a tone according to the motion of a suspended striker. I've since added a couple more wind chimes. I find restful the gentle discord of them all making music in a breeze whether I'm sitting on the deck or inside the house on a summer day hearing the jangly notes entering through screened windows and door.

Yet the wind chimes' tinkling is a slight matter compared to how momentous I find what the wind itself says. The currents of moving air that pass convey information I believe I need to attend to. When I overhear the wind's utterances to trees and water and sky, I acknowledge that the wind isn't speaking to me. I'm unable to understand the message, but the wind's tone emphasizes, I feel, the urgency and importance of what it communicates.

Perhaps my belief that the wind's messages are portentous even if indecipherable is a factor of my age. Literary Nobel laureate Bob Dylan in his 1962 protest song "Blowin' in the Wind" assures his audience that the wind contains the obvious answers to the rhetorical questions concerning social issues that his lyrics pose. Nearly 40 years later, in 2001's "Lonesome Day Blues," he regards the wind as less forthcoming:

Last night the wind was whisperin',
I was trying to make out what it was.
Last night the wind was whisperin' somethin',
I was trying to make out what it was.
I tell myself something's comin'
But it never does.

I love to stop what I'm doing outside to watch and listen to the wind as strong gusts stir the upper boughs of the evergreens that crowd the edges of Appledore's lawns. A gentler breeze can steadily ruffle the aspen leaves, while nearby evergreens stand absolutely still. In the latter case, I presume that the wind's message is not meant for the spruces and firs. Yet clearly they judge that what the wind is communicating is worth their complete attention.

In summer, when the sun has dropped below Perry Ridge and the air is beginning to cool, a hot breeze flows down the mountain toward my lower garden and the road. Such a current likely is driven by the temperature changes in Appledore's microclimate. But given how hot air usually rises, this late afternoon downslope breeze also represents for me wind's enigmas—and by extension, the wonders of this place I'm grateful to live in.

Again and again, the environmentalist scolds insist, "Humans are part of nature. We're not separate. Absorb that fact, you knuckle-heads, and all will be well for the biosphere."

I feel that if this claim were true, we would be able to comprehend what the wind imparts to the green world, to the rippled surface of the river, to great clouds soaring into the valley over the mountain rim. Perhaps only if we managed to lose the self-awareness that distinguishes our species, that intelligence based on words, could we understand the pronouncements of the wind.

Each of us does at last attain that state, however. In my poem "Release," published in my 2020 collection *Watching a Man Break a Dog's Back: Poems for a Dark Time*, I imagine my forthcoming absorption into the natural—when Appledore, like a pleasant dream ended by sunshine streaming into the bedroom here on a summer morning, will dissipate forever into air:

> I will merge then
> Into the textured density of trees—boughs, needles,
> Leaves, trunks massed along a hillside
>
> One August morning: I will be dispersed
> Throughout the sunlit floating
> Planes of green.
>
> I will enter this complexity
> That has no words, where tendril
> And filament draw up salts from earth,
>
> Draw water, where the fluttering greens
> Draw sustenance
> From light, where transpiration restores the air
>
> Without thought, without the letters of a name,
> Without the sounds of
> A language
>
> Drifting among the canopy
> —The vowels, sibilants, fricatives
> Translucent, ephemeral,
>
> Unknown as before I came to be: absent
> Amid the grace notes of pollen
> Tremulous on the wind.

ABOUT THE AUTHOR

Tom wayman's prolific literary career includes writing more than twenty poetry collections, three collections of critical and cultural essays, three books of short fiction and a novel, as well as editing six poetry anthologies. He received British Columbia's 2022 George Woodcock Award for Lifetime Achievement in the literary arts. In 2015, he was named a Vancouver Literary Landmark, with a plaque on the city's Commercial Drive commemorating his championing of people writing for themselves about their daily employment. His own work life involved a range of blue- and white-collar jobs across North America, including teaching in both alternative and mainstream post-secondary institutions. He won the Western Canada Jewish Book Awards prize for fiction in 2016 (for the short story collection, *The Shadows We Mistake for Love*) and for poetry in 2023 (for *Watching a Man Break a Dog's Back: Poems for a Dark Time*). Wayman lives in Winlaw, BC, and his website is www.tomwayman.com.